REFORM AND REGULATION
American Politics from Roosevelt to Wilson

Consulting Editor
Robert A. Divine
University of Texas at Austin

Reform and Regulation

American Politics from Roosevelt to Wilson

Lewis L. Gould
University of Texas at Austin

SECOND EDITION

ALFRED A. KNOPF New York

COVER PHOTO CREDIT: The Bettmann Archive

This new agency composite released for newspaper publication immediately before the 1912 election carried the following description: "All the States are represented in this picture, and the crowds shown were made in the States represented. The Presidential candidates are placed in the position where they are supposed to draw the largest number of votes. Mr. Taft in the East, Governor Wilson in the South and Middle West and Col. Roosevelt in the Western States."

COVER DESIGN: Katharine von Urban

Second Edition

9 8 7 6 5 4 3 2

Library of Congress Cataloging-in-Publication Data

Gould, Lewis L.
  Reform and regulation

  Bibliography: p.
  Includes index.
  1. United States—Politics and government—
1901–1909. 2. United States—Politics and
government—1909–1913. 3. United States—
Politics and government—1913–1921. 4. Progressivism (United States politics) I. Title.
E756.G63 1986   973.91   85-18080
ISBN 0-394-35413-3

Manufactured in the United States of America

FOREWORD

The resurgence of political history is one of the most intriguing developments in recent American historical scholarship. In the years immediately following World War II, scholars tended to dismiss the study of past politics as mundane and old-fashioned as they focused on cultural, psychological, ethnic, and intellectual approaches to the American experience. But the enduring importance of political events, brought home to scholars as well as journalists by the tumultuous events of the 1960s and the devastating Watergate scandal, led historians to examine the political past anew. Many borrowed ideas and techniques from social scientists to probe into such new areas as voting behavior, party fluctuations, and the role of ethnocultural factors in politics. Others relied upon more traditional studies of campaign rhetoric and the impact of charismatic leaders on the political process. The result was a new flowering of political history.

Critical Episodes in American Politics is a series of interpretive volumes designed to bring the new scholarship to bear on eight major episodes ranging from the origins of the first party system in the 1790s through the trauma of Vietnam and Watergate. Each author examines the political process at a critical time in the American past to demonstrate the way the democratic system functioned under great stress. Employing different techniques and approaches, each author seeks to explain the distinctive events in his period to give the reader an insight into both the strengths and weaknesses of the American political tradition.

In this volume, Professor Lewis L. Gould describes the dynamics of political change in the Progressive era by focusing on the way the two major parties dealt with the problem of regulating a modern industrial economy. He skillfully traces the divisions within both parties between those favoring and opposing greater federal supervision and shows how eventually the reformers lost out within the GOP and triumphed only briefly in the Democratic party under Wilson. Skeptical of political rhetoric, the author probes beyond Progressive slogans to lay bare the struggle for power between competing factions within the parties. He analyzes such diverse

leaders as Theodore Roosevelt, Robert La Follette, William
Howard Taft, and Woodrow Wilson to reveal their faults as well as
their virtues. The result is a compelling account of an era that wit-
nessed the birth of modern American politics.

ROBERT A. DIVINE

PREFACE TO THE SECOND EDITION

For this revised and enlarged edition, I have added material to the first chapter, included an epilogue, and inserted supplementary comments in the text. More important, the structure of the narrative has become chronological and less keyed to presidential administrations. I am grateful to the reviewers of the original book, to the readers at Alfred A. Knopf, to the initial editors, David Follmer and Naomi Schneider, and to Christopher Rogers for their helpful criticisms and suggestions. I owe thanks as well to Bill Childs, John S. Latcham, John Leffler, Michael McGerr, Fred Shoemaker, and especially Robert A. Divine for his patience and wise counsel. Karen Gould, who has helped me through two versions of the book, certainly deserves to have the volume dedicated to her.

LEWIS L. GOULD
Austin, Texas
January 1985

PREFACE TO THE FIRST EDITION

During the first fifteen years of the twentieth century, American politics took on a recognizably modern shape. After debating the extent to which the government should promote economic growth in the preceding century, the two major parties now discussed how far the nation and the states should regulate an industrial society. At the same time, the role and importance of partisan politics came under intense assault from critics and reformers who found the political practices of the Gilded Age anachronistic and constricting. The interaction of debate over government regulation with the attack on partisanship gave the politics of the Progressive era its unique character. This book endeavors to trace in an analytic narrative how the Republicans moved tentatively under Theodore Roosevelt toward an acceptance of the regulatory state and then rejected the idea by 1916. For the Democrats it was a matter of overcoming their states rights heritage and discovering the political potential of national power vigorously exercised under Woodrow Wilson. The study concludes with the presidential election of 1916, a contest whose issues and alignments anticipated the battles of the New Deal.

Throughout the account that follows there has been a conscious effort to avoid presenting political developments as the triumph of one virtuous individual, faction, or party over its misguided, evil, or foolish rivals. Historians have often accepted uncritically the partisan, occasionally melodramatic, statements of participants in the public affairs of these years as accurate judgments about the reality of party politics.

I am indebted to the National Endowment for the Humanities, the University Research Institute of the University of Texas at Austin, and the Dora Bonham Fund of the History Department, University of Texas at Austin, for assistance with the research that made this book possible. Some pages of the first chapter appeared in my "Popular Government and Political Reform: 1890–1920," *Current History*, 67 (1974), 16–17, and are reproduced here with permission. Professors Jerome Clubb and Howard W. Allen graciously permitted use of material from their work. Ambassador

Henry Cabot Lodge allowed me to quote material from his grandfather's letters, and Fanny Wickes Parsons permitted quotations from the letters of Herbert Parsons.

It is impossible to thank all the librarians who assisted me, but the Library of Congress deserves special recognition for the excellence of its Manuscript Division and the efficiency of that division's staff. Richard Holland of the Perry-Castañeda Library, University of Texas at Austin, provided timely assistance in acquiring microfilm sources. The critical readings of Herbert F. Margulies and R. Hal Williams caught errors and improved the analysis. Robert A. Divine was a model of editorial encouragement and patience. My wife Karen took time from her own research and writing to provide expert proofreading, constructive advice, and wise judgments. Quotations of Crown-copyright records in the Public Record Office appear by permission of the Controller of H. M. Stationery Office.

LEWIS L. GOULD
Austin, Texas
August 1977

CONTENTS

REFORM AND REGULATION
American Politics from Roosevelt to Wilson

CHAPTER 1

American Politics in 1900

From late summer to early November of 1900, the American political landscape echoed to the noise and hoopla of a presidential
election. The national headquarters of the two major parties
sent out millions of documents for distribution to the voters. Newspapers devoted extensive space to platforms, convention proceedings, and stump speeches, while readers contributed letters of
rebuttal or support. Speakers bureaus dispatched trained and
novice performers to large cities and country crossroads to further political education. Crude polls measured popular attitudes;
huge parades gave the faithful a chance to demonstrate enthusiasm for their party's candidate and reminded them to go to the
polls.

An engaging process, the campaign combined elements of festi-
val, championship sporting event, town meeting, and national debate. By the time President William McKinley confronted William
Jennings Bryan for the second time, the rituals of the campaign
seemed fixed and accepted. After the national conventions selected
the candidate and his running mate, a party committee "notified"
the fortunate hopeful, usually at his home, a month later. His
speech of "acceptance," along with the "letter of acceptance,"
which was released soon afterward, served as basic documents
around which the party focused its efforts. At the beginning of September the canvass commenced. Not all states voted on the same
day, and experts watched the vote of Maine in September, sharing
to some degree the faith of its citizens that "As Maine goes, so goes
the Nation." As September blended into October, the national
headquarters sent out contrasting predictions about which way key
states were leaning, while short and acerbic controversies erupted

3

over personalities and issues. Finally, in early November, the nation voted.[1]

In 1900 memories of the preceding election were fresh. "The Battle of the Standards" between McKinley and Bryan had brought voters to the polls in large numbers in 1896. Turnout exceeded 78 percent in the North. The excitement that surrounded the money question in a depression year, the evangelical ardor of Bryan's Democracy and its Populist allies, the social anxieties of McKinley's supporters at the challenge from the South and West, all made 1896 a year of color and drama, of climax and catharsis. Few politicians expected, given the general prosperity of the nation and the familiarity of the major candidates, that 1900 would match the frenzy and uproar of 1896. Yet there was apparent surprise at how calm the campaign in fact turned out to be. "I have never known a Presidential campaign so quiet," Senator Henry Cabot Lodge of Massachusetts told a friend, and a Democratic worker remembered it as "one of the dullest of the Bryan era."[2]

Some of the causes of the relative tranquillity of 1900 were unique to that contest. Times were good, the outcome of the race seemed predetermined, and the issues were not as dramatic or disputed as they had been four years earlier. But there were deeper forces at work, and students of American politics agree that 1896 was a genuine turning point. Before that contest, the arrangement of electoral strength that existed had its origins in the Civil War era. That political system, characterized by a close balance between Republicans and Democrats, broke apart under the stress of agrarian revolt and depression unrest in the 1890s. Politics after 1896 reflected the changed conditions and attitudes of this realignment within the party system. The election of 1900 mixed older practices and problems of the previous age of partisan warfare with the newer methods and issues of reform politics of the early twentieth century. As such, it provides a useful starting point for understanding how public life functioned in the age of Theodore Roosevelt and Woodrow Wilson.

The environment in which American politics operated before

---

[1] "How the Republican National Committee Works for Votes," 549–555, and Willis J. Abbot, "The Management of the Democratic Campaign," *The American Monthly Review of Reviews*, 22 (1900), 556–562.

[2] Henry Cabot Lodge to James Ford Rhodes, August 6, 1900, Henry Cabot Lodge Papers, Massachusetts Historical Society, Boston; Willis J. Abbot, *Watching the World Go By* (Boston: Little, Brown, 1933), p. 241.

1896 differed strikingly from conditions at the turn of the century. Republicans and Democrats battled on even terms, with no party enjoying a clear and unquestioned dominance. Presidential elections were close, and landslides nonexistent. Neither major party gained an absolute majority in the four races for the White House from 1880 through 1892. In Congress it was unusual for a single party to control both houses; it happened only four times between 1874 and 1896. Across the nation, most states, even some in the South, were hotly and narrowly contested between 1876 and 1892, with the results pivoting on a party's success or failure in turning out its adherents on election day.[3]

Historians often label the late nineteenth century as an age of dull and uneventful politics. The electorate of the time registered a contrary opinion. Turnout of the eligible white male voters reached levels in presidential and congressional contests that have not been equaled in modern times. When McKinley and Bryan squared off in 1896, more than 78 percent of the voters outside the South cast ballots. Popular participation in other partisan activities did not match the peaks of electoral turnout, but the public's interest in party fortunes between elections was far more intense than in contemporary America. Speeches, rallies, and literature found an audience that avidly followed and digested partisan arguments of great length and elaborate detail. Citizens also participated in the parades, campaign clubs, and military-style organizations that characterized "spectacular politics" in the North. As much as 20 percent of the voting public joined such diverse units as the Blaine and Logan Cadets of the Republicans in 1884 or the Michael C. Murphy Cleveland and Hendricks Legion that the Democrats organized in the first assembly district of New York City in the same year.[4]

---

[3] Richard Jensen, *The Winning of the Midwest: Social and Political Conflict, 1888–1896* (Chicago: University of Chicago Press, 1971), pp. 1–33; Paul Kleppner, "Partisanship and Ethnoreligious Conflict: The Third Electoral System, 1853–1892," in Paul Kleppner et al., *The Evolution of American Electoral Systems* (Westport, Conn.: Greenwood Press, 1981), pp. 113–146.

[4] Howard W. Allen and Jerome Clubb, "Progressive Reform and the Political System," *Pacific Northwest Quarterly*, 65 (1974), 140; Walter Dean Burnham, "The Changing Shape of the American Political Universe," *American Political Science Review*, 59 (1965), 7–28. The discussion of campaign styles is drawn from Michael Edward McGerr, "The Decline of Popular Politics: Political Style and Participation in the North, 1865–1928," doctoral dissertation, Yale University, 1984, pp. 37, 38, 40.

Table 1.1   Percentage of Estimated Eligible Voters in Northern States Who Voted for President, 1896–1916

Year	Percentage
1896	78.3
1900	71.6
1904	64.7
1908	67.9
1912	55.9
1916	59.7

Source: The information in this table is derived from Howard W. Allen and Jerome Clubb, "Progressive Reform and the Political System," *Pacific Northwest Quarterly,* 65 (1974), 140, and is reproduced with permission of the authors.

Strong party loyalty accompanied widespread popular involvement in Gilded Age political affairs. Most voters marked a straight ticket at the polling place. Party organizations provided ballots for their supporters, and ticket-splitting was difficult until the introduction of the Australian ballot. True independents were a small, often scorned, minority of the whole electorate. "Political parties are necessary to popular government," said William McKinley in 1892, "They are the agents of the popular will." Accordingly, it was the duty of party members to take part in the political process, especially during elections. "The man who, having the right to vote, is too lazy or too high-toned to mingle with his fellow citizens at the polls is the merest ape and echo of a citizen," remarked Jonathan P. Dolliver of Iowa during the presidential race of 1884. Criticism of partisan politics persisted and gained strength in the 1890s. For most of the late nineteenth century, however, loyal commitment to a political party was a basic requirement for success in public life.[5]

While agreeing that "The late nineteenth century voting universe was marked by a more complete and intensely party-oriented voting participation among the American electorate than ever before or since," scholars differ over the merits of this political system. Critics contend that the large turnout may have owed

[5] Thomas Richard Ross, *Jonathan Prentiss Dolliver: A Study in Political Integrity and Independence* (Iowa City: State Historical Society of Iowa, 1958), p. 59; *Speeches and Addresses of William McKinley* (New York: Appleton, 1893), p. 574.

something to voting frauds in the city and stuffed ballot boxes in the country. If partisanship was heated, this argument continues, issues were submerged as leaders sought safe positions on controversial matters to avoid upsetting the precarious balance of electoral forces. Politics served as a kind of popular entertainment before the advent of the mass media; spectacle masked an empty ritual of conflict between interchangeable political organizations. Detailed scrutiny of the rituals of spectacular campaigning has revealed their importance as a means of involving the voters in public affairs; it was "a process of communal self-revelation" that "marked the fullest acceptance of partisanship in popular culture."[6]

The performance of the voting public in the Gilded Age has also troubled historians. Recent research has revealed that voters often cast ballots on the basis of religious affiliation or loyalty to an ethnic group. What have been called "ethnocultural" issues—prohibition of alcohol, the closing of businesses on the Sabbath, whether schools should teach only in English or also in the language of immigrant students—were significant influences on electoral behavior. Parochial, localistic tensions frequently overshadowed national economic and social issues. Extensive exercise of the franchise did not bring the concern with class inequities, economic imbalances, and racial injustice usually presumed to follow an informed and involved electorate. Why were the industrial workers, lower-middle-class employees in small businesses, and the farming population unable to grasp their common interest in restraining the power of large corporations to dominate their lives?

To some extent they did. The degree of acquiescence in the existing economic order in the late nineteenth century was not complete. But many Americans still believed that expansion of the nation's wealth was a first priority. They had not yet come to perceive the results of industrialism as a threat, and they found partisan debate over the best means to stimulate economic development relevant and appropriate. The emphasis given to ethnocultural issues was the natural outcome of a situation in which religious views had more direct impact than in twentieth-century America, and in which the intimate social relations in the nation's commu-

---

[6] Burnham, "Changing Shape," 22, first quotation; McGerr, "The Decline of Popular Politics," 59, second quotation, 60, third quotation.

nities brought such questions to the surface repeatedly. It is unfair to indict Americans in this period for failing to view their problems as would historians committed to contemporary assumptions about social values.[7]

Whatever the merits of the Gilded Age political system, it broke down at the end of the 1880s. Politicians noted an easing of partisan fervor and commitment after the presidential election of 1888. A new stress on campaigns of education rather than spectacle accelerated the ebbing of partisanship. After the Republican victory in 1888, the public reaction against GOP legislative proposals such as the McKinley tariff and the Federal Elections bill in 1890, the local efforts of religious moralists in the Midwest, and farm discontent in the South and on the Great Plains produced Democratic successes in the elections of 1890 and 1892. Even as the Democrats verged on a majority status when Grover Cleveland took office in March 1893, a financial panic plunged the nation into four years of acute depression. In the ensuing social turmoil, the Republicans and the farmer-based People's party competed for the votes of those unhappy with Democratic rule. Despite some victories in Dixie and the Far West, the Populists were not able to establish themselves as a major national party. In the congressional elections of 1894 the Republicans made sweeping gains in Democratic areas, built a solid majority in the House of Representatives, and laid the basis for a dominance that would persist for four decades.[8]

Two years later the contest between McKinley and Bryan put the emerging Republican ascendancy to an exacting test. Winning the Democratic nomination with support from the South and West, and nominated also by the Populists, Bryan launched a vigorous personal campaign for the White House on a platform devoted to achieving the free and unlimited coinage of silver. This inflationary solution to the farmers' problem of debt and low commodity prices won "The Boy Orator of the Platte" wide popularity among the agrarian population, which had experienced the heavy burden of four years of slump. To his economic program, Bryan added a charismatic oratorical style and an ability to articulate the moral values of evangelical, Protestant America. He was a formidable candidate

[7] Geoffrey Blodgett, "A New Look at the American Gilded Age," *Historical Reflections*, 1 (1974), 234–235, makes this point with force and perception.

[8] R. Hal Williams, *Years of Decision: American Politics in the 1890s* (New York: Wiley, 1978), is the best single volume on the political events of the decade.

and, in the two months after his nomination in July, he looked like a winner.[9]

The Republicans had selected their most popular figure, William McKinley, and intended to play down the monetary question in favor of the unifying theme of a protective tariff. With a platform that endorsed the gold standard and an opponent committed to silver, McKinley became the champion of "sound money." As the Bryan enthusiasm surged in late summer, McKinley and his campaign manager, Marcus A. Hanna, prepared a counterattack. Equipped with ample campaign funds from a business community frightened of Bryan, the Republicans poured out literature that stressed the dangers of a free silver policy and proclaimed the virtues of the tariff. McKinley did not attempt to match Bryan's extensive tour of the country; instead, three-quarters of a million people heard his effective speeches from the GOP candidate's front porch in Canton, Ohio. Where Bryan was openly critical of residents of the Northeast and appeared to exclude nonrural and nonagrarian elements from his appeal, McKinley was more pluralistic and inclusive in his remarks. Other Republicans, terrified of Bryan's "radicalism," were much less tolerant, but the prevailing tone of the party's effort underscored the economic interdependence of the nation. By November, there was little surprise at McKinley's triumph.[10]

On its face, the result in 1896 was not a decisive Republican success or a landslide by modern standards. McKinley's margin in the electoral college was 271 to 176, and his majority was 600,000 ballots out of more than 14,000,000 cast. But the popular vote difference between the two candidates was the largest in a presidential election since Ulysses S. Grant's defeat of Horace Greeley in 1872. More important, the effects of this contest persisted in a fashion that historians and political scientists have described as the System of 1896, calling it "the most enduringly sectional political alignment in American history."[11] The crucial elements of this new political order were a South that was solidly Democratic and in

[9] Stanley L. Jones, *The Presidential Election of 1896* (Madison: University of Wisconsin Press, 1964), provides the most thorough coverage of the election.

[10] Jensen, *Winning of the Midwest*, pp. 283–296.

[11] Burnham, "Changing Shape," p. 25; E. E. Schattschneider, *The Semi-Sovereign People: A Realist's View of Democracy in America* (New York: Holt, Rinehart and Winston, 1960), pp. 78–96.

which interparty competition had been reduced to near the van-
ishing point, a heavily Republican bloc of states in the North and
Midwest with a much diminished Democratic strength, and a
smaller residue of other states where real partisan warfare still
continued.

This arrangement lasted until the upheaval of the Great Depression and the New Deal. A number of important characteristics
distinguished it from the political system that had preceded it. As
the two parties became less competitive across the nation, the emphasis shifted to intraparty strife in the selection of candidates. The
rise of the direct primary probably owed as much to the enhanced
significance of party nominations in determining who held office as
to a desire to involve citizens generally in the nominating process.
Voter turnout declined dramatically from Gilded Age highs as the
electorate withdrew its interest from partisan affairs. The fall in
turnout ranged from 10 to 15 percent of the eligible voters in the
first fifteen years of the new century. Independent voting became
more common, party loyalties became less intense, and a volatile
electorate made landslides a familiar part of the political landscape. In a period usually assumed to have fostered the expansion
of popular participation in political life, the exact opposite seems
to have occurred.[12]

In the System of 1896, the Republicans dominated. Their successes in the 1890s made them a choice of the majority of the
voters, creating allegiances that were not undercut until after 1929.
In eighteen states, having about 190 electoral votes, the Republicans were clearly ascendant between 1896 and 1930. During the
same period, the GOP had an edge in ten of the eighteen states
"characterized by active party competition," and these added another 115 votes to the party's potential base in the electoral college. In Congress, Republicans had solid majorities in the House of
Representatives between 1894 and 1910; only their own divisions
gave the Democrats an opening after 1910. From 1898 onward the
Senate was close to two-thirds Republican over the next dozen
years. Such preeminence was not undisputed. Though a few states
gave the GOP dependable, overwhelming majorities comparable to
what the Democrats received in the South, Republican "domi-

[12] Burnham, "Changing Shape," p. 10; Allen and Clubb, "Progressive Reform
and the Political System," pp. 139–145.

nance was almost always under internal attack and was shattered in 1912 by dissidence within the party itself."[13]

The election of 1896 and its consequences left the Democrats confined to their basic electoral foundation in the South. In twelve states of the Confederacy, and after 1912 in Arizona, the Democrats could count on about 125 electoral votes between 1896 and 1930; in the competitive states the party usually prevailed in eight border and western states with some 60 votes. The South furnished nearly 86 percent of all the electoral votes the Democrats won in the thirty-two years following 1896, and most of the party's congressional strength in both houses came from Dixie as the century turned. Outside the South, Democrats depended primarily on urban machines in northern cities as the principal source of votes. As long as the Republicans remained cohesive after 1896, their electoral advantages as a national party with a diversified appeal to a wide array of voters outweighed the Democrats' virtual monopoly of the South and subordinate status in other areas of the country.[14]

The problems of the Democrats as the election of 1900 approached reflected the difficulties the party would face for the next thirty years. Conservatives, who had followed Grover Cleveland for a dozen years after 1884, viewed the rise of Bryan and his disciples with continuing unhappiness and dismay. "I cannot see my great party in the hands of charlatans and put to the ignoble use of aiding personal ambition, without positive grief," Cleveland wrote in April 1900. This faction, concentrated in the Northeast, wanted a renunciation of the bimetallic, rural-oriented, sometimes anti-business proposals that Bryan put forward, but knew they were powerless to prevent a renomination of the 1896 standard bearer. Hopeful that the party would return to the creed of limited government and economic orthodoxy, the Democratic right wing intended to negotiate 1900 as smoothly as possible and strike to regain control in 1904.[15]

More practical and less principled, urban Democrats looked to

[13] Paul T. David, *Party Strength in the United States, 1872–1970* (Charlottesville: University Press of Virginia, 1972), pp. 34–39.

[14] Ibid., p. 36.

[15] Grover Cleveland to Charles S. Fairchild, April 12, 1900, in Allan Nevins, ed., *Letters of Grover Cleveland, 1850–1908* (Boston: Houghton Mifflin, 1933), p. 529.

the campaign with their gazes firmly fixed on the main chance. Their machines in cities such as New York, Boston, and Chicago depended on the votes of the Irish and other ethnic groups of recent immigrants who found Republican moralism distasteful and the machine organization's provision of rudimentary social services welcome. Easing the lot of constituents was not the machine's essential function; exploitation of the opportunities for legal and illegal profit from the needs of the expanding cities for sewers, electric lights, and transportation came first. However subsidiary the purpose of assisting the urban populace, the ability of such bosses as Richard Croker and Charles Murphy to supply these services gave them an electoral power that national party leaders could not ignore. As time went on, moreover, the interaction between urban conditions and the ambitions and concerns of younger machine politicians stimulated these aspiring leaders to sponsor social justice legislation to alleviate the situation of their constituents.[16]

The main core of the Democracy's strength in 1900, however, lay south of the Mason-Dixon line. After a generation of spirited Populist and Republican challenges, southern Democrats, primarily from areas of high black population, had repelled the attacks on their supremacy and had created a sectional bastion of one-party politics. This result was deliberate. Democrats used the poll tax, the white primary, restrictive legislation on voting, and violence to constrict the black vote and throttle their partisan opposition. Disenfranchisement and the tightening of the one-party system reduced the eligible electorate to virtually no blacks and to only one-half of the white population in the South, and caused an average fall in voter turnout of 37 percent. Among Democrats, there was disagreement about economic questions such as railroad regulation or corporate power, but an unbreakable consensus existed that the region's politics was for whites only.[17]

Leading the divided forces of the Democracy into the election

[16] John J. Broesamle, "The Democrats from Bryan to Wilson," in Lewis L. Gould, ed., *The Progressive Era* (Syracuse, N.Y.: Syracuse University Press, 1974), pp. 87–88.

[17] J. Morgan Kousser, *The Shaping of Southern Politics: Suffrage Restriction and the Establishment of the One-Party South, 1880–1910* (New Haven, Conn.: Yale University Press, 1974), pp. 224–237; Dewey W. Grantham, *Southern Progressivism: The Reconciliation of Progress and Tradition* (Knoxville: The University of Tennessee Press, 1984), pp. 36–107.

William Jennings Bryan
(1860–1925), circa 1906.
Photograph from *The World's
Work*, August 1906.

of 1900 was the party's preeminent national figure, William Jennings Bryan. Forty years old when he made his second run at the White House, "The Great Commoner," as he liked to be called, still showed traces, amid growing stoutness, of the slim, boyish orator who had entranced the delegates in 1896. A native of Illinois, he had absorbed the evangelical Protestantism of the middle border before launching a political career in Nebraska in the late 1880s. In his prime, Bryan was a compelling leader whose melodious voice and invigorating presence added excitement to his message of uplift and economic reform.[18]

Bryan's appeal fused traditional Democratic doctrines, a nostalgia for the disappearing America where rural values had prevailed, and a deep suspicion about industrialism and its effect on society. From Jeffersonian antecedents he derived his belief that virtue reposed in men and women who were close to the land; from Jacksonian precedents he drew an unhappiness with monopoly and a faith in the spoils system. As a critic, Bryan had a sharp eye for social evils and located sensitive spots in the new industrial order

[18] Louis W. Koenig, *Bryan: A Political Biography of William Jennings Bryan* (New York: Putnam, 1971), pp. 9–317, is the best study of Bryan's rise.

with practiced accuracy. His solutions for these genuine problems were less sophisticated, as his advocacy of free silver, government ownership of the interstate railroads, and arbitration of international disputes suggested. There was merit in the opinion of the British ambassador in 1914 that Bryan was "like a horrid mass of jellified sentimentality from which a sharp beak occasionally pokes out and snaps."[19]

Bryan spent his adult life as a professional politician, but his career is only occasionally appraised in the context of his primary activity. His assets in that role were obvious. He expressed the anxieties and emotions of rural, Protestant America with a sure touch. Loving the campaign trail, he used the Chautauqua lecture circuit in years when no elections beckoned. Newspapers found him good copy. He had always ready a statement on the events of the day or the future of his party. Bryan was the central figure among the Democrats for a decade and a half, and a significant force for a dozen years after 1912. No national convention from 1896 to 1924, no party program, no presidential aspirant could ignore Bryan's opinion or undervalue his approval.

Successful as a spokesman, Bryan was less adept as a party leader. He could be stubborn, as in his loyalty to free silver long after the issue lost its potency. He was also "an opportunistic crusader" who took up and discarded men and issues as the situation demanded.[20] Bryan's mind was a blunt instrument. Sensitive to the felt needs of his supporters, he never understood the East, urban problems, or the concerns of labor. He rarely engaged social problems with any subtlety, and remained faithful during his long career to the body of ideas he possessed when he first gained national notoriety. On balance, his influence on the party was constructive, but though he could lead the Democrats to the polls, he could not bring them either victory or a program with which to govern. "Bryan," concluded an angry Democrat in 1908, "is an ignorant man. You need in the White House a good brain, and you don't need a mouth. Bryan is a mouth."[21]

In the last quarter of the nineteenth century, the Democrats

---

[19] Arthur Willert to Geoffrey Robinson [Dawson], March 10, 1914, Archives of *The Times*, London.

[20] Charles Willis Thompson, *Presidents I've Known and Two Near Presidents* (Indianapolis: Bobbs-Merrill, 1929), p. 43.

[21] Koenig, *Bryan*, p. 431.

had used their doctrines of localism, negative government, and opposition to Republican moralistic programs to maintain a national following of impressive proportions. The disasters of the 1890s had discredited the leadership of the party's conservative wing and drastically reduced the size of the Democratic coalition. Defeat had not, however, produced agreement on the course to follow toward eroding the enemy's majority. "I can see nothing in the Republican victory," wrote a Bryan follower in February 1901, "to impel the Democracy to abandon its forward movement and tie itself slavishly to the limited social programme which a strict construction of the Constitution fixes." Opponents of Bryan, on the other hand, argued that the party had to "reestablish a reputation for conservatism, and not be known as a house of refuge for all radicals."[22]

Resolving this difference of opinion occupied the Democratic party for much of the next two decades. The problems were sizable. The party was deficient in votes, leadership, and programs. What it did have in abundance was flexibility. It could attack, oppose, and wait for its opportunity. Committed to no fixed set of principles, not required to govern, the Democrats could explore new ideas, nurture fresh leaders, and hope for the Republicans to err and perhaps divide. The early twentieth century would test Mr. Dooley's opinion that the party "'Tis niver so good as whin 'tis broke, whin rayspictable people speak iv it in whispers, an' whin it has no leaders an' on'y wan principal, to go on an' take it away fr'm th' other fellows."[23]

Republicans entered the campaign of 1900 united and cohesive. A visitor to their national convention found "a combination of political self-assurance and general altruism" among the delegates. "Business is certainly the dominant note in America this day, and far from being ashamed, these Republicans gloried in it."[24] In the four years after the election of 1896 the GOP had strengthened its hold on the voters who had chosen McKinley over Bryan. Although

[22] Willis J. Abbot, "The Lessons of the Election—A Rejoinder," *The Forum*, 30 (1901), 679; "Future of the Democratic Party," *The Literary Digest*, 21 (1900), 574.

[23] Finley Peter Dunne, *Mr. Dooley's Opinions* (New York: Harper & Bros., 1906), pp. 97–98.

[24] Walter Wellman, "The Kansas City Convention," *American Monthly Review of Reviews*, 27 (1900), 176–177.

the Democrats had a highly visible presence in northern cities such as New York and Boston, the Republicans, across the nation, had more imposing claims as the party of urban America. From 1892 through 1928 the Democratic vote in the ten largest cities of the country never surpassed 50 percent. But Republican dominance did not depend on supremacy among a few key voting blocs in the population. Among farmers, urban workers, middle-class entrepreneurs and professionals, and most religious and ethnic groups, with the exception of the Irish, the GOP enjoyed wide and persisting support. Under the leadership first of William McKinley, and then of Theodore Roosevelt, the Republicans constructed a majority coalition comparable to the achievement of Franklin D. Roosevelt in the 1930s.

The key elements in the Republican appeal were the memories of Democratic failure in the 1890s, the accomplishments associated with an active government promoting economic expansion, and a pluralistic posture toward the diverse ethnocultural components of white America. Just as the Democrats ran against Herbert Hoover in the 1930s, Republicans invoked the legacy of Grover Cleveland and hard times in elections after 1896. More positive was the GOP's endorsement of the use of governmental power to encourage enterprise and to diffuse economic benefits among the population. Where Democrats emphasized the autonomous individual in his role as consumer, Republicans depicted society as a web of interconnected producers who all gained from employment and prosperity. Finally, party spokesmen played down the party's earlier commitment to a crusading, heavily Protestant moralism, and adopted on these sensitive social issues a more tolerant and inclusive position. "The living present is ours," Henry Cabot Lodge told the national convention in 1900, "the present of prosperity and activity in business, of good wages and quick payments, of labor employed and capital invested, of sunshine in the market place and the stir of abounding life in the workshop and on the farm."[25]

The uncontested chief of the Republicans in 1900 was President William McKinley. As president and political leader, McKinley has never emerged from the shadow of Theodore Roosevelt. Yet it is impossible to grasp the course of American politics in the Progressive era unless McKinley's impact is clearly revealed. The

[25] *Official Proceedings of the Twelfth Republican National Convention, 1900* (Philadelphia: Press of Dunlap Printing, 1900), p. 86.

president was fifty-seven in 1900, and had reached the White House after a long career in the House of Representatives and two terms as governor of Ohio. Reticent and self-controlled, he left no large body of personal letters as clues to his motives and actions. His inability to prevent the Spanish-American War and his association with subsequent American imperialism incorrectly persuaded several generations of historians that he was a weak executive, a timid politician, and an unappealing personality.

Recent examination of McKinley's career has overturned these erroneous stereotypes. McKinley was the first modern president. He was the major architect of Republican success from 1894 onward; his diplomacy possessed ample amounts of skill and courage; he enhanced and broadened the powers of his office. Few presidents have enjoyed closer relations with Congress or had a greater ability to achieve their legislative goals. His foreign policy laid down the large initiatives that Roosevelt later consolidated. Deferential to the popular will in his speeches, McKinley used his public appearances, messages, and the press to shape the attitudes of the voters in the directions he wished. "He seems," wrote a French diplomat in 1901, "to possess a particularly sensitive eye for the movements of public opinion and the art of foreseeing and translating popular views before they have found their definite form."[26]

McKinley's political creed was more comforting than challenging, and did not travel well into the next century. His emphasis on sectional reconciliation found receptive audiences North and South, but took scant account of the black citizens who would be the victims of racial harmony. Though the president sensed the growing anxiety about the trusts and anticipated Roosevelt's program of publicity and legislative action, he did not place the problem of business consolidation in a moral context or give it greater weight than the maintenance of economic prosperity. More prone to pursue policies through an accumulation of small steps that collectively formed a pattern of action than to proclaim grand departures in ringing tones, William McKinley came to seem passive and pallid beside his robust successor. But Roosevelt's exuberant presidential style should not obscure how much his accomplishments

---

[26] M. de Margerie to Theophile Delcasse, September 9, 1901, Consular and Commercial Correspondence, Washington, Archives of the French Ministry of Foreign Affairs, Paris; Lewis L. Gould, *The Presidency of William McKinley* (Lawrence: Regents Press of Kansas, 1980).

owed to McKinley's efforts in shaping the presidency to meet the demands of the new century.

In the heat of an election campaign, few Republicans bothered to ponder the direction and thrust of the party. For Albert Shaw, editor of the influential magazine *The Review of Reviews*, the national convention provoked disquieting thoughts. "The Republican party was never outwardly so harmonious as it is now since it was organized half a century ago," he wrote an English friend, "and, apparently, it was never as strong as it is now. But it is a little too fat and sleek and prosperous, and its moral tone is not quite what it ought to be. It looks back with pride, rather than forward with aspiration."[27] Shaw's qualms reflected a genuine dilemma for the GOP. How did a political organization prevent its endorsement of economic enterprise from becoming simply support for business in its consolidated form? It was one thing to advocate a protective tariff to promote industrial growth and offset a Democratic depression. It was something else to perpetuate high duties when times were good, American industries were expanding and profitable, and consumers were restive about rising prices.

Since its creation, the GOP had been able to advocate policies, like the tariff, that employed the power of government to stimulate economic expansion. That commitment had made the Republicans the party of change, in contrast to the restrictiveness of the Democrats. With an industrial society now an accomplished fact, the issue of whether the government could regulate the economy to mitigate the effects of industrialism would confront Republicans with a new issue framed in a fresh context. "The Republican party may suffer innocently from a bad name," noted a journalist, "but I do not believe that one voter in ten in the United States honestly thinks that, if continued in power, it will wage successful war upon the trusts." It would not be easy to reconcile proposals to limit trust power or to curb business excesses with Senator Hanna's conviction "that a man had a right to do what he pleased with his own."[28]

Republican triumphs in the 1890s also bred conditions in which

[27] Albert Shaw to W. T. Stead, June 25, 1900, Albert Shaw Papers, New York Public Library, Astor, Lenox, and Tilden Foundations.
[28] Marcus A. Hanna to William E. Chandler, March 25, 1899, William E. Chandler Papers, Manuscript Division, Library of Congress; Henry L. West, "The Republican and Democratic Platforms Compared," *The Forum*, 30 (1900), 93.

factionalism flourished. In many states the general election became almost a foregone conclusion, and the real struggle turned on winning the GOP nomination. Younger party members, dissatisfied economic interests, and reform-minded Republicans chafed under arrangements that decided nominations in advance in caucuses where senior men dominated and debate was futile. "Under our system of party government," wrote Robert M. La Follette of Wisconsin in 1901, "the selection of the candidate is the vital question," and accordingly, the end of the caucus system was "decreed by the enlightened moral sentiment of the entire country." In Wisconsin, La Follette emerged as the leader of rebellious Republicans against the existing party organization between 1894 and 1901; in Iowa, Albert B. Cummins led a similar movement, and in Kansas, a Boss Busters League challenged the party hierarchy. Intraparty warfare was not new to the Republicans, but these groups had a moral emphasis that, in the minds of their sponsors, carried them beyond simple ambition into principle. Reconciling rectitude with party loyalty would, as events proved, be difficult for men who found less and less to admire in the Republican conviction that "no man is essential" to the party's success.[29]

At the end of the 1900 race, a midwestern editor, seeking an explanation for the quiet contest, concluded: "No clearly defined issue has been presented to the people, and it is already to be seen that the result of the election is not to be a test of sentiment on any one or more of the issues."[30] The three questions on which the campaign focused were the free coinage of silver, imperialism, and the trust problem. Silver was a hangover from 1896, and owed its place to Bryan's insistence that it be discussed. Better economic conditions, gold discoveries in the Yukon and South Africa, and the passage of the Gold Standard Act in 1900 had drawn off the emotions the monetary issue had stirred earlier. Nonetheless, Bryan compelled the Democrats to give it prominence and stressed it in his speeches. The Republicans responded by warning that "The menace of 16 to 1, therefore, still hangs over us with all its dire consequences to credit and confidence, business and activity."

[29] Ellen Torelle, comp., *The Political Philosophy of Robert M. La Follette* (Madison, Wis.: The Robert M. La Follette Co., 1920), pp. 39, 40; Jesse Macy, *Party Organization and Machinery* (New York: The Century Co., 1912), p. 258.

[30] Des Moines *Leader*, October 28, 1900.

With McKinley's victory, silver disappeared from the national agenda and went into the limbo of forgotten controversies.[31] Imperialism was a fresh addition to American presidential elections in 1900, and passions ran high over whether the nation's overseas expansion should be endorsed or repudiated. Bryan devoted his acceptance speech almost solely to an assault on Republican policy in the Philippines. "Better a thousand times that our flag in the Orient give way to a flag representing the idea of self-government than that the flag of this republic should become the flag of an empire." For his part McKinley rejected a "scuttle policy" and told his notification committee: "The Philippines are ours and American authority must be supreme throughout the archipelago."[32]

In fact, less distance separated the two candidates on this foreign policy question than their language indicated. After his spirited denunciation of what had occurred in the Philippines, Bryan proposed, if elected, to call a special session of Congress that would declare a national goal of providing "a stable form of government" in the islands, then to give them independence, and finally to set up an American protectorate for the new nation. Critics quickly noted that supplying a "stable" government and maintaining a protectorate resembled what the Republicans were doing, with the complication of Philippine independence. Bryan's program did not satisfy the more ardent opponents of the Philippine policy, such as the Anti-Imperialist League, and seemed to many voters less plausible than the course the government was already pursuing overseas.[33]

Imperialism did not survive the 1900 election as a major issue in American politics. Over the next decade the results of expansion continued to furnish sources of controversy such as tariff reciprocity with Cuba or the Panama Canal, but the essential accomplishments growing out of the Spanish-American War won popular endorsement. Because of the efforts of the opponents of imperialism, especially with regard to the conduct of the war in the Philippines, as well as the sense of restraint within the McKinley and

[31] *Republican Campaign Textbook, 1900* (Philadelphia: Press of Dunlap Printing, 1900), p. 438.

[32] Ibid., p. 439, McKinley quotation: *National Democratic Campaign Book Presidential Election 1900* (Washington, D.C.: Globe Printing Co., 1900), p. 30.

[33] *National Democratic Campaign Book*, p. 31; "The Progress of the World," *American Monthly Review of Reviews*, 22 (1900), 262–268.

Roosevelt administrations, there was also little disposition to go beyond what had taken place between 1898 and 1901. For the next decade the American public was not compelled to face the responsibilities of world power that increasingly troubled national leaders like Roosevelt, and could devote its political attention to questions of domestic reform.

In mid-September Bryan shifted his focus from imperialism to the trusts. He told a crowd in Kansas that "The Republican party to-day stands sponsor at the cradle of more trusts than ever sprang into existence before."[34] Though Republicans replied that Bryan was threatening the continuance of prosperity and that their party would take appropriate action against combinations, the Democratic candidate had touched a sensitive nerve of the GOP. By 1900 the spread of industrial consolidation had received elaborate attention in the press and popular magazines. Conferences, speeches, and a government inquiry produced evidence about a wave of corporate mergers that began in 1895. Businesses were being absorbed into larger companies at a rate of nearly 300 a year in the decade 1895 to 1905; in 1899, the peak year of the process, more than 1,200 companies became part of expanded enterprises.

For the Democrats, the Republican record on the trusts made a tempting target. "The Republicans have had the President and the Senate and the House, and the Republican president has been in power for three years," said Bryan, "and as yet he has never made one specific suggestion looking toward the destruction of the trusts." Democratic proposals included "more stringent" laws to publicize corporate affairs, and the enforcement of existing antitrust statutes. To Republican pleas that court decisions called into question the power of Congress to act, Democrats replied that the interstate commerce clause should be brought to bear on combinations. The GOP blunted the Democratic offensive with attacks on the record of Grover Cleveland and his administration in enforcing the Sherman Antitrust Act of 1890, and criticism of the Ice Trust, whose organizers in New York City included prominent Tammany Hall Democrats. "Wild and frantic denunciations" like Bryan's, contended Theodore Roosevelt, did not hurt the trusts, but "simply

---

[34] *Washington Post*, September 19, 1900; "Size of the Trust Problem," *The Literary Digest*, 18 (1899), 359–360.

postpones the day when we can make them amenable to proper laws."[35]

Because of their growing identification with the business community and their hold on the national government, the Republicans found the trust issue a source of mounting concern during the McKinley administration. "It is untrue that the republican party stands as the godfather of combination," wrote a troubled midwestern party member in 1898, "but it is perhaps distracting that the longest steps in this direction have been accomplished during republican administrations."[36] The president criticized combinations in his first inaugural address, but the Justice Department did not take serious steps against mergers in the succeeding four years. By 1899 McKinley was sufficiently aware of the problem to seek congressional action in his annual message, and Republicans unsuccessfully offered a constitutional amendment in the House of Representatives to "give Congress power to regulate trusts" in June 1900. The same month the party's platform favored "such legislation as will effectively restrain and prevent the abuse of corporate combinations." Republican literature made the most of these relatively modest steps, but party orators in 1900 preferred to stress prosperity and mute the trust question. "Let the American people have the good sense," said Theodore Roosevelt, "to keep in office the man under whose administration we have accomplished our present prosperity."[37]

Beyond its direct impact on the GOP, the trust issue had dangerous implications for the basic foundation of Republican policy, the protective tariff. The Dingley Tariff of 1897 had raised customs duties, and critics associated the spread of mergers with the higher rates. As consumer prices began to rise, there was evident discontent when trusts sold goods abroad at lower prices than Americans paid in the domestic market. "Tariff laws should be amended," declared the Democratic platform, "by putting the products of trusts

[35] *Washington Post,* September 19, 1900; *National Democratic Campaign Book,* p. 6; *Republican Campaign Textbook,* pp. 113–114; *The Works of Theodore Roosevelt: Campaigns and Controversies,* 20 vols. (New York: Scribner, 1926), XIV, p. 348.

[36] C. E. Faulkner to Joseph L. Bristow, January 17, 1898, Joseph L. Bristow Papers, Kansas State Historical Society, Topeka.

[37] Des Moines *Leader,* September 8, 1900; *Republican Campaign Textbook,* pp. 112–113, 422.

upon the free list to prevent monopoly under the plea of protec-tion."[38] In meeting these attacks, the Republicans had several choices. They could do nothing, or as Hanna put it, "let well enough alone," and leave the tariff untouched. Or the party could revise downward, a course that involved repudiation of the Dingley Act, a bitter congressional fight, and no guarantee of a satisfactory result.

William McKinley found both options unpalatable. He sought to remove the sting from the tariff issue through reciprocity treaties with foreign competitors to lower rates on selected products in a controlled, gradual manner. This method preserved the structure of the protective system, avoided a wholesale party debate on revi-sion, and joined the tariff changes to the expansion of American markets. In 1899 and 1900 the administration negotiated pacts with Argentina, France, and several other nations, and laid them before the Senate. They were not taken up in 1900, and McKinley pre-pared to push them after his second term began.

The president's strategy on the trust issue was thus two-pronged. To meet the appeals for direct action, he supported ini-tiatives to bring greater publicity about the affairs of large cor-porations and, like Roosevelt, distinguished between trusts and combinations whose economic practices and results were "good" and those whose methods and impact were "bad." At the same time, he did not ignore his party's vulnerability on the tariff. If Re-publicans criticized trusts, they would need a response to the charge that protection promoted combination. Reciprocity pro-vided precisely that kind of answer. By the end of 1900 it was evi-dent that the party needed a coherent program on the trusts. As an associate informed a prominent midwestern senator: "Some thing more has got to be done to restrain them than has been done within the past four years, or the Republican party's hide will be on the fence again as sure as you live."[39]

In the second McKinley-Bryan encounter, the Republicans eas-ily overcame the burdens of the trust issue and rode to victory on voter satisfaction with prosperity and the party's record since 1896.

[38] *National Democratic Campaign Book*, p. 6; "Mr. Havemeyer, the Tariff, and the Trusts," *The Literary Digest*, 18 (1899), 720–721.

[39] George Tichenor to William Boyd Allison, December 14, 1900, Box 341, Wil-liam Boyd Allison Papers, Iowa State Department of History and Archives, Des Moines.

McKinley won 292 electoral votes to Bryan's 155, received 51.7 percent of the vote to his opponent's 45.5 percent, and increased his 1896 majority by nearly 200,000 votes. The turnout, however, fell off almost 7 percent to 71.6 percent; 1900 was the last time the turnout figure in the North exceeded 70 percent of the eligible electorate. The GOP began McKinley's second term with a 46-seat margin in the House and a comfortable 24-seat bulge in the Senate. "If we use our power in a sensible and conservative manner," observed Senator Charles Warren Fairbanks of Indiana, "we shall be able to maintain our supremacy for years to come."[40]

The relative calm that marked the election of 1900 and the early months of McKinley's second term was illusory. Beneath the placid surface of the political scene were forces that made the period 1900 to 1916 as eventful as the 1890s had been. With the approach of the new century, the 76 million Americans had good reason to celebrate the nation's material prosperity. After twenty-five years of falling prices and hard times, economic well-being had reappeared after 1897, and the Republicans ran hard in 1900 on the record of high employment, humming factories, and resurgent agriculture. The indices of a later generation underlined the rosy picture. National income stood at $17 billion in 1900, up from $7 billion thirty years earlier; the average per capita income of $227 was the highest in the world. Inventions and technological developments promised more abundance for all citizens, as the 1 million telephones in homes and 4,000 new automobiles on the road indicated. "Circumstances—education, the claims upon vitality, the natural pride of a self-governing people," wrote a British visitor in 1904, "have raised the standard of American life to a height hitherto unrealized in civilized society."[41]

For many Americans in 1900, however, wealth and income offered inadequate guides to the true state of the nation's condition. Writing well before the election of 1900, the journalist Ray Stannard Baker warned: "We can feed ourselves, we are great and powerful; but we have our own galling Negro problem, our rotten machine politics, our legislative bribery, our municipal corruption, our giant monopolies, our aristocracy of mere riches, any one of

---

[40] Charles Warren Fairbanks to T. S. Browning, November 19, 1900, Charles Warren Fairbanks Papers, Indiana State Historical Society Library, Indianapolis.

[41] Archibald R. Colquhoun, *Greater America* (New York: Harper & Bros., 1904), p. 34.

which is a rock on which the ship of state, unless skillfully navigated, may go to its destruction."[42] Baker's words captured the mood of foreboding in middle-class Americans that lay behind the apparent optimism and confidence that greeted the twentieth century. While the depression of the nineties reshaped electoral alignments, it also altered attitudes toward social problems, the range of government power, and the proper role of the political party.

Partisan politics between 1900 and 1916 took place in an "age of reform" whose essential character remains a subject of intense debate. The issues that dominated the public dialogue of the period, however, grew out of the preceding decade and are more easily defined. The 1890s were a time of sharp economic conflict and political unrest. Labor disputes such as the Homestead Strike of 1892 and the Pullman Strike of 1894 led many middle-class citizens to see the dark shapes of proletarian revolution and socialism on the horizon. Organized labor, embodied primarily in the American Federation of Labor, was growing; the A.F. of L. had more than a million and a half members by 1904. What should government do when capital and labor faced off in a strike? Meanwhile, millions of unskilled and unorganized workers, many of them women and young children, labored long hours for six or seven days a week in dangerous workplaces. Should society remain deaf to "the bitter cry of the children," or should it wield the power of the state to pursue health and economic justice for the poor and helpless?[43]

If organized labor represented a collective force that challenged older values of individualism and self-reliance, the business corporation, growing in size and power, was equally worrying. Its consolidation into trusts and holding companies seemed to imperil the opportunity and livelihood of small entrepreneurs. Where major businesses at the end of the Civil War might employ several hundred workers, single railroads as the 1890s began had more than 100,000 men on their payrolls. United States Steel came into existence in 1901 as the first billion-dollar American corporation.[44] Linked to politics through campaign contributions and other corrupting influences, businesses, Americans increasingly believed by

---

[42] Ray Stannard Baker, *American Chronicle* (New York: Scribner, 1945), p. 90.

[43] John Spargo, *The Bitter Cry of the Children* (New York: Quadrangle Books, 1968 edition).

[44] Thomas K. McCraw, "Business & Government: The Origins of the Adversary Relationship," *California Management Review*, 26 (1984), 42.

1900, sought profit at the expense of the consumer and the competitor. One of the key elements of the early Progressive coalition were residents of such cities as Chicago and Milwaukee who banded together to protest inadequate public services and unjust taxation that flowed, in their opinion, from corruption and favoritism toward public utilities and other corporations by urban governments.

A general sense of questioning and reappraisal pervaded America as the old century closed. The rapid rise and decline of Populism revealed a volatility and discontent in the South and West that emphasized an apparent instability in the nation's institutions. These fears lingered even after agrarian unrest ebbed. The successes of the war with Spain prompted further apprehension about the future. Did imperial adventures and wars in the Caribbean and Philippines undermine democratic ideals at home? Could a nation rule subject peoples and remain self-governing? Most of all, there was the larger issue of coming to terms with an industrial society. Were class warfare, a loss of autonomy, and the dominance of great corporations inescapable results of the material bounty of industrialization?

In shaping answers to these issues, Americans retained and worked within the existing political structures. It is thus true that reform in the early twentieth century "did not stimulate and was not caused by an outpouring of mass support or by a sharp and lasting reorientation of popular partisan attitudes." Progressivism, as it came to be known, was a series of campaigns of political leaders within the cities, the states, and the nation to formulate new policies and create new procedures for making decisions on public questions. While it primarily occurred "within the framework of existing political practices and patterns," it did compel party leaders to reexamine the premises of their programs.[45]

The dominant policy question of the late nineteenth century had been how best to promote the growth of an industrial economy and to distribute its benefits. By 1900, groups in the business community and the society at large were asking government to regulate the workings of the economy to achieve equity as between competing forces or to pursue a more just allocation of benefits and resources. In the Midwest, for example, merchants and shippers

---

[45] Allen and Clubb, "Progressive Reform and the Political System," p. 145.

sought to have the Interstate Commerce Commission influence railroad rate-making to keep transportation costs low and to reduce the perceived advantages of rival companies in the East and Far West. Faced with higher prices, consumers wanted government to restrain the power of the meat packers, or Beef Trust, in the interest of lower food costs.

Interest groups, newly conscious of their identity, also asked for government action on all levels. Advocates of the prohibition of alcohol, especially the recently organized Anti-Saloon League, wished to see the liquor traffic curbed and in the long run abolished. Feminists wanted votes for women, both on the merits as a democratic idea and also to expand the constituency for other reforms such as prohibition and social justice. Farmers forsook the mass appeal of Populism and targeted specific legislative initiatives—railroad regulation, banking reform, and agricultural subsidies. Particular issues called forth a corresponding lobbying group to push the campaign in legislatures and on Capitol Hill. The National Child Labor Committee, created in 1904, grew out of campaigns in the South that depicted cotton mill communities where young boys and girls worked as "the poorest place in the world for training the citizens of a democracy." Eventually the NCLC worked for a national law or constitutional amendment to remove teenagers and children from mills and factories. Reflecting this newer attitude, a Texas progressive wrote that governments were created "for the protection of the weak against the encroachments of the strong."[46]

Reformers believed government should do more; they wanted political parties to have less to do with government. The Gilded Age had been a high point of partisanship. By 1900 attacks on party feeling from liberal reformers, combined with the emphasis on educational campaigns, ended the devotion to party organizations as newspapers, advertising, and pamphlets superseded spectacles and marches. "The people have grown tired of the same campaign speeches, a repetition of bonfires, noise of the anvil and fireworks and all that went to awaken enthusiasm," wrote a California reporter in 1900. The political party once again came under critical scrutiny as a perceived obstacle to sound government. Partisanship

[46] Grantham, *Southern Progressivism*, p. 192; Lewis L. Gould, *Progressives and Prohibitionists: Texas Democrats in the Wilson Era* (Austin: University of Texas Press, 1973), p. 26.

The direct primary impresses the political boss. Cartoon from the
Cleveland *Dispatch*, as printed in the *American Monthly Review of
Reviews*, July 1912.

itself became a term of derision and scorn. Where the independent
voter was a derided outcast in the 1880s, he was the example to be
followed twenty-five years later.[47]

So much of the reform impulse involved an assault on party
power. "The political party which is strongly intrenched in
power," said Robert La Follette, "behind a blind partisan majority,
scorns public opinion and claims its share of graft to enrich bosses
and maintain the party machine." Direct primaries were designed
to take the nomination process away from "bosses" and put selection in the hands first, of party members, and in time of the people
at large. The initiative, the referendum, and other devices of direct
democracy stripped legislative functions from lawmakers beholden
to parties and returned them to an independent-minded electorate.

[47] McGerr, "The Decline of Popular Politics," p. 217.

On the local level, commission and city-manager governments in the cities reflected the view that party government made for bad streets, inadequate transportation, and unresponsive machines in city hall. Similar impulses underlay the shift to expert, nonpartisan regulatory agencies as a method of supervising corporate behavior and handling complex social problems. Just as there was no Republican or Democratic way to pave a local highway, there was no partisan solution to regulating railroads or overseeing corporations. "The people have come to see," commented the *Saturday Evening Post* in 1905, "that parties are to a great extent the tools of the unscrupulous who make of politics a profession."[48]

Many aspects of the indictment of parties had merit. The way in which elections were financed, for example, tended to corrupt the businesses that provided the funds and the politicians who received them. "Corporations have, and ought to have, many privileges," wrote Governor Albert B. Cummins of Iowa in 1902, "but among them is not the privilege to sit in political conventions or occupy seats in legislative chambers."[49] Democrats and Republicans acted in unresponsive ways on sensitive issues, and did not place the public interest, however loosely defined, ahead of the immediate concerns of their organizations. Political parties by 1900 needed new ideas and new leaders, and the assault on excessive partisanship stemmed from basically healthy motives. As Woodrow Wilson noted in his first inaugural address in 1913, in words most reformers would have endorsed irrespective of their political allegiance: "The success of a party means little except when the nation is using that party for a large and definite purpose."[50]

Not all the manifestations of discontent with political parties and clamor for increased government action corresponded with what would be deemed socially desirable seventy-five years later. Some reformers in the cities disliked the way urban political machines used the votes of immigrants and ethnic groups as a power base; as a result, their calls for change had an ethnocultural and

---

[48] Torelle, *The Political Philosophy of Robert M. La Follette*, p. 32; *Saturday Evening Post*, 177 (March 18, 1905), 12.

[49] Richard L. McCormick, "The Discovery That Business Corrupts Politics: A Reappraisal of the Origins of Progressivism," *The American Historical Review*, 86 (1981), 264, quotes Cummins.

[50] Arthur S. Link, ed., *The Papers of Woodrow Wilson, Volume 27, 1913* (Princeton, N.J.: Princeton University Press, 1978), p. 148.

class dimension. Prohibition, restriction of immigration, and racial proscription were ways that some progressives, North and South, sought to reaffirm older values and to reassert a common purpose in the face of an industrializing and urbanizing social order. Many reformers pursued change at the expense of blacks, Mexican-Americans, and other national groups; most simply left minorities off the agenda. The rhetoric of reform also clothed the efforts of business groups in the South, Far West, and agrarian Middle West to realign economic forces to the disadvantage of the East and in favor of their region or section.

The two major parties between 1900 and 1916 thus quarreled within and among themselves over the reach of governmental authority and, simultaneously, met flanking attacks on their authority and legitimacy in debating these matters. Politics, many Americans decided, was too important to be left to the politicians. The efforts to resolve the question of how much power government should have over an industrial society, while limiting the scope of political parties to influence that decision, gave American politics in these years its special importance and enduring fascination.

CHAPTER 2

Roosevelt, Hanna, and the Republicans

Presidential politics in the United States never ends. By the late spring of 1901 the question of the Republican nominee for 1904 already spurred pundits to assess the prospects of aspirants to succeed President McKinley. Those mentioned included Vice-President Theodore Roosevelt, Senator Mark Hanna of Ohio, Senator Fairbanks, and Governor Leslie M. Shaw of Iowa. Some politicians even suggested that McKinley might seek a third term in defiance of the custom that then set a two-term limit. To this the president responded on June 11, 1901, that he would not accept a third nomination. With this announcement Roosevelt, in particular, accelerated his efforts to line up support for 1904.

William McKinley's goal for his second term was ratification of the tariff reciprocity treaties in the Senate. Already convinced that "This trust question has got to be taken up in earnest and soon," the president intended to press both issues, but gave priority to the reciprocity policy with which he had been identified for a decade.[1] To persuade senators to act on these pacts, McKinley used public statements, trial balloons in the press, and broad hints from friends to prepare the lawmakers for action when Congress convened in December 1901.

In June, Senator Hanna called the president "a strong advocate of reciprocity" who would "consider treaties along the line of mutual interest between this country and another." A month later the president of the American Protective Tariff League told reporters

[1] James Creelman, "Mr. Cortelyou Explains President McKinley," *Pearson's Magazine*, 19 (1908), 570.

that "the time has come when the policy of this administration will favor more positively than hitherto the negotiation of treaties of reciprocity with the purpose of enlarging our foreign markets." Early in August the chairman of the Senate Committee on Foreign Relations visited McKinley in Ohio, discussed the tariff and reciprocity, and remarked that there were "some things we ought to do which will amount to a partial revision of the tariff." The senator's comments, wrote a British diplomat, "have been taken as an indication that there will be a renewal on the part of the Executive to recommend Congress to take action upon some of the Reciprocity treaties which have been 'hung up' in the Senate owing to the influence of certain protected industries."[2]

To underscore his interest in reciprocity, McKinley intended to make several speaking tours in 1901 in which he would rally opinion behind the treaties. He assured French visitors before departing on a nationwide trip in April that he planned to take every opportunity "to defend the policy of commercial reciprocity." Before his wife's illness cut short the tour, the president told a Memphis audience he favored a policy "that shall open up to the widest markets in every part of the world for the products of American soil and American manufacture." After his summer vacation, McKinley returned to his theme in an address at Buffalo, New York, on September 5, 1901. He predicted: "By sensible trade arrangements which will not interrupt our home production, we shall extend the outlets for our increasing surplus." Reciprocity, he argued, "is the natural outgrowth of our wonderful industrial development under the domestic policy now firmly established."[3]

The opening steps of McKinley's campaign for the reciprocity treaties coincided with mounting uneasiness among midwestern Republicans over the tariff. During the session of Congress in the winter of 1901, Representative Joseph W. Babcock of Wisconsin introduced a measure to lower rates on iron and steel in response to the creation of the United States Steel Company. It was Congress's

[2] *American Economist,* 27 (1901), 281, 28 (1901), 7; *New York Daily Tribune,* August 6, 1901; Gerard Lowther to Lord Lansdowne, August 9, 1901, FO5/2463, Public Record Office, London.

[3] Jules Cambon to Theophile Delcasse, May 6, 1901, Commercial and Consular Correspondence, Washington, Ministry of Foreign Affairs Archives, Paris; "President McKinley's Tariff Views," *Public Opinion,* 30 (1901), 739; Charles S. Olcott, *William McKinley,* 2 vols. (Boston: Houghton Mifflin, 1916), II, p. 382.

duty, he asserted, "to interfere and protect, so far as possible, the interests of the people against this enormous steel combination." In midsummer Babcock contended that "it is a part of the policy of protection to protect the consumer," a sentiment which found an echo in the Iowa Republican state convention in early August. That platform called for "any modification of the tariff schedules that may be required to prevent their affording a shelter to monopoly." Aware of views like this "Iowa idea" within the GOP, McKinley spent the summer preparing "a series of speeches in which he proposed to develop progressively his ideas on the extension of our foreign trade through the means of reciprocity treaties, and had directed the collection of data on the trusts."[4]

The speech at Buffalo was intended to be the first of several addresses in which McKinley applied public pressure on the Senate. But an assassin's bullet wounded the president on September 6, and he died a week later, on September 14, 1901. With his death, the momentum of his reciprocity campaign stopped, as did other public business, while the nation and the Republicans waited to see how Theodore Roosevelt would handle the duties of his new office. "You will have hard work to keep the pace with Roosevelt," wrote a conservative Republican to a supporter of the new president, "and sometimes I fancy you must be frightened at the spirit you have helped to unchain."[5]

After he had visited McKinley's successor, a journalist described the impact of the vigorous new personality in the White House. "You go into Roosevelt's presence, you feel his eyes upon you, you listen to him, and you go home and wring the personality out of your clothes."[6] Roosevelt had the same effect on the history of the early twentieth century. Now that he has passed into national folklore, his political career is encrusted with legends that have gathered around him. After World War II, when strong presidents came back in fashion, Roosevelt's historical star rose. He was ac-

[4] Joseph W. Babcock to Robert M. La Follette, February 13, 1901, Robert M. La Follette Papers, Wisconsin State Historical Society, Madison; *New York Daily Tribune*, August 1, 1901; Creelman, "Mr. Cortelyou," p. 572; *Iowa State Register*, August 8, 1901.

[5] Eugene Hale to William E. Chandler, September 29, 1901, William E. Chandler Papers.

[6] Mark Sullivan, *Our Times: The United States 1900–1925*. Vol. III: *Pre-War America* (New York: Scribner, 1930), p. 81.

corded a place as the precursor of Woodrow Wilson, Franklin D. Roosevelt, and their imperial successors. His carefully preserved correspondence, sometimes tailored to persuade history of his position, gave scholars a ready and fascinating access to the Progressive era. As a result, Roosevelt's self-appraisal of his role in the American past has been generally accepted as a correct and discerning one.

Much of this evaluation is correct. Roosevelt enhanced the power of the presidency, he displayed uncommon gifts as an electoral politician, and he posed the right questions about public policy in the new century. To understand Roosevelt's impact on national politics, however, requires comparable attention to his weaknesses as a party leader. His abilities to deal successfully with Congress and to manage the GOP were less formidable than is often claimed. Ever the rhetorical champion of courage and commitment in politics, he could be as evasive and opportunistic in practice as any of his enemies. Roosevelt thrived on melodrama, but it is wrong to treat his presidency as an extended morality play.

When he became president, Theodore Roosevelt was not yet forty-three years old. Youthful exuberance marked his twenty years in political life. Friends called him "the meteor of the age," and a senator described him as "A steam engine in trousers." A French visitor to the White House reported: "His countenance is frank and bold; his vigorous neck is left free by the slope of the low collar. His eyes are perpetually moving behind his spectacles or eye-glasses." A state legislator at twenty-two, he had been a civil service commissioner, police commissioner of New York City, and an assistant secretary of the navy under McKinley. In his spare time he ran unsuccessfully for mayor of New York in 1886, wrote a shelfful of historical works, and ranched in the Dakotas. When the Spanish-American War erupted, he helped raise a regiment of Rough Riders and performed valiantly in battles against the Spanish in Cuba. "The only trouble" with the conflict, he later said, "was that there was not enough war to go around."[7] For the Republican party in New York, facing a difficult contest in the fall of 1898, the new hero

[7] George H. Lyman to Henry Cabot Lodge, November 13, 1901, Henry Cabot Lodge Papers, first quotation; Francis Leupp, *The Man Roosevelt* (New York: Appleton, 1904), p. 290, second quotation; Andre Tardieu, "Three Visits to Mr. Roosevelt," *The Independent*, 64 (April 16, 1908), 861, third quotation; *New York Tribune*, July 25, 1902, last quotation.

made an ideal candidate for governor. In a hard campaign he won a relatively narrow victory and took office in January 1899.

Roosevelt did well as governor, and soon there was talk of his presidential ambitions. Since McKinley was assured of a second nomination in 1900, the choice was between the vice-presidency and another term in Albany. Friends like Henry Cabot Lodge told him to go on the ticket with McKinley. But fears of being bored or sidetracked and a desire for reelection moved him toward a gubernatorial race. In the end, the inability of the McKinley administration to find an alternative, the opposition of the Republican organization in New York to Roosevelt's gestures toward antitrust regulation, and the enthusiasm of western Republicans produced an irresistible tide to nominate him in June 1900. By the time McKinley was shot, Roosevelt was well into the preliminary planning for a race in 1904.

After he took the oath of office, Roosevelt assured Americans "that it shall be my aim to continue absolutely unbroken the policy of President McKinley for the peace, the prosperity, and the honor of our beloved country." Such a pledge was easy for Roosevelt to make because, with only minor variations of emphasis, he stood within the mainstream of Republican policy as the McKinley administration had developed it. His views on the tariff were vague and conventional, and his stress on publicity as an answer to the trust problem paralleled ideas already common among Republicans. "I cannot say that I entered the presidency with any deliberately planned and far-reaching scheme of social betterment," he wrote in his autobiography, except to make the government "the most efficient possible instrument" to aid the American people "to better themselves in every way, politically, socially, and industrially."[8]

Roosevelt's style and demeanor worried some Republicans more than his cautious positions on public issues. James G. Blaine suggested in 1889 that he could be "too quick in execution," and President McKinley eight years later found him "always in such a state of mind." Professional politicians, remembering Roosevelt's near bolt of Blaine in 1884 or his early flirtation with free trade

[8] Henry F. Pringle, *Theodore Roosevelt: A Biography* (New York: Harcourt, Brace, 1931), p. 223; *The Works of Theodore Roosevelt: An Autobiography*, 20 vols. (New York: Scribner, 1926), XX, p. 376.

ideas, shuddered when he seemed lukewarm on questions of party loyalty. Businessmen who knew of his lack of rapport with their calling were apprehensive about his criticism of corporate behavior while he was governor. After summarizing Roosevelt's virtues, an aide at the British Embassy noted that he was regarded as having "more than an ordinary share of impulsiveness," and "a firm determination to impose his will upon others."[9]

The Republican party had gained a leader with a superlative feel for the movements of popular opinion and a masterful ability to captivate voters. He understood that the nation possessed a great interest in the daily affairs of the president, and he fed the people's desire for news and color. He quickly changed the name of the president's residence from the Executive Mansion to the White House. Similarly, his daughter Alice became the object of unrelenting press attention for her high-spirited antics. Roosevelt conceded that "I can be President of the United States, or I can control Alice. I cannot possibly do both."[10]

Roosevelt courted the press, took favored reporters into his confidence, and adroitly managed an expanded coverage of presidential activities. He knew that he could usually establish the terms of a public debate, and he exploited fully the president's prerogative to have the last word in most controversies. McKinley had toured the nation more than any other predecessor. Roosevelt built on this example and expanded it, using public appearances to gather support for his policies and to enhance his own appeal. The presidency, he observed in a famous phrase, was a bully pulpit.

The more subtle devices by which presidents construct their political followings also received Roosevelt's detailed attention. Aware of how ethnic loyalties influence American voting decisions, he distributed appointments with an eye to religious affiliation and national origin. "The President is of the opinion that there should

[9] John A. S. Grenville and George Berkeley Young, *Politics, Strategy, and American Diplomacy: Studies in Foreign Policy, 1873–1917* (New Haven, Conn.: Yale University Press, 1966), p. 217; *Taft and Roosevelt: The Intimate Letters of Archie Butt, Military Aide*, 2 vols. (Garden City, N.Y.: Doubleday, Doran & Co., 1930), II, p. 441; Gerard Lowther to Lord Lansdowne, September 19, 1901, FO5/2548, Public Record Office.

[10] Nathan Miller, *The Roosevelt Chronicles* (Garden City, N.Y.: Doubleday & Co., 1979), p. 260.

be a Catholic on the Board of Indian Commissioners," the secretary of the interior was informed; the secretary of the navy was asked for "a list of the chaplains in the navy and their creeds," with the number of current vacancies. Although publicly committed to the proposition that each individual was "to have a square deal, no more and no less, without regard to his creed," Roosevelt went further in the direction of ethnic inclusiveness than even the tolerant McKinley had gone.[11]

Some of the ways in which Theodore Roosevelt captivated American society were planned; others arose from the excitement and appeal he naturally exuded. The first president to be a true celebrity as well as a chief executive, he made news by being himself, and the newspapers covered him as though he were a force of nature. When Roosevelt was "in the neighborhood," wrote an unfriendly journalist, the public could "no more look the other way than the small boy can turn his head away from a circus parade followed by a steam calliope."[12] Like a parade, he kept the nation fascinated and entertained with an ample quota of controversies and squabbles during his presidency. He advocated simplified spelling ("thru" for through), quarreled with an old friend Maria Storer in famous "Dear Maria" letters, and battled "nature fakirs" about writings that depicted animals as having feelings and motives akin to those of humans.

Success with the electorate did not follow Roosevelt into his relations with the Republican party and Congress. The party leadership in the lower house was not impressive, but Senator Nelson Aldrich of Rhode Island and a small group of his colleagues shaped and directed the flow of legislation in the Senate. The balance of power, long in favor of the legislative branch, had already begun to move toward the presidency by 1901. McKinley's amiable relations with Capitol Hill had obscured how much he influenced the way laws were made. Republican lawmakers still assumed, however, that the president was no more than their equal partner in the governing process, and observers wondered how relations between

[11] George B. Cortelyou to Ethan Allen Hitchcock, November 15, 1901, Ethan Allen Hitchcock Papers, Record Group 316, National Archives, Washington, D.C.; William Loeb to William H. Moody, March 4, 1903, William H. Moody Papers, Manuscript Division, Library of Congress; Oscar S. Straus, *Under Four Administrations* (Boston: Houghton, Mifflin, 1922), p. 182.

[12] Mark Sullivan, *Our Times: Pre-War America*, p. 73.

Roosevelt and the Congress might develop. "I shall not feel sorry," decided a reporter, "if some of the great old personages in the Senate, made up largely of stuffing with patronage and money, find their innards ripped up in due time."[13]

As a champion of presidential power, Roosevelt would have encountered congressional resistance to his policies in any event, but the Roosevelt style compounded this with Capitol Hill. The president rarely deferred to legislative sensibilities. A senior senator visiting the White House might hear business discussed before onlookers in the anteroom, or have his presentation of a patronage problem forestalled by a presidential monologue. Roosevelt made it no secret that he regarded some legislators as "bigoted," or "fools and scoundrels," or "crooks."[14] However accurate these epithets were in particular cases, they did not promote better relations with the legislative branch. Congress came to resent the lecturing tone of the president's messages, the accelerated pace of government action, and the reduction of power inherent in Roosevelt's administrative policies and expansion of executive authority.

Roosevelt's liabilities in handling Congress also surfaced in his management of the GOP. Fancying himself adept at persuading men to do what he wanted them to do, he could be swayed by flattery, and had only modest skill in assessing men's intentions. "As high-minded and pure-minded as he is," concluded Albert B. Cummins, "he is about the poorest judge of men and their motives I have ever met."[15] The president prided himself on seeking a broad range of advice, but he usually relied in the end on those who said what he wanted to hear. Serious disagreement, as in the cases of Nicholas Murray Butler, Elihu Root, and William Howard Taft, produced a rupture. To those who crossed him, the consequences could be spiteful and petty reprisals. Always aware of the difference between right and wrong and confident that he would not confuse them, Roosevelt exhibited a flexibility and suppleness in his

[13] Murat Halstead to Albert Halstead, November 23, 1901, Halstead Family Papers, Cincinnati Historical Society.

[14] Entry for April 17, 1908, George von Lengerke Meyer Diary, Manuscript Division, Library of Congress; Mortimer Durand to Edward Grey, April 6, 1906, FO371/12861, Public Record Office; Chauncey M. Depew, *My Memories of Eighty Years* (New York: Scribner, 1922), p. 169.

[15] Albert B. Cummins to L. W. Lewis, November 28, 1905, Albert B. Cummins Papers, Iowa State Department of History and Archives.

personal relations that critics viewed as expediency and deceit. When he retired from the presidency, Roosevelt believed his policies and methods had bolstered his party. An equally plausible case can be made that, beyond divisiveness over specific issues, his personality contributed a good deal to the irritation and discord inside Republican ranks.

With nomination and election in 1904 as his primary political goal, Roosevelt had to choose whether to extend McKinley's policy of tariff reciprocity or move to other issues. In his first eighteen months, the new president decided to push the trust question and built the most distinctive program of his first term on control of corporate power. This stance did not involve in substance any marked departure from previous Republican actions. The idea of greater publicity was widely shared, and the party platform in 1900 had advocated the creation of a Department of Commerce. Despite the furor over the Northern Securities case and the prosecution of the Beef Trust, there was no dramatic increase in antitrust cases in Roosevelt's first term. What Roosevelt did was to proclaim first, that his activities represented a divergence from earlier precedents, and second, to assert in more theoretical and elaborate terms than McKinley the authority of the government to regulate corporate behavior. He proposed several remedies for the trust problem. Publicity through government agencies that could elicit relevant facts from business was essential. So too was the demonstration that the government had the power to restrain excesses. Finally, the president should endeavor "to make big man and little man alike obey the law."[16]

It was necessary first, however, to shift the focus of political debate. Soon after becoming president, Roosevelt began preparing his annual message to Congress for its December delivery. He circulated drafts of his statement on corporations to cabinet members, friends in the business community, and influential politicians. To some associates, even the mention of the problem was unwise, but Roosevelt insisted on including references to the trusts. He believed, the press said, "that the time is ripe for a judicious agitation of the subject so that in the end some method may be arrived at which will cure the manifest evils of the trusts without in any way

---

[16] Theodore Roosevelt, *Addresses and Presidential Messages of Theodore Roosevelt, 1902–1904* (New York: Putnam, 1904), p. 50.

attacking the natural right of capital to combine in a legitimate manner." Mild in its language and recommendations, the message carefully balanced praise and criticism, arguing that "Publicity is the only sure remedy which we can now invoke" to deal with the trusts.[17]

Ten weeks after his message raised public awareness of the issue, the president seized the opportunity to demonstrate the supremacy of the government over large corporations. In the spring of 1901 a battle among railroad interests in the Northwest had produced a brief stock market panic, and the settlement of the struggle involved the creation of the Northern Securities Company in the fall. This holding company embraced the railroad interests of such business giants as James J. Hill, J. P. Morgan, and E. H. Harriman. When the company was chartered, the governor of Minnesota, a state that the new combination's rates would directly affect, began a campaign against the merger. "I shall leave no stone unturned to prevent this contemplated consolidation," said Governor Samuel R. Van Sant. In early 1902 Minnesota sued the Northern Securities Company in the Supreme Court. Attorney General Philander C. Knox told representatives of the state: "If you find your proposed remedy to be ineffective for any reason and if you can show me how I can be of any service to you, I will be glad to take the matter up." When it appeared likely the Court would dismiss the Minnesota suit and thus encourage other mergers, Roosevelt and Knox decided to act. On February 18, 1902, a press release from the Justice Department revealed the government's intention to take the railroads to court for violations of the Sherman Act. That suit ended in victory for the administration's position two years later.[18]

Two months after the Northern Securities case was begun, popular agitation against meatpacking companies over rising prices led to a congressional investigation and broad newspaper coverage of the Beef Trust. Once again the Justice Department acted, with a suit against leading beef companies in mid-May 1902. "The moral effect of this injunction is in the highest degree important," re-

---

[17] *Chicago Tribune*, October 15, 1901; Roosevelt, *Addresses and Presidential Messages*, p. 296.

[18] *New York Daily Tribune*, November 18, 1901, quotes Van Sant; George P. Wilson to William B. Douglas, February 5, 1902, Attorney General Correspondence, 43. E. 3. 10F, Minnesota State Archives, Archives/Manuscripts Division, Minnesota Historical Society, St. Paul, quotes Knox.

marked a Republican editor. "It will encourage other efforts to restrain the greed of combinations." In a series of late summer speeches in 1902, Roosevelt presented the assumptions behind his antitrust policy. "The great corporations which we have grown to speak of rather loosely as trusts are the creatures of the State," he told a Providence, Rhode Island, audience, "and the State not only has the right to control them, but it is in duty bound to control them wherever the need of such control is shown."[19]

The anthracite coal strike, which came to a head in the early fall of 1902, did not relate directly to the trusts, but Roosevelt's personal intervention to end the walkout of mine workers further confirmed his standing as an objective arbiter between capital and labor. Fifty thousand members of the United Mine Workers left their jobs in the Pennsylvania coalfields in May 1902 to obtain pay hikes of 10 to 20 percent, employer recognition of their union, and an eight-hour day. The railroads that owned the anthracite coal mines refused to negotiate, and the prospect of a cold winter aroused public apprehension about a prolonged deadlock. In October Roosevelt brought owners and workers together at the White House, and he later made it clear that he would use the army to mine the coal. Presidential pressure brought the owners to agree to a commission that ultimately awarded coal workers a 10 percent pay increase, a reduction in hours, but no union recognition. What Roosevelt had done was an extension of the mediation, led by Hanna, that had ended an earlier strike in 1900. But the contrast with Grover Cleveland's actions in the Pullman Strike of 1894 was obvious. The GOP quickly pointed out these facts to the voters. "The coal strike is ended," said a Wisconsin Republican, "and this seems to have removed the last doubt which would have existed as to a Republican House of Representatives."[20]

The results of the congressional elections in 1902 underlined the popular approval of Roosevelt's trust policies and actions. In a House of Representatives enlarged after the 1900 census, the Democrats gained 27 seats and reduced the Republican majority to 30, but the number of GOP members also rose by 11. The usual pattern of losses for the party in power in off-year elections had been at

[19] "Effects of the Beef Trust Injunction," *Literary Digest*, 24 (1902), 727; Roosevelt, *Addresses and Presidential Messages*, p. 15.

[20] Henry Casson to Elisha W. Keyes, October 16, 1902, Elisha W. Keyes Papers, Wisconsin State Historical Society.

least disrupted, and increased Republican totals in key states
seemed to augur well for 1904. Anticipating a difficult struggle in
August, the party came out of the contest with a "very satisfactory"
victory that was credited "to the personal popularity of the President."[21]

Roosevelt completed the substantive part of the trust program
in his first term when Congress convened a month after the elections. The lawmakers passed the Elkins Act to curb railroad re-
bates, and enacted a bill to speed up the Justice Department's
prosecution of antitrust suits. To the bill establishing a Department
of Commerce, the president achieved the addition of an amendment to set up a Bureau of Corporations. The bureau was em-
powered to gather information about corporate activity and to
publish what it and the president deemed appropriate. More conservative than other congressional proposals to regulate the trusts,
the bureau gained credibility when Standard Oil publicly opposed
it. For Roosevelt, the new agency fitted in with his distinction between good and bad trusts and his reliance on publicity. But with a
presidential election year ahead, the administration put antitrust
aside after March 1903 until the president was safely returned.

The combined effect of the Northern Securities case, coal strike
mediation, and congressional actions in 1903 improved the Republican party's electoral prospects. It was no longer so easy for the
Democrats to allege that "the Republican party always legislates to
aid the rich and oppress the poor." Within the party, however, the
issue of government regulation of business posed difficult questions.
To those Republicans, especially in the Midwest, who distrusted
corporate power, Roosevelt's vigorous public action aroused expectations of further advances that would prove hard to fulfill.
Conservatives in the GOP felt increasing alarm over the implications of the party's trust policy. Their qualms would not receive a
public airing until the 1904 election was won, but an ominous note
could be detected in remarks that Roosevelt "says and does things
that make business men uneasy."[22] Finally, it proved difficult to
detach the tariff from the trusts, and the president's evasiveness on
protection stored up problems for his party.

[21] Michael Herbert to Lord Lansdowne, November 7, 1902, FO5/2488, Public
Record Office.

[22] John J. Jenkins to Roosevelt, October 6, 1902, Theodore Roosevelt Papers,
Manuscript Division, Library of Congress; Sereno S. Pratt, "The President and
Wall Street," *The World's Work*, 7 (1904), 4400.

The fate of McKinley's reciprocity treaties provided the first test of Roosevelt's tariff views in the autumn of 1901. The protective tariff was the essential element in the GOP's economic program. "When the Republican party ceases to maintain protection in its strength and vigor, it will cease to be the Republican party," proclaimed a newspaper in 1904. To its advocates, a majority of the party, protection as exemplified in the Dingley Act did more than encourage American enterprise and insulate labor from foreign competition. It symbolized what the Republicans stood for—"an industrially independent, and therefore self-contained, prosperous, rich and all powerful nation." Unlike these partisans, Roosevelt found the tariff boring, and he never devoted time to mastering its details. After a youthful dalliance with free trade, he settled back into orthodox protectionism. Remembering how Grover Cleveland had split the Democrats in the 1890s over the Wilson-Gorman Tariff, Roosevelt preferred to dodge the question, prevent a party rupture, and spend time on issues that engaged his interest. To those of his circle who had doubts about protection, he made sympathetic noises; in practice, he did virtually nothing to resolve the tensions building within the GOP over revision of the Dingley Act and the future of the tariff.[23]

Roosevelt, during his early weeks in office, assured friends and journalists that he would continue McKinley's campaign for reciprocity, that it would be "the corner stone of the commercial policy of the administration." Protectionists in Congress, however, quickly realized that Roosevelt was nervous about the prospects of a battle over reciprocity and that his real concerns lay elsewhere. By mid-October supporters of the tariff were telling him that reciprocity was unwise and should be avoided. "Roosevelt Alters Ideas," noted the *Chicago Tribune* on November 9, and a letter from Senator Aldrich, long a foe of the treaties, on November 15 made up the president's mind. "All I shall do about the treaties will be to say I call the attention of the Senate to them," he replied, and that is all he did. The upper house silently rebuffed this lukewarm overture.[24]

---

[23] "Roosevelt and Fairbanks," *Literary Digest*, 29 (1904), 2; National Association of Manufacturers, *Proceedings of the National Reciprocity Convention, Washington, D.C., November 19 and 20, 1901*, Washington, 1901, p. 26.

[24] *Chicago Tribune*, October 1 (quotation), November 9, 1901; Nelson Aldrich to Roosevelt, November 15, 1901, Roosevelt Papers; Roosevelt to Aldrich, November 18, 1901, in Elting E. Morison, et al., eds., *The Letters of Theodore Roosevelt*, 8 vols. (Cambridge, Mass.: Harvard University Press, 1952), III, p. 199.

The decision to shelve reciprocity had important consequences for the GOP. Aside from the disagreement inside the party over tariff revision, institutional reasons now precluded a satisfactory resolution of the issue during Roosevelt's first administration. Of the four annual sessions of Congress in a presidential term, two had statutory limits on their duration. Beginning in December of even-numbered years, they had to adjourn on March 4 of the next year. In three months it was impossible to deal with a complex issue like the tariff. The remaining two sessions began in odd-numbered years and had no limit on their length. The session that ran into a presidential year, however, was unlikely to produce much legislation because of the proximity of the election. When Roosevelt deferred action on reciprocity in 1901, then, he virtually guaranteed that there would be nothing done on the tariff until after 1904 and probably not before the 1905–1906 session. In the meantime intraparty friction mounted.

The president could not escape one part of the reciprocity question. Economic conditions in Cuba persuaded American officials on the island and in the administration that reciprocity with the United States was essential. In the winter of 1901–1902 legislation to grant tariff concessions on Cuban sugar and tobacco was introduced. It promptly encountered opposition from western producers of beet sugar, tobacco growers in the South, and protectionist Republicans who disliked any breach in the tariff wall. Elaborate parliamentary infighting during the spring of 1902 ended in defeat for the Cuban bill, despite heavy pressure from Roosevelt. Over the next eighteen months the president secured what he wanted through a treaty with the new Cuban Republic, but the drawn-out process reinforced his wariness about the tariff's effect on Republican unity. "I do not wish to split my own party wide open on the tariff question unless some good is to come."[25]

To prevent a rupture, Roosevelt sided with the protectionist wing of the party for the rest of his term. In the 1902 election, tariff revision sentiment appeared anew among Wisconsin and Iowa Republicans. The Speaker of the House, David B. Henderson, declined renomination from his Iowa district in September on the stated ground that he could not agree with the low-tariff views of

[25] Roosevelt to Nicholas Murray Butler, August 12, 1902, Morison, *Letters*, III, p. 313.

his constituents. Roosevelt conferred with Aldrich, Hanna, and the Senate leadership and arranged to defuse the issue. The president's speeches on trusts, before an injury and the coal strike took him off the stump, rejected any connection between consolidation and the tariff. "The real evils connected with the trusts," he said, "cannot be remedied by any change in the tariff laws." He proposed a nonpartisan tariff commission as an alternative to congressional action, but this idea never received much more than rhetorical attention from the White House once the election had passed. Despite warnings that tariff revision "will not down any easier than Banquo's ghost," Roosevelt persisted in a course premised on his conviction that "this tariff question is, of course, . . . one of expediency and not of morality."[26]

The most significant center of Republican sentiment for tariff revision as 1903 began was Iowa. Governor Albert B. Cummins won prominence as the leading exponent of the Iowa Idea, which sought the removal or suspension of tariff duties whenever "a monopoly is attained in any protected commodity." In 1902 the Iowa state convention had renewed its previous endorsement of the plank criticizing tariff rates that offered a "shelter" to monopoly. Protectionists responded that such a policy "would lead to inevitable economic ruin," and Roosevelt worried that revision agitation in the Midwest might cost him votes in the Northeast. Through his postmaster general and the Iowa congressional delegation, the president encouraged negotiations with Cummins to ensure that the state convention in 1903 wrote a tariff plank along a "conservative line." After protracted discussions the Iowa governor, anxious for his own renomination, agreed to wording that omitted references to the tariff's sheltering impact on monopoly and accepted Roosevelt's program of trust regulation. The Iowa Idea, the press concluded, had been "shelved."[27]

During a national tour in the spring of 1903, Roosevelt and his close associates gave additional comfort to the high-tariff cause. At

[26] Roosevelt, *Addresses and Presidential Messages*, p. 69, first quotation; James R. Garfield to Roosevelt, September 17, 1902, Box 155, James R. Garfield Papers, Manuscript Division, Library of Congress; Roosevelt to Joseph B. Bishop, April 27, 1903, Morison, *Letters*, III, p. 471.

[27] Cummins to Lyman Abbott, November 17, 1902, Henry Clay Payne to Cummins, March 7, 1903, Cummins Papers; "Address before Michigan Club," Detroit, March 6, 1903, J. H. Gallinger Papers, New Hampshire Historical Society, Concord; "The 'Iowa Idea' Shelved," *Literary Digest*, 27 (1903), 34–35.

Minneapolis in April he warned the nation against "the ruinous policy of readjusting its business to radical changes in the tariff at short intervals," and repeated that "No change in tariff duties can have any substantial effect in solving the so-called trust problem." In speeches to a protectionist audience, Secretary of War Elihu Root and Senator Lodge also advanced similar arguments. By the summer the secretary of agriculture, himself an Iowan, observed that "it is generally agreed that there shall be no tariff agitation until after the presidential election, which is the point the President undoubtedly wanted to make."[28]

Through the remainder of 1903 and into 1904 flurries of tariff revision activity appeared over reciprocity with Canada and reduction of the duty on cattle hides, but the plank in the Republican platform for 1904 gave Roosevelt and party leaders the most concern as the election campaign approached. Supporters of protection wrote endorsements of the Dingley Act into platforms in Massachusetts, Michigan, and even Iowa. Only Wisconsin persisted in its sentiment for lower duties. Although Roosevelt told Root in June that if elected he intended "to try to give effect" to the views of the "large and fervent minority" in the GOP that wanted revision, his counsel to the drafters of the platform indicated that the party ought not to go beyond "saying that the door for tariff revision shall be kept open." He concurred with Lodge's advice that a specific promise to revise the tariff in 1905 "would be an exceedingly dangerous thing to do." The platform thus asserted that tariff rates "should be readjusted only when conditions have so changed that the public interest demands their alteration, but this work cannot safely be committed to any other hands than those of the Republican party."[29]

During his first four years as president, Roosevelt prevented an immediate rupture within the GOP because he accepted control of the tariff issue by the protectionist wing. To that extent, his strategy bought time and allowed for concentration on domestic and foreign matters closer to his interests. The long-run effects, how-

---

[28] Roosevelt, *Addresses and Presidential Messages*, pp. 143, 144; James Wilson to William Boyd Allison, July 23, 1903, Box 205, Allison Papers.

[29] Roosevelt to Root, June 2, 1904, Roosevelt to Henry C. Hansbrough, June 14, 1904, Morison, *Letters*, IV, pp. 813, 834; Lodge to Roosevelt, June 6, 1904, Roosevelt Papers; *Republican Campaign Text-Book, 1904* (Milwaukee: Press of the Evening Wisconsin, 1904), p. 486.

ever, were more serious. The protective policy stood at the center of party doctrine. Disagreement about its value could, if unresolved, erode the foundations of Republican unity. The more that the leaders and the rank and file explored their differing perceptions of the tariff's fairness to the competing sectional and economic groups within the party, the more difficult it became to sustain cohesion and common purpose. Instead of considering the merits of the issue, deciding on his own position, and leading Republicans to accept or reject it after full evaluation and debate, Roosevelt temporized and equivocated. As his second term proved, the tariff's divisive effects might be suppressed, but for the GOP between 1904 and 1912, they would not go away.

When the Republican National Convention assembled in June 1904, Theodore Roosevelt was assured of a unanimous nomination. Almost three years after becoming president, he could point to a record of accomplishment that included, beyond the trust issue, domestic successes in maintaining the open shop in the Government Printing Office, effective handling of scandals in the Post Office, and the launching of conservation policies in the West. On the diplomatic side, the Alaska boundary controversy with Canada had been settled, and a forceful foreign policy had been pursued in the Caribbean. Reminding an audience in Chicago in April 1903 of his stand in opposition to German action against Venezuela in late 1902, he remarked: "There is a homely old adage which runs 'Speak softly and carry a big stick; you will go far.' " Later in 1903 he wielded American power to secure the Panama Canal Zone for the United States, a stroke that public opinion overwhelmingly endorsed. "I think I can truthfully say," Roosevelt wrote on the eve of his nomination, "that I now have to my credit a sum of substantial achievement—and the rest must take care of itself."[30]

To gain the nomination, however, Roosevelt had not been content since September 1901 to let political considerations take care of themselves. From the early weeks of his presidency he had devoted much time and thought to lining up delegates in what has been called "his happiest campaign."[31] Although there were inevi-

---

[30] Roosevelt to George O. Trevelyan, May 28, 1904, Morison, *Letters*, IV, p. 807; Roosevelt, *Addresses and Presidential Messages*, p. 121.

[31] John Morton Blum, *The Republican Roosevelt* (Cambridge, Mass.: Harvard University Press, 1954), p. 38.

table pitfalls and reverses along the way, it was also an easy campaign to win. With the possible exception of Mark Hanna's endorsement, the president faced no serious challenges and encountered no formidable opposition. In most states he deferred to the established party leaders and gave, at best, slight encouragement to groups that challenged the power of entrenched party organizations.

By the end of 1902 the record of Roosevelt's year in office had squelched the hopes of several potential rivals. Leslie M. Shaw had come into the cabinet as secretary of the treasury and was looking toward the election of 1908. Senator Fairbanks was "almost as timid as was the boy who was afraid to say boo to the goose," and seemed, if possible, even more colorless beside Roosevelt than he had been before McKinley's death. Thirteen state conventions endorsed the president's nomination in 1902. Their 286 delegates gave him much more than half the 498 needed to nominate in what a political aide called "the finest compliment that has ever been paid to an American President."[32]

Roosevelt acted as his own campaign manager in pursuing the nomination, but he also relied on a number of subordinates who handled the details of the search for delegates. Postmaster General Henry Clay Payne, a replacement for a McKinley holdover, had wide contacts in the business community, and he understood the demands of Republican politics in the South. James S. Clarkson was resurrected from obscurity to be surveyor of the port of New York, where he advanced the president's interest among ethnic groups in that state, used his friendships with southern Republicans to good effect, and served as a source of political intelligence. Intimates such as Senator Lodge, President Nicholas Murray Butler of Columbia University, and Joseph B. Bishop of the New York *Commercial Advertiser* provided continuous advice and acted as spokesmen for Roosevelt's cause.

An important region for delegates was the South. Although they supplied almost no electoral votes to the Republican column, the southern and border states possessed one-quarter of the votes in the national convention. The Republican parties below the Mason-Dixon line were but shadowy replicas of real political organiza-

---

[32] James S. Clarkson to A. B. Humphrey, September 20, 1902, Louis T. Michener to Clarkson, October 15, 1902, James S. Clarkson Papers, Manuscript Division, Library of Congress.

tions. Predominantly black, notoriously purchasable, and a perennial patronage problem, their influence stemmed from what they could do for presidential candidates. The condition of the party disturbed Republican leaders constantly, but their options seemed limited. Reliance on black votes offered little hope of building a strong GOP structure, especially during a period of black disenfranchisement. An abandonment of black politicians in Dixie, however, might imperil the allegiance of black Republicans in the North. One alternative was to assemble a coalition of white Republicans, Gold Democrats, and "respectable" blacks, a combination that appeared more decorous than existing alignments and one that might offer a promise of future power.

In the segregated America of the Progressive era, racial justice, based on a commitment to human equality, had few adherents. The 10 million black Americans were concentrated in the South in a rigid, oppressive caste system. Few could vote, most were illiterate, and many were victims of coercion and violence. Lynch mobs killed a thousand blacks in the decade and a half after 1900. The Democrats, North and South, were resolutely racist, and the Republican heritage of Reconstruction provided a goad to action to only a few in the GOP. The Republican leaders—William McKinley, Theodore Roosevelt, and William Howard Taft—were not among them.

Roosevelt shared with McKinley a desire to upgrade the quality of southern Republicanism, but his efforts in that direction also had to adjust to the demands of his nomination campaign. The result was a policy that mixed equal portions of opportunism and principle. In some southern states the president appointed those who favored his candidacy, irrespective of their racial views or skin color. In others, such as Alabama and South Carolina, he sought, with the aid of Booker T. Washington, to select those Gold Democrats and blacks who would raise the level of party personnel. Roosevelt never supported the total exclusion of blacks from Republican affairs in the South, but his criticism of previous practices and his selection of prominent white appointees gave tacit encouragement to the lily-white cause in North Carolina and Louisiana. Aware of his White House dinner with Booker T. Washington, his defense of a black postmistress in Mississippi, and his lengthy fight to confirm a black official in South Carolina, the South and blacks generally both regarded Roosevelt as a greater friend of blacks than he actually was. The common theme of Roosevelt's southern strategy did not lie in his oft-stated claim to be the heir of Abraham Lincoln, nor in his desire to create a better Republican party in the region. These goals were pursued, reconciled, or abandoned in light of how well they served the larger aim of his nomination. In fact, his treatment of the problem had proved by 1904 to be an overwhelming success, as the GOP in the South easily ratified his candidacy.

If it had been only a matter of beating competition like Shaw or Fairbanks, or gathering up southern delegates, even Roosevelt would not have mustered much anxiety about the prospects for his nomination. The great question mark for the president, however, was the allegiance of Mark Hanna. After the 1900 election there had been talk of Hanna's candidacy in 1904, and it was natural to view the Ohio senator as a logical rival to the new chief executive. For those who believed that Hanna had been the real political power of the McKinley years, a contest between the two party leaders seemed inevitable. In the end, of course, Roosevelt triumphed and had the nomination in his pocket when Hanna died in February 1904.

Putting Roosevelt's victory in proper perspective requires a bal-

Marcus Alonzo Hanna (1837–1904), from *The Battle of 1900* (American Bible House: Chicago, 1900).

anced appraisal of Hanna's standing in the GOP between 1901 and 1904. It is first necessary to recognize that McKinley had been the dominant figure in the Hanna-McKinley relationship and that much of the senator's direct political influence rested on authority President McKinley allowed him to have. A good deal of Hanna's clout simply disappeared on September 14, 1901. Evidence that the senator had built up a network of state organizations loyal to him is also fragile. Three states, Colorado, Missouri, and Kansas, have been identified as those where Roosevelt's patronage policies undermined pro-Hanna factions. In Colorado, the connection between Hanna and the dominant Republican element was extremely tenuous. In Kansas, the individuals described as Hanna sympathizers had already been eclipsed by their rivals, and the Missouri leadership leaned toward Fairbanks in 1901. Challenges from Senator Joseph B. Foraker and other Republicans in Ohio meant that Hanna's grip was not completely secure in his home state. Hanna had many friends both in the North and South within the GOP, and he spoke for a large body of conservative business opinion. His opposition could have posed great difficulties for Roosevelt. It is wrong, however, to regard him as having sufficient political weapons to mount a successful assault on a sitting president who had made more than a creditable record in office.

Theodore Roosevelt wanted passionately to have Hanna's endorsement for the nomination. It would supply a seal of approval from the McKinley camp, and would relieve the president's lingering apprehension that his most cherished goal might slip away. Because he shared to some extent the view that Hanna's power pervaded the GOP and was prone to see conspiracy and cohesion among those he deemed his enemies, Roosevelt readily accepted the information, gossip, and rumor that reported Hanna intrigues against him. Members of the presidential entourage and politicians with ambitions for White House favor soon learned that warnings of Hanna opposition to their goals could be a rapid route to Roosevelt's favor.

Hanna's motives in this period are less readily discovered than Roosevelt's. The senator was in poor health, had little desire for the presidency, and recognized that public opinion saw him as the symbol of Republican deference to the trusts. A nomination that came to the preeminent representative of corporate power after Roosevelt had been repudiated would be worthless. Hanna liked

Theodore Roosevelt speaking in Providence, Rhode Island, 1902. Reproduced with the permission of the Theodore Roosevelt Collection, Harvard College Library.

being a senator, wanted to continue his work on industrial harmony with the National Civil Federation, and told a conservative associate in August 1902 "that I am not a candidate and will not be a candidate." While he denied presidential ambitions for himself, Hanna also refused to endorse Roosevelt, arguing in the same letter that it was "out of place to permit so much discussion about the future selection of the candidate for the Republican party."[33] Hanna may have been sincere in his claim that the chairman of the national committee should be neutral and that early endorsements were inappropriate, but critics remembered that he had not been so patient in McKinley's behalf before 1896. For the president and his friends, Hanna's reluctance to be enlisted on Roosevelt's team provided evidence either of interest in the nomination or, at the very least, participation in a campaign to select someone else.

The senator and president cooperated with a reasonable degree of amity throughout 1902. During the coal strike Hanna's efforts at conciliation were significant, and he generally supported Roosevelt's legislative program. By early 1903, however, the White House circle learned of "lots of Hanna talk" in New York and the

[33] Marcus A. Hanna to N. B. Scott, August 20, 1902, Hanna-McCormick Family Papers, Manuscript Division, Library of Congress.

Midwest, and the senator's continued assertions that he was not a candidate did not resolve the presidential doubts. On the way home from his western trip in June 1903, Roosevelt planned to attend the wedding of Hanna's daughter. Friends urged that "The whole situation should be talked out" there.[34]

Matters came to a head before that meeting could take place. As the Ohio Republican state convention approached, allies of Hanna announced that the gathering would not endorse Roosevelt's candidacy a year in advance and would confine itself to state issues and Hanna's race for reelection. Hanna may have intended this procedure as a fulfillment of a promise to conservative Republicans in New York and Pennsylvania to "keep the Ohio situation open in 1903." To Senator Foraker, these remarks provided an opportunity to demonstrate his loyalty to Roosevelt and to gain an upper hand over his intraparty rival. He told the press that the president was "the best known and the most popular man in the United States" and that the convention should support his nomination.[35] Whether Roosevelt encouraged Foraker, or whether the senator had ambitions to gain luster for a race of his own in 1908 is not clear, but his action was a masterful stroke.

Hanna attempted to offset Foraker's maneuver in public statements and a wire to Roosevelt that depicted the endorsement issue as being forced on him and the state convention. To approve the president's candidacy a year in advance was premature, Hanna contended, and the proposal grew out of Foraker's desire to humiliate him. It would embarrass him in his senatorial race. Roosevelt found Hanna's interview "insincere" and thought the senator was "showing his hand definitely in Ohio." Reporters received a statement, and Hanna was sent a wire on May 25 that announced "those who favor my administration and nomination" would support endorsement resolutions "and those who do not will oppose them." When the issue was framed in this public way, Hanna had no alternative but submission. The senator's friends resented the way Roosevelt's statement had obscured his rival's position, and they were pleased that Foraker did not share a close connection with the presidential campaign. There was little doubt, however, that

[34] Michener to Clarkson, March 12, 1903, Clarkson Papers; John J. McCook to Roosevelt, May 22, 1903, Roosevelt Papers.

[35] Philadelphia *Press*, June 20, 1903, clipping in Roosevelt Papers; Joseph B. Foraker, *Notes of a Busy Life*, 2 vols. (Cincinnati, 1916), II, p. 110.

Hanna's "back-action-double-spring feat" had settled the nomination for 1904.[36]

Roosevelt now had the substance of power, but he still sought a public affirmation of support from his supposed opponent. At their June meeting he believed, probably incorrectly, that Hanna had agreed to come out openly in his behalf. A willingness to serve again as chairman of the Republican National Committee would, in the president's mind, be a suitable indication of loyalty. During the rest of 1903 relations between the two men once again deteriorated. A stock market panic in the summer produced new uneasiness about Roosevelt on Wall Street; Hanna opposed the promotion of a White House intimate, General Leonard Wood; and the senator's successful race for reelection sparked new talk about his candidacy. Worst of all in the president's view, there was no sign of Hanna's willingness to continue as chairman of the national committee through 1904.

Hanna listened politely to colleagues and business leaders who told him that "if we renominate Roosevelt, it means defeat," but would not allow his own candidacy to be launched. He assured J. P. Morgan and others "that he would not advocate the nomination of Roosevelt before the convention, thus giving them the opportunity to endeavor to get another candidate."[37] While this stance hardly represented what Roosevelt wanted, it had the practical effect of aiding the president. As long as Hanna remained a possibility, the anti-Roosevelt effort could not focus on other candidates. When death removed the Ohioan in February 1904, the field was clear for the incumbent.

If Hanna had lived, the Roosevelt camp would have insisted on receiving his declaration of support. In December 1903 the president's men began gathering endorsements from prominent Republicans. A month later they assembled "a little organization to combat some of the work that is being done against the President." At the same time, speeches from William Jennings Bryan and William Randolph Hearst reminded businessmen who were cool to

[36] Roosevelt to Lodge, May 23, 1903, Roosevelt Papers; *New York Daily Tribune,* May 26, 27, 1903; Orville H. Platt to Albert J. Beveridge, May 30, 1903, Orville H. Platt Papers, Connecticut State Library, Hartford.

[37] N. B. Scott to Hanna, December 23, 1903, Hanna-McCormick Family Papers; Bascom N. Timmons, ed., *A Journal of the McKinley Years by Charles G. Dawes* (Chicago: Donnelley, 1950), p. 362.

Roosevelt that there were Democrats who might be more trouble-some than the Republican leader. Two weeks before Hanna's death, a friend of Roosevelt's reported that "The Anti-Roosevelt-Morgan-Hanna-N.Y. Sun house of stacked cards has been caving in, & some of the financial house cats are crawling out of the ruins as fast as possible."[38]

As an intraparty struggle, the Roosevelt-Hanna battle was no contest. The senator did not seriously challenge the president, and the latter's nomination was never in doubt. The episode did encourage factional warfare in several states and contributed to the divisiveness within the GOP from 1904 onward. It also revealed Roosevelt's weaknesses as a manager of the party. Obsessed with securing his own nomination, he failed to exercise a cool judgment about the strengths of his own position and devoted excessive attention to the Hanna problem. In the process, he demonstrated a tendency to accept advice and political intelligence uncritically, a propensity to overdramatize and personalize opposition to his goals, and a willingness to identify the interest of the party with his own ambition.

Hanna's death did not cause Roosevelt to alter the conservative course he had followed since 1903. In a series of well-publicized actions, he indicated his desire for a platform that was regular on the tariff, laudatory of the Republican record, and noncommittal on future policies. The search for a successor to Hanna as national chairman was also conducted in a semi-public manner, and the president's overtures to Elihu Root and Cornelius N. Bliss, a wealthy New Yorker, underscored his orthodoxy. The ultimate choice, Secretary of Commerce and Labor George B. Cortelyou, who had been McKinley and Roosevelt's secretary, caused some grumbling among Republicans who saw the candidate as intent on being his own campaign manager. In the event, Cortelyou proved to be an efficient and adroit operator with impressive fundraising abilities and a common interest with Roosevelt in attracting a wide range of voting blocs to the ticket.

On the question of the vice-presidency, Roosevelt moved cautiously and in the end accepted advice that the convention be permitted to pick the running mate. Allowed to express its own

---

[38] William Loeb to James R. Sheffield, January 11, 1904, James R. Sheffield Papers, Yale University Library; Sheffield to Roosevelt, January 30, 1904, Roosevelt Papers.

Roosevelt harvests Republican delegates. Brooklyn *Eagle*, from Albert Shaw, *A Cartoon History of Roosevelt's Career* (New York, 1910).

feelings, the party did not spend much time on an elderly Illinois congressman about whom the president had made mildly favorable statements. Instead, the GOP chose the cautious midwesterner, Charles W. Fairbanks, to allay "the general feeling of distrust" on Wall Street and elsewhere "among those conservative men of property who have heretofore been pillars of party support." Party rebels also received scant sympathy from the White House. In Illinois, Roosevelt backed the faction of Chicago boss William Lorimer against his opposition; in Wisconsin, the president cared less for the merits of the dispute between the nascent progressive Robert M. La Follette and his conservative enemies than that "the Wisconsin people settle their differences without dragging in the National Convention, to the certain detriment of the ticket."[39]

The Republican convention in Chicago was a routine and lifeless affair. It nominated Roosevelt and Fairbanks without opposition, adopted the president's handmade platform, and dispersed. Despite the optimistic signs for his election, Roosevelt warned his friend Lodge that "we have a hard and uphill fight ahead of us."[40] The Democrats, their flirtation with Bryan and social protest temporarily adjourned, selected a New York state judge, Alton B.

[39] Roosevelt to Lodge, June 13, 1904, Morison, *Letters*, IV, p. 833; Frank H. Platt to Charles W. Fairbanks, June 23, 1904, Charles W. Fairbanks Papers, Lilly Library, Indiana University, Bloomington.

[40] Roosevelt to Lodge, July 14, 1904, Morison, *Letters*, IV, p. 858.

Parker, to head their ticket. The issue they planned to run on was Roosevelt himself. The choice for the voters, wrote a Vermont attorney, lay between "the hair trigger man and the judicial mind."[41] For Roosevelt, such a campaign enhanced his strengths and masked his political weaknesses. His first term, as he promised when assuming office, had carried out the broad policies of his predecessor. In terms of actual achievement, it was a second term for McKinley. But to the presidential office Roosevelt also brought public vigor and highly visible executive assertiveness. The Democrats preferred not to quarrel with what Roosevelt had done; they attacked instead his methods of using power. It was a fateful judgment that brought the opposition to a low point in its political fortunes and elevated Theodore Roosevelt to the greatest electoral triumph of his career.

[41] Henry A. Fisk to Elmer Adams, July 29, 1904, Elmer Adams Papers, Archives/Manuscripts Division, Minnesota Historical Society.

CHAPTER 3

The Campaign and Election of 1904

Even before William Jennings Bryan's decisive loss to William McKinley in 1900, conservative Democrats discussed how best to "reorganize" their party to return to the precepts of Grover Cleveland. With the result in November, a swing to the right became the dominant theme of Democratic history through 1904. "It is time now for the Democrats of all the States to return from following after strange gods," said a New Orleans editor in July 1901, "and stand again for the faith delivered to them by the fathers of American liberty."[1]

The "reorganizers" were a loose coalition of one-time Cleveland men, southern congressional leaders, and eastern conservatives who regarded Bryan as the spokesman, in Cleveland's words, of "undemocratic forces" whose union with the Populists had been "immensely costly in defeat." They advocated "The establishment of equal rights, the abolition of special privileges in the maintenance of self government," and viewed an emphasis on tariff reform, sound money, and opposition to Republican power as more productive of political success than the expanding of government power to deal with social problems or the trusts.[2]

Making common cause with the conservatives of the North were southern Democrats who were becoming increasingly sensitive to the race issue. When the president entertained Booker T.

---

[1] "Ohio Democrats Silent about Bryan and Silver," *The Literary Digest*, 23 (1901), 64.

[2] "The Plight of the Democracy and the Remedy," *Public Opinion*, 29 (1900), 805; "More Democratic Harmony," *Public Opinion*, 34 (1903), 391–392.

Washington at the White House, a Memphis newspaper spoke for opinion in Dixie: "The most damnable outrage that has ever been perpetrated by any citizen of the United States was committed yesterday by the President when he invited a nigger to dine with him at the White House." The appointment of a black man to be collector of the port at Charleston, South Carolina, evoked similar protests. Roosevelt's "negro appointees will be killed," said a New Orleans paper, "just as the negro appointees of other Republican presidents have been put out of the way."[3] Regional bitterness also existed over what was perceived to be Republican militancy in Congress to enforce the Fourteenth Amendment. That most of this alarm was illusory made it no less real in Democratic councils. The South wanted to support a winning candidate who would remain true to Jeffersonian principles of state rights and to a limited government that let Dixie handle racial matters.

With the Northeast and the South in tandem, the Bryan wing of the party was on the defensive in 1901 and 1902. State conventions ignored or repudiated the 1900 platform in 1901, and the off-year elections confirmed the rise of the conservatives. "Ohio sweeps the Populistic and Socialistic rubbish out of the way, clearing the road and the atmosphere at the same time," ran a typical conservative editorial in 1901. The feuding continued into 1902. At a dinner in June ex-president Cleveland told the guests: "We were never more ready to do enthusiastic battle than now, if we can only be marshaled outside the shadow of predestined defeat." To this sally Bryan replied that "Cleveland stabbed his party to prevent its return to the paths of virtue."[4]

Despite this bickering, the Democrats looked forward to success in the congressional contests of 1902. They hoped to exploit popular discontent with the tariff, use the record of military atrocities in the Philippines against the GOP, and secure more than the usual gains for the opposition in such nonpresidential balloting. "Quietly, systematically," wrote a Texas senator, "but tenaciously we are forging an indictment that ought to convict the Republicans

[3] Pearl Kluger, "Progressive Presidents and Black Americans," Ph.D dissertation, Columbia University, 1974, p. 42, quotes the Memphis newspaper; Willard B. Gatewood, Jr., *Theodore Roosevelt and the Art of Controversy: Episodes of the White House Years* (Baton Rouge: Louisiana State University Press, 1970), p. 106, quotes the New Orleans paper.

[4] "Cleveland, Bryan and Democratic Discord," *The Literary Digest,* 25 (1902), 1; "Ohio Democrats Silent about Bryan and Silver," p. 64, first quotation.

if the American people are not ready to surrender everything to greed."[5]

The anti-imperialism campaign fizzled in the face of voter apathy and forceful rebuttals from Roosevelt and Elihu Root. In the struggle over Cuban reciprocity, the Democrats voted to protect their constituents in ways that mocked their professed allegiance to tariff reform. Most important, Roosevelt's intervention in the coal strike took away the trust issue and the initiative. As a result, the Democratic gain of 27 seats in the House appeared to be a defeat instead of a victory. "Doubtless there has never been a time in America," wrote the *Springfield Republican*, "when the opposition party understood itself less than it does to-day; there never was a time when it was more variedly discordant and more magnificently unled."[6]

The Democrats entered 1904 without either a strong candidate or a compelling issue. Senator Arthur P. Gorman's attempt to defeat the treaty with Panama, which conveyed a canal zone to the United States, collapsed when public opinion supported the pact. In the end almost half the Democrats in the Senate voted for the treaty. Gorman realized that his effort to build a presidential campaign on rejection of the treaty had "ended in a smash."[7]

With no serious foreign policy differences and with Roosevelt preempting the trust issue, the Democratic party seemed intent on making the president himself the issue in 1904. "The republican president disregards treaties, statutes and constitution and exercises arbitrary power with as little concern as the czar of Russia," said an Indiana Democrat. In language that captured the irritation and frustration with which the opposition viewed Roosevelt, the New Orleans *Times-Democrat* predicted that "The fundamental values of the republic can not survive if this pigmy autocrat be allowed to work his own sweet will through another four years of licensed egotism."[8]

The Democrats had only a number of flawed hopefuls to run

---

[5] Charles A. Culberson to Edward M. House, April 15, [1902], Edward M. House Papers, Sterling Memorial Library, Yale University, New Haven.

[6] "Condition of the Democratic Party," *The Literary Digest*, 25 (1902), 623.

[7] John R. Lambert, *Arthur Pue Gorman* (Baton Rouge: Louisiana State University Press, 1953), p. 307.

[8] *Des Moines Register Leader*, May 13, 1904, quotes the Indiana Democrat; " 'Caesarism' in the White House," *The Literary Digest*, 28 (1904), 579.

against a popular incumbent amid general prosperity. On the conservative side, Richard Olney, Cleveland's secretary of state, George Gray, a federal judge from Delaware, and Senator Gorman, before his Panama fiasco, all possessed scattered support. There was even talk of a fourth race and a third term for the aging Cleveland. That prospect outraged those on the left of the party. Cleveland was a man, said Bourke Cockran of New York, "whose friendship means destruction, whose touch means paralysis, and whose support means dishonor." If Cleveland were nominated, Bryan added, the party would have to assume "the burden that he and his plutocratic associates ought to bear with them into oblivion."[9]

As for the Bryan faction, its leader mentioned as possibilities a number of well-known and obscure men in the party. He intended to "show that we have plenty of material and don't have to go to the reorganizers for material," Bryan wrote. New York newspapers called the list "The Little Unknowns from Nowhere," and there were those who speculated that Bryan had ambitions for yet another nomination.[10]

The two serious contenders in 1904 were, on the left, the newspaper publisher William Randolph Hearst and for the reorganizers, Alton Brooks Parker. Hearst's candidacy possessed a strange and unreal quality. Barely forty-one years old, he had made his name as the millionaire owner of newspapers that relied on lurid stories and timely exposés for their large circulation. He was elected to Congress in 1902 and had shown himself to be an awkward speaker with an uncertain command of the issues. It was his scandal-ridden personal life that most outraged conservatives. He was, argued the New York *Post*, "a low voluptuary trying to sting his jaded senses to a fresh thrill by turning from private to public corruption."[11]

Nevertheless, Hearst used his fortune, his dominance of the National Association of Democratic Clubs, and the absence of a radical competitor to take an early lead in 1904. Despite his personal wealth, he assailed the trusts and championed organized labor in a

[9] "The New Cleveland Boom," *Public Opinion*, 34 (1903), 614; "Survey of the World," *The Independent*, 56 (1904), 875.

[10] Paolo E. Coletta, *William Jennings Bryan.* Vol. I: *Political Evangelist* (Lincoln: University of Nebraska Press, 1964), p. 311.

[11] "Mr. Hearst's 'Boom' and His Fitness," *Current Literature*, 36 (1904), 382.

Alton B. Parker (1852–1926) in his judicial robes. *Literary Digest*, July 1904.

way that appealed to the party's liberal members. The strategy also indicated that the Democrats might in the future find votes by courting the urban, working-class electorate. If Hearst had gained the support of Bryan, his candidacy might have moved from the potential to the possible category. The Great Commoner would say no more than that Hearst was "one of the men who are to be considered." Lacking Bryan's endorsement, the Hearst boom faltered in the spring under the counterattacks of the conservatives. "Hearst has no more chance of being nominated," remarked a southerner, "than he has of being carried to heaven in a wicker basket handmade by Bryan." A month before the convention, the publisher conceded that he would not be the nominee.[12]

Alton B. Parker's star rose steadily in the first half of 1904. Friends in New York sent out copies of Parker's opinions and pictures of the judge taken at his country residence. "He was," wrote one of these men, "chastely portrayed in all the stock situations that the voters seem to desire." By the time the Democrats met in

---

[12] "Is Mr. Bryan for Mr. Hearst?" *Public Opinion*, 36 (1904), 423; Louis W. Koenig, *Bryan: A Political Biography of William Jennings Bryan* (New York: Putnam, 1971), p. 375.

St. Louis in early July, the nomination of the fifty-two-year-old New Yorker was assured. The primary strength of the Parker candidacy lay in his presumed ability to carry his home state, which he had demonstrated in his successful race for the New York Court of Appeals in 1897. He was also conservative, "no roving comet seeking change and adventure through the corners of the universe." Because of his place on the bench, he had been silent on substantive and divisive issues, though it was known he had voted for Bryan in 1896 and 1900.[13]

Parker's political assets attracted the attention of former governor David B. Hill, William F. Sheehan, and the wealthy campaign contributor August Belmont. The judge did nothing in public while they pushed him forward as someone calm and reticent, in contrast to Roosevelt's impetuosity and clamor. The Atlanta *Journal* called Parker "the safe and sure leader who must be opposed to the unsafe and erratic Mr. Roosevelt." Parker would be "safe" as well on the race issue for the South, and he tacitly assured business of his dependability.[14]

But it was not all smoothness and harmony to Parker's first-ballot triumph. There was opposition from Tammany Hall in New York City, where the machine's leader believed "There is nothing in Parker to campaign on." The rest of the country exhibited no great enthusiasm for the jurist. "We cannot succeed with Parker because he is a cipher," one Democrat concluded, and the New York *Sun* tartly noted that Parker, an "estimable and symmetrical gentleman," presented "to the inquiring vision all the salient qualities of a sphere."[15]

Bryan's opposition to Parker was relentless, and his harsh language underlined the New Yorker's closeness to the Cleveland tradition. "If the party is to return to its wallow in the mire of plutocracy," Bryan remarked, "it might just as well openly declare

---

[13] Fred C. Shoemaker, "Alton B. Parker: The Images of a Gilded Age Statesman in an Era of Progressive Politics," M.A. thesis, Ohio State University, 1983, pp. 37, 41; author's copy courtesy of Mr. Shoemaker.

[14] "Parker Presidential Prospects," *The Literary Digest*, 28 (1904), 504.

[15] Daniel S. Lamont to Grover Cleveland, February 11, 1904, Grover Cleveland Papers, Manuscript Division, Library of Congress, quotes the Tammany leader; Daniel E. Sickles to Ernest Harvier, March 7, 1904, Daniel E. Sickles Letterbook, Duke University Library; "Democratic Objections to Democratic Possibilities," *The Literary Digest*, 28 (1904), 398.

its purpose and renominate Mr. Cleveland." Unwilling to have control of the party pass to those who had scorned him in 1896 and 1900, Bryan pursued divisive tactics that prevented cohesion on the left and unity behind the candidate of the right.[16]

In the end, however, Parker's managers were able to win in New York. Under the direction of Hill, the Democratic state convention gave the judge the solid vote of the entire delegation. The platform shied away from controversial questions such as the monetary issue or municipal ownership of public utilities. "The silent candidate," contended the Chicago *Post*, "had been presented to the country on a blank form of platform." During May, Parker gathered in the Connecticut and Indiana delegations and convinced the reorganizers, North and South, that he alone could prevent both a Hearst-Bryan alliance and a Roosevelt victory in November. Still Parker kept silent. "You may be right in thinking that an expression of my views is necessary to secure the nomination. If so, let the nomination go," he told a reporter privately.[17] Actually Parker's nomination depended on his silence. If he became outspoken, he might inflame his enemies. His silence left them with only a vacuum to oppose.

Parker's selection at St. Louis was the only easy result of a tumultuous Democratic convention. Fighting with immense energy to retain his policy positions in the platform, Bryan kept the convention in turmoil over whether to include a plank labeling the money question no longer a political issue. He finally agreed to omit the matter altogether, but secured an antitrust provision to his liking and a stronger tariff reform plank. The thrust of the document, however, was more conservative than had been the platforms for the past two elections. An anti-Bryan journal decided that "a convulsed party is casting out Bryanism." For the Great Commoner himself, the high point came when he told weary delegates: "You may dispute over whether I have fought the good fight, you may dispute whether I have finished my course, but you cannot deny that I have kept the faith."[18]

The convention named Parker as the nominee on the first ballot early on July 9 and reassembled that afternoon to select his running

---

[16] "Survey of the World," *The Independent*, 56 (1904), 975.

[17] Shoemaker, "Alton B. Parker," pp. 46, 48.

[18] *The Nation*, 79 (1904), 25; Koenig, *Bryan*, p. 388.

mate. As the nominating speeches ended and the roll call began, the delegates learned that the candidate had wired them about his position on the money issue and the platform's silence about it. Adjourning until the evening, the Democrats gathered to learn of Parker's "gold telegram." In the message Parker said that he regarded "the gold standard as firmly and irrevocably established." He intended to act on that basis as president and would decline to run if the delegates took a contrary view. After a passionate debate, including a contribution from Bryan, who had risen from his sickbed with pneumonia, the convention responded to its nominee that because "the monetary standard" was not "a possible issue in this campaign," the platform had been mute. Parker could thus adopt whatever position he chose and remain the nominee. Over Bryan's objections, the convention sent its answer to the candidate. The delegates then nominated the eighty-two-year-old, wealthy, and presumably generous Henry Gassaway Davis of West Virginia to run with Parker. "It was a great convention," wrote August Belmont, who thought "that everything is looking very well for the election."[19]

A feeling of optimism about the election characterized the Democrats in the month following the convention. Parker's telegram won eastern applause, and it seemed momentarily as though the party could prevail. Of the 239 electoral votes needed, the South would furnish at least 150. Since Parker would, so the thinking went, carry New York as well as New Jersey and Connecticut, the Democrats could then add the border states of Delaware, West Virginia, and Maryland to have approximately 225 votes. Indiana's total of 15 would put Parker over the top. Supplied with funds from Davis and eastern conservatives, running as a sane and reliable candidate in contrast to Roosevelt, and offering "conservative and constitutional Democracy against radical and arbitrary Republicanism," the Democrats began the campaign, as Cleveland put it, "not in gloom and fear, but in hope and confidence."[20]

Parker's speech of acceptance, delivered at his home in Esopus

---

[19] August Belmont to Edward M. House, July 22, 1904, House Papers; Milton W. Blumenberg, comp., *Official Report of the Proceedings of the Democratic National Convention Held in St. Louis, Mo., July 6, 7, 8, and 9, 1904* (New York: Publisher's Printing Co., 1904), pp. 277, 279.

[20] "Democratic Views of the Campaign Issues," *The Literary Digest*, 29 (1904), 95; "Chances of Democratic Victory," *The Literary Digest*, 29 (1904), 125.

on August 10, disappointed the expectations the gold telegram had raised. He said that the common law provided all the weapons the states needed to combat the trusts, advocated self-government for the Philippines, and otherwise offered a drab collection of party clichés. "Judge Parker's speech of acceptance fell upon his party like a wet blanket," said *Harper's Weekly*. The candidate decided, imitating McKinley, to make a front porch campaign, but the public response was tepid, and few visited him at his isolated residence.[21]

The course of the campaign from mid-August through the end of October rapidly dispelled any Democratic prospects of victory. Despite adequate funds, the national committee did not function with anything like the efficiency of the Republicans under Cortelyou. A southern senator, "with blood in his eye," offered bitter criticisms of "what he called the mismanagement of the Democratic campaign." The inroads the Republicans made into normally Democratic ethnic groups, like the Irish Catholics, were not successfully countered, and apparently scant effort was made to mobilize the party faithful.[22]

If they did not vote for Roosevelt, Democrats of the Bryan stamp stayed home. Bryan himself campaigned for Parker in the Middle West, but spent much of his time speaking for other Democrats or on the lecture circuit. Hearst gave Parker only modest coverage in his newspapers. Defections on the left caused Parker's total to run a million votes behind the Democratic count in the preceding two elections. Prosperity also worked for the incumbent. "The greatest load we have to carry is the era of distress that existed during the second Cleveland administration," wrote a western senator to Parker, and nothing in the Democratic campaign was directed sufficiently toward relieving this enduring burden.[23]

The underlying assumptions of the Parker campaign also proved to be incorrect. It was not possible to defeat the GOP by being the more conservative party; that course allowed Roosevelt and the Republicans to win the left and middle of the two-party spectrum by default. When they focused the campaign on the issue

[21] Shoemaker, "Parker," p. 46.

[22] A. B. Atkins to Roosevelt, September 9, 1904, Roosevelt Papers.

[23] Francis G. Newlands to Alton B. Parker, July 20, 1904, Francis G. Newlands Papers, Sterling Memorial Library, Yale.

of Roosevelt's character, the Democrats gave their opponents a chance to unite behind an incumbent president and avoid substantive issues. The assaults on Roosevelt simply bounced off the overwhelming popular support for his leadership. Finally, Parker's safety and sanity, as the Democrats styled them, came across as dullness and shallowness. Obscurity and silence had won Parker the nomination, but they made him an easy adversary for the best popular politician of the day.

The Republican canvass in 1904 combined an attractive, popular presidential candidate with a highly effective use of the advertising and merchandising techniques that had transformed American campaign styles since the late 1880s. The emphasis shifted from rallies, spectacular events, and public enthusiasm to an attempt to reach the voters through newspapers, pamphlets, and other literature. Vast quantities of documents entitled "A Square Deal for Every Man" and "Our Patriotic President" went out from GOP headquarters. "A special corps of trained writers" supplied Republican newspapers with a reliable flow of campaign information and editorials. Overseeing the operation was George B. Cortelyou, whose organizational skills had been perfected in the White House and at the Department of Commerce and Labor. "He is much more industrious than Hanna was, & is making a splendid 'still hunt.' Nothing very much will be away," a seasoned Republican operative said of the new chairman.[24]

Although the Republicans maintained a speakers bureau, the old-style stump orator found his services less in demand. A newspaper depicted a typical speaker of the 1890s vintage who complained that the nation was "swayed now by half a dozen bulging browed youths, a set of encyclopedias and a report of the Bureau of Statistics." Professionals realized that the public was losing its taste for Gilded Age oratory. "If there is anything worth listening to in the speech the people know that the papers give it what it merits." Rallies became less important in themselves and were more designed to achieve the maximum of journalistic attention.[25]

[24] William C. Beer to Martha Beer, September 20, 1904, Beer Family Papers, Sterling Memorial Library, Yale, comments on Cortelyou. Louis A. Coolidge to George D. Perkins, September 8, 1904, George D. Perkins Papers, Iowa State Department of History and Archives.

[25] *New York Herald,* October 9, 1904, clipping in Roosevelt Papers; McGerr, "The Decline of Popular Politics," p. 223.

Under Cortelyou's direction and Roosevelt's guidance, the Republican canvass also sent out appeals to a diverse array of ethnic, economic, and religious groups. There was an Austro-Hungarian Republican League, a National Roosevelt League for German-Americans, and French-Canadians for Roosevelt clubs in Rhode Island. Black voters in the North were asked to remember "the silent legions which sleep to-night in Northern churchyards and in the forgotten buried trenches on the Southern battlefield." Civil War veterans learned of how Roosevelt's pension orders had lowered the benefit age to sixty-two. The National Committee organized First Voters Clubs, and the National League of Republican Clubs did similar work among independent electors.[26]

The most specific targets of the GOP's coalition-building effort were the members of the nation's religious bodies. Fairbanks worked effectively "stirring up the Methodist brethren in various quarters." Jewish leaders applauded what the administration had done to protect American Jews of Russian origin traveling in their native country and to protest the mistreatment of Russian Jews generally. All Jews, said one New York spokesman, "whatever their origin, glory in the president's sympathy for our people in Russia." Roosevelt's ethnocultural strategy emerged most clearly in his appeal to Catholics. The president's handling of the complex issues of Church lands in the Philippines and his appointment of Catholics to various positions in the government proved to several Catholic newspapers that he was "a man without prejudice, sectarian bias or intolerance." In early November a journalist surveyed opinion in New York City and predicted that "the Republican ticket will this year be voted by a larger number of Irish-Americans than has been the case since the days of Blaine."[27]

In the public phase of speeches, campaign literature, and statements, the Democratic strategy of stressing Roosevelt's conduct of the presidency meant that they excluded more cutting social and

[26] *New York Tribune*, September 1, 23, 1904; David Mulvane to Knute Nelson, August 27, 1904, Knute Nelson Papers, Archives/Manuscripts Division, Minnesota Historical Society; Eugene F. Ware to Roosevelt, September 13, 1904, Roosevelt Papers; W. C. Beer to E. W. Lampton, November 4, 1904, Beer Family Papers, quotation.

[27] Fairbanks to Roosevelt, August 22, 1904, Roosevelt Papers, first quotation; *New York Tribune*, September 4, 30, 1904, second and third quotations; *Philadelphia Press*, November 2, 1904, clipping in Roosevelt Papers, last quotation.

economic issues. This line of attack allowed Roosevelt and his party to sound the twin themes of Republican achievement and Democratic disarray and to escape the need to articulate more positive proposals. The president's letter of acceptance contained only brief and passing references to his intention to deal with railroad problems or revision of the tariff. "We base our appeal upon what we have done and are doing, upon our record of administration and legislation during the last seven years, in which we have had complete control of the Government. We intend in the future to carry on the Government in the same way that we have carried it on in the past."[28]

Custom still dictated that an incumbent president refrain from participation in the active phase of the campaign. "I wish I were where I could fight more offensively," Roosevelt said. "I always like to do my fighting in the adversary's corner." The burden of speech-making fell on Fairbanks, party officeholders, and administration officials. Their addresses rebutted Democratic assaults on Roosevelt and defended the party's record in ringing and conservative terms. "If Republican policies are approved at the ballot box in the coming election," the vice-presidential candidate told a Connecticut audience, "commerce will not need to furl her sails and industry will not need to meet surprises which change of administration sometimes brings." A New England senator claimed that Roosevelt had been "tried and found true and faithful, and able," and the people "like him, believe in him, admire him, and are growing more and more to love him." The Republicans were, others said, "the party of facts," or "a party fit to govern." They rode "in the chariot of American glory; the Democratic party in the hearse of dead and discredited theories."[29]

From the beginning of the campaign the Republicans displayed amused shock at their bright prospects. "I was afraid when the campaign began that possibly Parker might develop some unexpected strength," wrote Jonathan P. Dolliver in September, "but so far he appears to be a blank cartridge." There were, of course, dif-

[28] Roosevelt to Joseph G. Cannon, September 12, 1904, Morison, *Letters*, IV, p. 921.

[29] Roosevelt to Lodge, July 14, 1904, Morison, *Letters*, IV, p. 858, first quotation; *New York Tribune*, September 3 and 9, 1904; speech at Providence, Rhode Island, October 13, 1904, Orville H. Platt Papers; Linden Bates, *The Party of Facts* (New York, 1904), last quotation.

ficulties. Factionalism in Wisconsin and Utah agitated the party leadership, and the struggle in states like Indiana was protracted. As the state with the largest bloc of electoral votes, and Parker's home state, New York gave Roosevelt and the GOP the greatest concern. Apprehension over the fate of the ticket there caused the president to urge in late summer, without result, that Elihu Root run for governor. By the early part of October, Roosevelt was sufficiently worried to ask Secretary of State John Hay to make speeches in New York. He also engaged in conversations with railroad magnate E. H. Harriman about fundraising. For the most part, few spectacular incidents occurred, and the common theme of participants and spectators was the "amazing quietude" of the electorate. "This is the most apathetic campaign ever heard of since James Monroe's second election," concluded Albert Shaw. It was, he continued, "as different from what we are accustomed to in September and October of a presidential year as black is different from white."[30]

The change in campaign style and the difference in the public response to elections went along with the decreasing emphasis on partisanship as a central aspect of political life. Fewer voters wore buttons or discussed the election in public. The focus of the campaign in 1904 on the president and his personality was part of a trend toward seeing these elections more as a contest of individuals than an encounter of contrasting party ideologies. In the attempt to make an appeal to the personal convictions of independent voters, the advertising style also transformed contests into less interesting and involving experiences. While some voters were pleased with the quiet and rationality of the new procedures, others appear to have turned to alternative diversions to partisan activity which proved more engrossing than the routinized rituals of campaigning. In 1904, turnout and participation continued their drop from the levels of the 1890s.

A climactic episode underscored Parker's weaknesses as a candidate and also foreshadowed an issue that would emerge soon after the election ended. To inject life into his flagging canvass, Parker

---

[30] Jonathan P. Dolliver to S. W. Rathbun, September 6, 1904, Jonathan P. Dolliver Papers, State Historical Society of Iowa, Iowa City; Albert Shaw to W. T. Stead, October 7, 1904, Shaw Papers; John Hay to Joseph Hodges Choate, September 23, 1904, Joseph Hodges Choate Papers, Manuscript Division, Library of Congress, second quotation.

began in late October to make an issue of the size of the Republican campaign fund and to accuse Cortelyou, who had had access to corporate records as secretary of commerce and labor, of pressuring business to make donations to the party treasury. The trusts, remarked the Democratic candidate, were being allowed "to buy protection" and as a result were "not now opposed to the continuance of the present administration." The issue, said the newspapers, was "Cortelyou and Corruption." Parker acted on information from a wealthy Democrat, who got it from a third party, that Roosevelt had met secretly with wealthy businessmen to secure campaign funds.[31]

Parker's charges outraged Roosevelt. "I used to think Parker only a fool," the president told Cortelyou, "but I guess he is as much of a knave as his associates." He ordered Cortelyou to return a $100,000 contribution from Standard Oil, and he bombarded the chairman with letters denying the Democratic allegations. Nevertheless, he did not probe deeply into his party's fundraising practices. Cortelyou and his treasurer, Cornelius N. Bliss, were accepting corporate donations and did not tell the president of the full scope of their activities. Roosevelt also corresponded and met with such potential benefactors as Harriman and others.[32]

On November 3, Parker renewed his accusations, referring to Cortelyou's "organized importunity." Roosevelt could restrain himself no longer. He issued a statement that appeared on November 5. What Parker had said was "unqualifiedly and atrociously false." Roosevelt would be, if elected, "unhampered by any pledge," and promised only that "I shall see to it that every man has a square deal, no less and no more." The president hoped that he could make "the refutation reach as large an audience as the slander."[33]

This presidential intervention threw the burden of proof back on Parker in the last two days of the contest. Since he was unable to consult the Republican financial records, and his wealthy informant had sworn him to secrecy, he could only point to a set of circumstances and suggest the possibility of misconduct. The

[31] *Washington Post,* October 24, 1904; New York *World,* October 26, 1904, clipping in Roosevelt Papers; Shoemaker, "Parker," p. 81.

[32] Roosevelt to Cortelyou, October 29, 1904, Morison, *Letters,* IV, pp. 1004–1005.

[33] *Washington Post,* November 1, 5, 1904; Roosevelt to Root, November 5, 1904, Morison, *Letters,* IV, p. 1014.

Democratic response fell flat, and the Republicans rejoiced. The *Chicago Tribune*, a Republican paper, said that Parker had descended "from a high plane . . . to the level of the cheap politician." The last-minute exchange probably influenced few votes in 1904, but the sensitivity with which both sides viewed the episode indicated that public opinion was already attuned to the issue of corruption and business influence in politics that would gain notoriety over the next year.[34]

President Roosevelt voted at his home in Oyster Bay, New York, on November 8, 1904, and then returned to Washington to await returns. By quarter after ten that evening, a landslide was in the making. The president crossed the street to his private office in the Executive Office Building, where reporters awaited him. "Ranged in a semi-circle" around his desk, the newsmen listened as Roosevelt dictated a statement. After expressing gratitude at the verdict of the people, he added that the three and one-half years he had already served "constituted my first term. The wise custom which limits the President to two terms regards the substance and not the form. Under no circumstances will I be a candidate for or accept another nomination."[35]

The announcement was no sudden decision. Roosevelt had discussed the subject with at least one senator, and probably remembered the strong public response to McKinley's statement about a third term in 1901. The action also refuted Democratic charges about his dictatorial ambitions. Although his motives were laudable and his resolve in maintaining his position consistent and unswerving, the political effect of the statement was in the long run disastrous, and Roosevelt came to wish he had never said anything about the matter.[36] The declaration had two unfortunate consequences. To the degree it was believed, and Roosevelt reaffirmed its substance constantly during the next three years, it made him a lame-duck president and gradually diminished his influence with Congress. For those who wanted Roosevelt to run again or for those who feared he might, no denial was sufficiently final to still their hope or apprehension. Ambiguity about the president's position

---

[34] *Chicago Tribune*, November 4, 1904, quoted in Shoemaker, "Parker," p. 83.

[35] *New York Tribune*, November 9, 1904.

[36] Roosevelt to Winthrop Murray Crane, November 12, 1904, Morison, *Letters*, IV, p. 1032; Meyer Diary, September 12, 1908, Library of Congress.

persisted until 1908, but he could not use it with much impact unless he wished to undermine his own statement.

The possible consequences of Roosevelt's statement were not explored in the aftermath of the overwhelming triumph that the president and his party achieved in 1904. Roosevelt received 7,628,875 votes, or 56.4 percent, to Parker's 5,084,442 and 37.6 percent. Roosevelt's 336 electoral votes were the most any candidate had ever won, and he carried thirty-three of the forty-five states. His victory in Missouri represented a small Republican break in the Solid South; his majorities in industrial states such as Ohio and Pennsylvania were massive. The ethnocultural strategy also paid rich dividends for the ticket. Roosevelt ran strongly in normally Democratic ethnic areas in Wisconsin cities like Milwaukee, La Crosse, and Madison. In Chicago, Germans, Swedes, Jews, Italians, and Poles moved away from their usual Democratic loyalties to support the Republican standard bearer. His "tolerance, democracy, and contemptuous disregard of lines of wealth, race and color," reported a national magazine, "won the admiration of Jews, Germans, Italians, and all other ingredients entering into the American composite, and, for the first time in the party's history, carried a majority of the Irish vote to the Republican side."[37]

While 1904 was the first true landslide of the twentieth-century variety, it did not come about because of an outpouring of voters. The number of Americans marking ballots fell by more than 400,-000 from the 1900 total, and the estimated turnout in the northern states went from 71.6 percent four years earlier to 64.7 percent in 1904. The Democratic total dropped by 1,300,000 votes. Some of those votes went to Roosevelt, some to the Socialist candidate, Eugene V. Debs, who received slightly more than 400,000 votes, and some Democratic voters simply stayed home.

The ability of the Democrats to elect governors in five states (including Massachusetts, Minnesota, and Missouri) that Roosevelt won offered additional evidence of the loosening bonds of party loyalty. Ticket-splitting meant that the Republican ascendancy in this period was strongest for presidential candidates, while "the

---

[37] *Leslie's Weekly*, November 17, 1904, clipping in Roosevelt Papers; Roger E. Wyman, "Middle Class Voters and Progressive Reform: The Conflict of Class and Culture," *American Political Science Review*, 68 (1974), 496; John M. Allswang, *A House for All Peoples: Ethnic Politics in Chicago, 1890–1936* (Lexington: University Press of Kentucky, 1971), pp. 29–33.

Democratic party was stronger in its parts than as a whole (or as a
national coalition)." The tendency to vote for candidates as individuals rather than as representatives of parties meant that personal-
ism was replacing partisanship as a motive for casting a ballot. For
all its apparent dullness, the presidential election of 1904 was a
contest where the shift occurred from the older style of politics to
the newer emphasis on the charismatic and individual traits of the
chief executive.[38]

Conservative Democrats were surprised at the magnitude of
the Roosevelt victory and Parker's defeat. The president appeared,
wrote Henry G. Davis, "to have a hold upon the people which to
me seems strange." The strategy of the reorganizers left the Democrats with only the 140 electoral votes that the South furnished.
Elsewhere Parker's conservatism resulted in decisive defeats in
New York, New Jersey, Indiana, and Connecticut, the states where
he had been presumed to be a strong contender. For his part, Bryan
seized on the outcome as evidence of the Democratic mistake in
abandoning his policies. "It looks as if the party sold its birth right
& then failed to receive the pottage." Within a few months, Bryan
had reemerged as the Democratic leader and the acknowledged
frontrunner for the nomination in 1908.[39]

Naturally delighted with their success, Republicans asked
themselves: "What are we going to do with our victory?" Its "very
character," suggested Senator Dolliver, "imposes upon us many
difficult responsibilities as a party." For Roosevelt, it was gratifying
to be president "in his own right," and he told visitors that "he
would feel at liberty to have his own policies."[40] The effect of Roosevelt's first term, however, had been to clear the political agenda
of most of the issues of the McKinley era. "It is a significant measure of the stagnant political thought of the time," observed a mag-

[38] Walter Dean Burnham, "The System of 1896: An Analysis," in Paul Kleppner
et al., *The Evolution of American Electoral Systems* (Westport, Conn.: Greenwood Press, 1981), pp. 171, 174 (quotation), 175.

[39] Henry Gassaway Davis to John W. Daniel, November 9, 1904, John W. Daniel
Papers, Duke University Library; William Jennings Bryan to James S. Hogg, No-
vember 24, 1904, James S. Hogg Papers, Eugene C. Barker Texas History Center,
University of Texas at Austin.

[40] Orville H. Platt to Nelson Aldrich, November 12, 1904, Platt Papers, first quo-
tation; Dolliver to J. W. Blythe, November 12, 1904, Dolliver Papers; entry for
November 8, 1904, Diary, John Hay Papers, Manuscript Division, Library of
Congress; Foraker, *Notes of a Busy Life*, II, p. 203, last quotation.

azine editorial in June 1904, "that a campaign should turn on the personal characteristics of the President—one might even say, on his personal manner." It remained to be seen in what direction Roosevelt would seek to implement his own policies. There would be pressure to revise the tariff, and midwestern governors were coming to Washington to confer with him about railroad regulation. Many followers of politics believed that a realignment of parties impended. A conservative Republican senator looked for "populism, socialism, rheumatism, etc." on one side opposed to "conservatism," while Roosevelt's friends urged him to foster a "liberal Republicanism" that would be fair "to corporate wealth and organized labor, but entangled in neither."[41]

The election of 1904 brought one era of Republican history to an end and opened a new, more dangerous period for the party. The program of tariff protection, economic prosperity, expansive foreign policy, and ethnic inclusiveness that had built party majorities in the decade after 1893 had now been carried out. In place of the nineteenth-century issue of how best to promote the growth of the economy, the newer problem of how far the government should regulate an industrial society was gaining attention. Also the methods of political organization and operation by which the Republicans had achieved and maintained their dominance were receiving critical scrutiny. Even as Theodore Roosevelt savored his triumph in November 1904, these fresher issues of reform and regulation demanded action. In meeting the challenges these problems presented, Republicans would find much about which to disagree, and the first two years of Roosevelt's second term would leave the party much weaker and more divided than anyone could have anticipated in the euphoria that followed the 1904 victory.

[41] "Mr. Roosevelt's 'Safeness,' " *The World's Work*, 8 (1904), 4832; John Coit Spooner to John Hicks, November 11, 1904, John Coit Spooner Papers, Manuscript Division, Library of Congress; Benjamin Ide Wheeler to Roosevelt, November 13, 1904, Roosevelt Papers.

CHAPTER 4

Roosevelt and Regulation

The Republicans had only a few weeks to enjoy their 1904 success before the pressures in the party to act on crucial issues resumed. Recognizing that the first year of a presidential term was the only time when decisive action could occur in Congress, advocates of tariff revision and railroad regulation sought to launch these initiatives during the last session of the Fifty-eighth Congress, which was scheduled to assemble in December 1904. Roosevelt had to make important choices about his legislative agenda, and the decisions rendered in the last months of his first term affected the timing and direction of his second.

The most immediate and controversial problem was the hardy perennial, the tariff. From eastern friends of revision such as Nicholas Murray Butler and Elihu Root came suggestions for early action, including a special session of Congress in March 1905 "unhampered and undelayed by the performance of any other duty whatever." Midwestern party leaders from Iowa, Minnesota, and Wisconsin shared the view of an Indiana Republican that "the people are as much opposed to a tariff for monopoly as they are to a tariff for revenue only." In the week after the election, Roosevelt responded to revision sentiment and asked influential congressmen and senators to explore the chances of an extra session "at the earliest possible date." To give public endorsement to this policy, the president drafted language about the tariff for inclusion in his annual message. "We beat the Democrats on the issue that protection was robbery," Roosevelt wrote, and if the GOP failed to revise the tariff, "we will be putting a formidable weapon in the hands of our opponents."[1]

---

[1] Root to Roosevelt, November 16, 1904, Roosevelt Papers; R. L. McCabe to Fairbanks, November 2, 1904, Fairbanks Papers, Lilly Library; Roosevelt to Or-

As he had in the past, Roosevelt backed away from revision almost as soon as he had advanced. On November 18, 1904, Senator Orville H. Platt talked with him and argued against a special session in 1905. When a newspaper reported the next day that there would be a special presidential message on the tariff, the White House announced that Roosevelt "will not discuss tariff revision or reciprocity in his annual message." As an alternative, he wrote the Speaker of the House, Joseph G. Cannon, on November 30 about a special message that would call for a joint commission of senators and representatives to investigate the tariff and report on revision to a special session "to be held as early as possible." The public discussion of this possible initiative roused the high-tariff wing of the party to action, and the prospect of revision and a special session soon receded. At a conference with Cannon and other legislative leaders in early January 1905, tariff revision was "postponed until fall."[2]

The idea of a special session in 1905 was now dead, but its official burial did not come until the end of the summer. Since the Republican leadership had little stomach for a tariff battle in the election year of 1906, the decision to defer action on revision meant that the question could not come up for serious congressional consideration until after the presidential race in 1908. Whoever Roosevelt's successor was, he would have to confront the accumulated tensions of the tariff controversy at the outset of his administration. Once again, the president had chosen to secure short-range political benefits and to free himself to pursue subjects of more personal interest, like railroad regulation, in preference to a resolution of the tariff split within the GOP. "On the interstate commerce business, which I regard as a matter of principle, I shall fight," he observed in January 1905. "On the tariff, which I regard as a matter of expediency, I shall endeavor to get the best result I can, but I shall not break with my party." For a politician with Roosevelt's meager grasp of the tariff expediency had a certain logic, but his convenient formulation ignored the degree to which

---

ville H. Platt, November 22, 1904, Roosevelt to Joseph Wharton, November 22, 1904, Morison, *Letters*, IV, p. 1039.

[2] James R. Garfield Diary, November 16, 1904, Garfield Papers; New York *World*, November 19, 1904; New York *Press*, November 20, 1904, first quotation; Roosevelt to Cannon, November 30, 1904, Morison, *Letters*, IV, p. 1053, second quotation; *New York Tribune*, January 8, 1905, third quotation.

protection was the most salient and significant ideological principle of his party.[3]

The flurry of talk about the tariff in the short session of 1904–1905 contributed to a growing suspicion and discord between Capitol Hill and the White House that characterized Roosevelt's second term. Hoping that "we can go slow now for awhile," GOP leaders were ill-prepared for the quickened pace Roosevelt set shortly after the election. They had believed the president would moderate his style once he was elected on his own. For his part, Roosevelt thought of his victory as a mandate to press ahead more vigorously and actively. In the three months following the election, he took an increasing and lively interest in the patronage, to the dismay of Congress, and advanced a number of suggestions about social legislation on which lawmakers might act, including corporal punishment for wife-beating in the District of Columbia. The president received public plaudits from William Jennings Bryan and other Democrats for, in Bryan's words, having "symptoms of reform that I for one had no suspicion of."[4]

Congress responded to presidential assertiveness with some public opposition and even stronger private misgivings. "There are a large number of men in both Houses who think they see in the attitude of the President an intention to force his views, instead of his recommendations on Congress," a reporter noted. A sharp fight took place over the extent of executive power in February when the Senate amended a general arbitration treaty to ensure itself a role in the treaty-making process. Both sides publicly minimized the effect of the quarrel, but the episode rankled. The Senate, wrote the president, "is such a helpless body when efficient work for good is to be done." One of the most conservative Republican senators, on the other hand, predicted that "Unless some restraint can be placed on the White House the Republican party will be divided into hostile camps before 1906."[5]

Among the many subjects that Roosevelt raised in his 1904

[3] Roosevelt to Lyman Abbott, January 11, 1905, Morison, *Letters*, IV, p. 1100.

[4] Orville H. Platt to Beveridge, November 14, 1904, Platt Papers; Paolo Coletta, *William Jennings Bryan: Political Evangelist, 1860–1908* (Lincoln: University of Nebraska Press, 1964), p. 354.

[5] New York *Herald*, January 7, 1905; Roosevelt to James B. Bishop, March 23, 1905, Morison, *Letters*, IV, p. 1144; J. H. Gallinger to James O. Lyford, February 12, 1905, James O. Lyford Papers, New Hampshire Historical Society.

message the most explosive was his call for increased railroad regulation through strengthening the powers of the Interstate Commerce Commission to review and rule on the reasonableness of railroad rates. "The government," he wrote, "must in increasing degree supervise and regulate the workings of the railways engaged in interstate commerce." The alternative would be "an increase of the present evils on the one hand or a still more radical policy on the other."[6] During the next twenty months the question of railroad regulation became the major policy issue for both parties. Involving the nature and scope of governmental supervision of a crucial sector of the economy, the struggle that produced the Hepburn Act of 1906 brought to the fore the clash of interests and ideology that would, in particular, vex the GOP for more than a decade.

Roosevelt's decision to push for railroad regulation grew out of information he had gathered from the Bureau of Corporations and the Interstate Commerce Commission about railroad practices and abuses. He was also aware of the public clamor on the issue, though he characteristically denied that it had prompted his action. Knowing that sponsorship of a stronger Interstate Commerce Commission would be popular in the Midwest and South, the president also saw in the program a chance to apply the Square Deal to a specific economic problem. In his message he asked that the commission secure the power when a rate was questioned and "found to be unreasonable, to decide, subject to judicial review, what shall be a reasonable rate to take its place." He proposed that the commission's rate would go into effect at once and would remain in force until a court had ruled on it. With this idea, he joined those critics of railroads who wished to shift the burden of challenging a rate decision to the railroads and away from their customers.[7]

By the time Roosevelt threw his support behind the national campaign for railroad regulation, it had built up a good deal of momentum. The major economic force seeking enhanced power for the Interstate Commerce Commission among Republicans were shippers in the Middle and Far West, with such states as Iowa,

[6] *The Works of Theodore Roosevelt: State Papers as Governor and President, 1899–1909,* XV, p. 226.
[7] Ibid.

Minnesota, and Wisconsin in the lead. With similar pressures
emanating from the South, Democratic senators and congressmen
from that region added their voices and votes to the regulatory
cause. The commission itself, its authority reduced by court decisions in the 1890s, wanted more power to oversee the railroads.
Newspaper coverage of its proceedings and annual reports kept the
issue before the public. For citizens generally, especially those who
encountered the industry only as passengers, the continuing unease
about business consolidation and rising consumer prices made
plausible the rhetoric that blamed the railroads for a higher cost of
living and unfair practices. "The railway business of this country
has become a monopoly in fact," wrote Robert M. La Follette in
March 1905, and a New York newspaper concluded: "The country
is a unit in its demand for a square deal from the railroads and it is
in no mood for delay."[8]

At its core the railroad issue involved a dispute between competing economic groups over the price of rail services and the
manner in which the roads conducted their business. Critics of the
lines argued that rates were too high, that the railroad managers
discriminated among cities and regions, and that it was unfair for
the rail companies to be the sole judges of the merits of rate disputes. "Rates made by the railway company are made by a party
prejudiced in its own interests," charged La Follette, "and, therefore, certain to be unjust to the public." To these indictments the
railroad companies replied that rates were too low rather than too
high, that discriminations flowed from the nature of doing railroad
business, and that attacks on railroads had selfish purposes. In answering La Follette, an industry leader claimed that the aim of the
campaign to increase the power of the Interstate Commerce Commission was "to enable some Government tribunal to assume the
affirmative direction and rearrangement of the railroad policies of
the country, to make radical changes in the system of railroad rates,
to attempt to 'build up local points,' and to try to rearrange the
present relative importance of the ports and the commercial and
industrial centres of the country."[9]

[8] Robert M. La Follette, "Fair Railroad Regulation," *Saturday Evening Post*, 177
(March 4, 1905), 20; *New York Press* quoted in "The President and the Rebate
Question," *Literary Digest*, 30 (1905), 82–83.
[9] La Follette, "Fair Railroad Regulation," *Saturday Evening Post*, 177 (April 15,
1905), 4; Walker D. Hines, "Unfair Railroad Regulation: The Case for the Companies," *Saturday Evening Post*, 177 (April 1, 1905), 18.

Both sides of the argument had merit. By 1904 the railroads were a different industry than they had been in the flamboyant, speculative days of the Gilded Age. General rates were stable and not exorbitant; the management of most lines acted responsibly on the basis of legitimate economic considerations; and the business as a whole provided good service to those traveling and shipping. "The real effort" behind the regulation campaign, believed a Connecticut attorney with railroad stock holdings, "is to force a general reduction of railroad rates, on the Bryan doctrine, that those who have got something presumably got it wrongfully, and so it is not worthwhile to be particular how it is to be got from them."[10]

Opponents of railroad practices, on the other hand, possessed enough evidences of rebating, discrimination against regions like the South and Midwest, and heavy-handed railroad tactics to present a case for a more rigorous Interstate Commerce Commission that persuaded midwestern Republicans and southern Democrats. More important, they contended that it was unjust to have the commission declare a rate unreasonable only to have the challenged rate remain in effect "until the case has run the gamut of three federal courts, and has been finally settled by the Supreme Court of the United States." A preferable alternative would be to have "some tribunal which is at once impartial and powerful enough to do justice between the Railroad and the Citizen." In practice this would mean that the Interstate Commerce Commission could set a reasonable rate, have it go into effect at once, and put the burden of proof on the railroad to have the rate overturned. "There is no disposition anywhere to deprive the railway companies of their day in court," commented an Iowa editor; "All that is demanded is that the shipper will have his day in court while he is yet alive."[11]

In the month and a half after Roosevelt's message was delivered, the administration sought to get a railroad bill through the short session of Congress. By mid-January a measure bearing White House approval had been introduced, and when it encountered difficulties a compromise bill received committee endorsement in the House on January 31, 1905. This Esch-Townsend bill, named

[10] John W. Alling to Orville H. Platt, January 31, 1905, Platt Papers.

[11] *Des Moines Register and Leader*, February 2, 1905; Ray Stannard Baker, "The Railroad Rate: A Study in Commercial Autocracy," *McClure's Magazine*, 26 (1905), 59.

after its midwestern authors, won the overwhelming approval of the full House on February 9, 1905, by a vote of 326 to 17. The president hoped that the Senate would rapidly pass the House version "and end the present agitation and uncertainty," but the upper chamber's Republican leadership, particularly Senator Nelson Aldrich and his associates, would not be hurried. The approaching end of the session on March 4, the fight over the arbitration treaties and other measures, and the complexity of the question strengthened the hand of conservative lawmakers who contended that the Esch-Townsend bill "ought not to be passed in the Senate without full opportunity for consideration and debate." The Senate would not go beyond having the Interstate Commerce Committee hold hearings on the railroad bills after adjournment.[12]

Roosevelt's strategy for helping his railroad proposals included a barrage of press coverage about presidential support for the legislation. More directly, he informed the Union League Club of Philadelphia on January 30, 1905, that "Neither this people nor any free people will permanently tolerate the use of vast power conferred by vast wealth, and especially by wealth in its corporate form, without lodging somewhere in the Government the still higher power of seeing that this power, in addition to being used in the interest of the individual or individuals possessing it, is also used for and not against the interests of the people as a whole." This speech led the Washington press to decide "that there is a serious conflict on between the President and Congress, and that the President has decided to force the fighting."[13]

To what extent did the Roosevelt campaign also rest on the real or implied threat of tariff revision in the absence of congressional support for railroad regulation? Were his "tariff negotiations . . . less an objective than a device?"[14] Public discussions of protection may have marginally accelerated the movement of the railroad bill through the House, but the backing for it was so pervasive that it is doubtful Speaker Cannon, an alleged object of a tariff feint, could have bottled up a railroad measure in any event. In the context of

[12] New York *Herald*, February 9, 1905 (first quotation); Platt to Wilbur F. Day, February 15, 1905, Platt Papers.

[13] *Washington Post*, January 31, 1905; New York *Herald*, February 1, 1905; Joseph B. Bishop, *Theodore Roosevelt and His Times Shown in His Own Letters*, 2 vols. (New York: Scribner, 1920), I, p. 427.

[14] Blum, *The Republican Roosevelt*, 77.

Roosevelt's consistent handling of the tariff throughout his presidency, his maneuvers in these months do not appear to be so much a part of a shrewd and subtle design, as further evidence of his gingerly treatment of an issue he never mastered. With or without presidential action on the tariff, railroad legislation was to be the prime issue in 1905 and 1906, and the combination of White House support *and* popular interest were the key elements in Roosevelt's success.

By the time Congress adjourned in early March 1905, the implication of what had taken place since the election had intensified Republican fears about the party's future course. Roosevelt's proposals, remarked a St. Louis paper, "offer a strong test to the old hands-off conservatism and those elements which largely dominated the party organization and throve by fealty to privileged property interests." A conservative leader and railroad spokesman thought that "the President has marked out a course so radical as to be fairly revolutionary of the business of the country."[15]

In the spring of 1905 Roosevelt stood at the height of his popularity. Already he had begun the negotiations with the two sides in the Russo-Japanese War that would lead to a peace conference in Portsmouth, New Hampshire, in August and the termination of the conflict. For his peacemaking efforts, the president received the Nobel Peace Prize in 1906. His emergence as a world statesman, exemplified in such episodes of his second term as the Algeciras Conference over Morocco in 1906 and the round-the-world cruise of the American fleet in 1907–1909, solidified his standing with the people. Americans, a politician observed, "pay no attention to any mistakes the President may make, but magnify his virtues with joy and gladness." So it was a confident, assured chief executive who departed at the beginning of April 1905 "for a week's horrid anguish in touring through Kentucky, Indian Territory and Texas; and then I hope for five weeks' genuine pleasure in Oklahoma and Colorado on a hunt."[16]

The nation across which the president traveled to his vacation was giving evidence of a powerful new political mood. This fresh

[15] J. W. Blythe to George D. Perkins, December 13, 1904, Perkins Papers; *St. Louis Republic,* December 7, 1904.

[16] C. B. Landis to Joseph B. Foraker, July 31, 1907, Joseph B. Foraker Papers, Cincinnati Historical Society; Roosevelt to John Hay, April 2, 1905, Morison, *Letters,* IV, p. 1156.

attitude formed the setting within which the campaign over railroad regulation and other battles of Roosevelt's second term were
fought. In June 1905 a New York minister wrote Senator Dolliver
that "The whole country is keenly sensitive to the perils of corporate wealth and the decline of the great convictions."[17] By 1906
public outrage at the extent of business involvement with unsavory
political practices gave a powerful thrust to progressive reforms
throughout society.

A triggering episode was the investigation of gas and insurance
companies in New York, under the leadership of a young attorney
named Charles Evans Hughes. The probe revealed business practices, among them bribes, payoffs, and large campaign contributions, "so shocking that the feeling aroused has been most
profound."[18] Other states experienced similar revelations and consequent political repercussions. California, Colorado, and South
Dakota were western examples; Texas, Mississippi, and Alabama
marked the South's participation. Senators, congressmen, and state
and local officials came under legal scrutiny, and some received
prison sentences for their misdeeds.[19]

Feeding popular anxiety were the journalistic exposés of the
muckrakers in popular periodicals such as *McClure's*, *World's
Work*, and *Collier's*. Lincoln Steffens, Ida Tarbell, and Samuel
Hopkins Adams uncovered urban corruption, dissected the amass-
ing of great fortunes, and warned their readers of the dangers of
shoddy industrial and food products. Underlying these spectacular
manifestations of public concern was the rise in consumer prices;
persistent inflation would be a fact of life throughout the decade.

The outpouring of feeling against a perceived alliance between
business and politics produced support for legislation to regulate
both corporations and parties between 1905 and 1908. Twelve
states passed laws to supervise lobbyists from 1903 to 1908;
twenty-two prohibited corporations from making campaign contributions. Thirty-one states in the same period adopted the direct
primary. On the regulatory side, state railroad commissions and

[17] Newell Dwight Hilles to Jonathan P. Dolliver, June 9, 1905, Dolliver Papers.
[18] Seth Low to James Bryce, October 26, 1905, James Bryce Papers, Bodleian Library, Oxford.
[19] Richard L. McCormick, "The Discovery That 'Business Corrupts Politics': A
Reappraisal of the Origins of Progressivism," *American Historical Review*, 86
(1981), 261–263.

state boards to oversee insurance companies proliferated. In these years the state and national governments turned to regulatory agencies and bureaucratic commissions to provide a continuing oversight function for key areas of an industrialized economy and society. The popular mood of upheaval spent much of its energy quickly, and it never involved an assault on capitalism as such. Still, it provided a favorable environment in which, for a time, the process of shaping an expanded system of governance could go forward.[20]

These political changes from 1905 onward ended the relative unity of the Republican party over the preceding eight years, and brought on mounting and ever more bitter factionalism. In states as diverse as California, Oregon, New Hampshire, Kansas, South Dakota, Iowa, and Wisconsin, insurgent party members challenged the existing GOP leadership for control of the organization and the power to shape policy. Their grievances and enemies were often similar. Railroads became the target for reform and regulation in Kansas, California, New Hampshire, and Iowa. Rebellious Republicans questioned the fairness of tariff policy to their regional interests, and quarrels over protection agitated the upper Midwest. To advance their cause against the entrenched party command, these progressives, as they began to style themselves, advocated direct primaries, reform of campaign practices, and a general reduction in the power of the formal party machinery.

In their public statements, the progressives depicted their goals and methods in lofty terms. The nation confronted "intricate and vital" problems, wrote Governor Cummins of Iowa, and the question was "What kind of men will solve these problems? Will they be men who are selected by the selfish, aggressive interests that must be regulated by the law, or shall they be men who are selected by the body of the people, and who therefore can enjoy complete independence of thought and liberty of action?"[21]

Progressivism within the GOP, embodied in men like Cummins and La Follette, was in reality a more familiar blend of honesty and expediency than the language of its adherents might suggest. Their economic goals had a distinctly sectional flavor, and their loyalty to

---

[20] Ibid., pp. 265–268.

[21] Cummins to Eugene Ganoe Hay, November 30, 1906, Eugene Ganoe Hay Papers, Manuscript Division, Library of Congress.

procedural innovations in the political process owed equal amounts
to a desire to accelerate change and a perception that rewriting the
rules of the game would hurt their enemies most. When a majority
of the Republicans supported the progressive program, then a direct primary confined to party members only was preferred to the
caucus and convention system. If, as time passed, a majority of Republicans seemed likely to oppose reform, the votes of Democrats
would be welcomed in the more flexible and less partisan open primary for selecting candidates. Gradualistic, moderate, and cautious, Republicans of this stamp did not wish "to destroy special
privilege; they simply wished to clasp it to their own bosoms." Yet
while their policy differences with party conservatives were more
narrow than they might appear to be on the surface, the reformers
did not lack for either conviction or intensity. "The Republican
party," observed Cummins in 1906, "must be dominated by the
spirit of progress. While not yielding to the demands of insane radicalism, it must not be terrorized into inaction by the threats of
those who have all they want, and more than they deserve."[22]

The leading example of this new Republican force in 1905 was
Robert M. La Follette of Wisconsin. Elected to the Senate early in
that year after four years as governor, Battle Bob had gained a reputation as a foe of corporations and spokesman for midwestern reform. After a decade of rebellion against the Republican state
organization, he won the governorship in 1900. In two terms he and
his progressive allies enacted laws to establish a direct primary,
regulate Wisconsin railroads, and impose higher taxes on corporations. La Follette established close ties between the state government and the University of Wisconsin. His drawing on academic
expertise to help mold his programs became known as the Wisconsin Idea. La Follette was fifty when named to the Senate; his thick
hair and fighting stance, combined with his combative oratory, belied his short, slight stature. He possessed the power and drive of
the confirmed crusader. Having learned "never to know defeat in a
good cause," he relied on a dogged persistence that made him an
effective legislator and reform leader.[23]

[22] Richard C. Baker, *The Tariff under Roosevelt and Taft* (Hastings, Neb.: Democratic Printing Co., 1941), p. 196; Cummins to Albert J. Beveridge, November 12,
1906, Cummins Papers.
[23] Ellen Torelle, comp., *The Political Philosophy of Robert M. La Follette*, p. 20.

Robert M. La Follette
(1855–1925), from *La Follette's Autobiography* (Madison, Wisconsin, 1913).

La Follette's sincere belief that he did the people's work sustained him through the vicissitudes of a long public career. With his passion for justice and fairness went self-righteousness, ambition, and an ample store of ruthlessness. La Follette wanted to be president, and viewed himself as a man of destiny for the GOP. Consequently, he did not always scruple about the means that might take him to the White House. Roosevelt's status as the national embodiment of Republican innovation forced La Follette to defer to him, and the Wisconsin senator chafed at the ascendancy of a man he regarded as opportunistic and a covert conservative. The tension of the La Follette–Roosevelt relationship would be, in time, as significant for the party as the friendship between Roosevelt and William Howard Taft.

During the spring and summer of 1905, both sides in the railroad struggle courted public support for the impending legislative contest when Congress reassembled in December. Although railroads underwrote an expensive lobbying and publicity campaign to shape editorial opinion and influence popular attitudes, their heavy-handed and over-organized effort changed few minds. The Senate hearings in the spring gave industry advocates another platform to air their opposition to the regulation that the Esch-Town-send bill proposed. As a means of swaying sentiment, however, these ventures had mixed results. A prominent Kansas Republican believed that speeches from railroad leaders had "a tendency to enfuriate [sic] and irritate public feeling rather than allay and mollify the anti-railroad sentiment that now prevails." By the time Congress convened, it was clear, as Senator Lodge noted, that "There is going to be a railroad rate bill."[24]

Theodore Roosevelt worked hard to achieve this result. Returning from his hunting vacation, he renewed his support for regulation in speeches at Denver and Chicago in May. At the same time, the attorney general supplied the Senate committee with an opinion that the president's proposals were constitutional. During the summer the Justice Department filed suits against rebaters in the Middle West. The president's campaign against the railroads was not entirely evenhanded. When rebating charges forced Secretary of the Navy Paul Morton, a former railroad executive, to resign, Roosevelt intervened to make certain that the probe of Morton's conduct was gentle. On the publicity side, the White House encouraged reporters to detail railroad misdeeds in the popular magazines. Finally, during a tour of the South in October, Roosevelt set forth anew the premises and specifics of his regulatory goals.[25]

When the first session of the Fifty-ninth Congress gathered in December 1905, Roosevelt's annual message called for railroad legislation as part of his greater purpose "to assert the sovereignty of the National Government by affirmative action." Simultaneously, another wave of federal antirebating suits were filed in courts in Pennsylvania, New York, and Chicago. The president backed away slightly from his earlier proposal to have a rate that the Interstate Commerce Commission had imposed go into effect immediately; now it would do so "within a reasonable time." But on the whole, the message laid out a broad array of regulatory solutions for the railroad problem. The rate-making authority of the ICC would be enhanced, railroad accounts ought to be open to inspection, and private car railroad lines should receive more supervision. In re-

[24] Joseph L. Bristow to Chester I. Long, May 10, 1905, Chester I. Long Papers, Kansas State Historical Society; Lodge to Henry L. Higginson, December 1, 1905, Lodge Papers.

[25] *New York Tribune*, May 10, 11, June 17, July 15, 17, 1905; Ari and Olive Hoogenboom, *A History of the ICC* (New York: Norton, 1975), pp. 50–51.

viewing Roosevelt's other suggestions about child labor laws, government regulation of insurance companies, employer liability laws for the District of Columbia, and a pure food and drug measure, the New York *World* called the message "the most amazing program of centralization that any President of the United States has ever recommended."[26]

For the next six months, the congressional struggle over railroads dominated the national political scene. An understanding between Roosevelt and Speaker Cannon that the tariff would not come up smoothed the way of the railroad bill in the House. The Hepburn bill, sponsored by William P. Hepburn of Iowa, sailed through the lower house on February 8, 1906, by a vote of 346 to 7. In the House and Senate, the president found that the Democrats offered the railroad bill strong support. In the upper house, however, the conservatives, under Aldrich's lead, used the parliamentary devices at their command to modify what Henry Cabot Lodge called "an extreme and dangerous measure." Through three months of debate and maneuver, the Roosevelt forces sought to collect a majority from both parties for the substance of what the administration desired and to block conservative attempts to obtain the broadest possible judicial review of the Interstate Commerce Commission's actions. In the end, the scope of court review remained vague, and the Aldrich forces could believe, as Senator Albert J. Beveridge noted, that they "won out in the fight for broad review."[27]

Beveridge quickly added, however, that "if it had not been for Theodore Roosevelt there would not have been any railroad legislation of any kind." The president could claim the bulk of the credit for the Hepburn Act that provided the ICC with power to set maximum rates, to review rail company accounts, and to supervise the railroad industry extensively. It was, the president told his son, "a fine piece of constructive legislation, and all that has been done tends toward carrying out the principles I have been preaching." The Hepburn Act represented the major domestic legislation of

[26] *The World* is quoted in *Current Literature*, 40 (1906), 11; *State Papers as Governor and President*, p. 273 (Roosevelt quotations); *New York Tribune*, December 12, 13, 15, 1905.

[27] Lodge to Henry White, February 26, 1906, Lodge Papers; Albert J. Beveridge to Albert Shaw, May 20, 1906, Albert J. Beveridge Papers, Manuscript Division, Library of Congress; Blum, *Republican Roosevelt*, pp. 87–105.

Roosevelt's presidency. From his first moves in late 1904, he had pursued his campaign with determination and patience. More significant than the substance of the law was the demonstration of how a president could utilize the powers of his office to push legislation through Congress.[28]

On two other controversial subjects in 1906, Roosevelt added the weight of the presidency to efforts for greater federal regulatory power. When the publication of Upton Sinclair's *The Jungle* precipitated a popular clamor about unsanitary and filthy conditions in the meatpacking industry, the White House supported a meat inspection amendment to the agricultural appropriation law that passed Congress in late June. Amid the uproar over this problem, the faltering campaign for a pure food bill also gathered momentum, and when Roosevelt "threw his influence into the balance" the lawmakers agreed to a compromise measure on June 30. Considering the three regulatory acts of the session, the president concluded that "taken together" they were "a noteworthy advance in the policy of securing Federal supervision and control over corporations." To a journalistic commentator, they also revealed "a marked tendency toward the centralization of power in the United States and a corresponding decrease in the old time sovereignty of the states, or of the individual."[29]

Once Congress adjourned, preparations began almost immediately for the fall elections. The Republicans faced the usual difficulties of midterm contests for the party in power, and also confronted resurgent Democrats "buoyant with hope, and planning for victory" after the disaster of 1904. Reports circulated privately in July that the Republicans might find their House majority of more than 100 seats "wiped out or certainly cut down to a margin of 10 or 15 unless something happens to save the day."[30]

Leading the Democratic rebound was William Jennings Bryan. Before he left on a world tour in the late summer of 1905, Bryan

[28] Beveridge to Shaw, May 20, 1906, Beveridge Papers; Roosevelt to Kermit Roosevelt, June 13, 1906, Roosevelt Papers.

[29] Roosevelt to Lyman Abbott, July 1, 1906, Morison, *Letters*, V, p. 328; John Braeman et al., *Change and Continuity in Twentieth Century America* (Columbus: Ohio State University Press, 1964), p. 75; Oscar E. Anderson, Jr., *The Health of a Nation: Harvey W. Wiley and the Fight for Pure Food* (Chicago: University of Chicago Press, 1958), p. 190.

[30] William C. Beer to D. E. Thompson, July 25, 1906, Beer Papers; Joseph B. Foraker to A. Maurice Low, May 30, 1906, Foraker Papers.

staked out a position designed to place him and the Democrats to the left of Roosevelt and the Republicans on the questions of reform and regulation. He identified "plutocracy" as the basis of Republicanism, called for decisive action against the trusts, and asked whether Roosevelt had "the courage to be a reformer." Congressional Democrats also depicted themselves as better friends of Roosevelt's programs than the Republicans. In the struggle over the Hepburn Act, the Democrats were more unified than in previous years and gave the president consistent backing on crucial votes. "At this moment," a New York congressman observed in May 1906, "the only support in either House of Congress which Mr. Roosevelt can depend on with certainty is the Democratic vote."[31]

Democrats also hoped that the emergence of organized labor as a political force would bolster their electoral hopes in 1906. The American Federation of Labor, composed of skilled workers in craft unions, had attained a membership of nearly 1,700,000 by 1904. The A.F. of L. did not seek to organize unskilled employees, it was restrictive in its racial policies, and it was more conservative than counterparts on the left like the Industrial Workers of the World. However, it did want federal legislation to offset anti-union injunctions from the courts and to protect the right to strike. By 1906, at the suggestion of its president, Samuel Gompers, the federation sought to use its potential power at the polls to advance its aims. When Speaker Cannon and the Republican Congress proved unreceptive in the spring to the A.F. of L.'s ideas, Gompers advocated "the positive defeat" of Republican congressional candidates "who have been hostile or indifferent to the just demands of labor."[32]

In this early demonstration of interest group politics, the unions first focused on an unsympathetic GOP incumbent in Maine's September balloting. To counter the threat the Republicans sent in Cannon, Taft, and other speakers, and the local candidate survived the labor assault. "We have got to meet these movements which

---

[31] William Jennings Bryan, "Has the President the Courage to Be a Reformer?" *Public Opinion*, 38 (1905), 559; W. Bourke Cockran to Montague White, May 17, 1906, W. Bourke Cockran Papers, New York Public Library, quoted in David Sarasohn, "The Democratic Surge, 1905–1912: Forging a Progressive Majority," Ph.D. dissertation, University of California at Los Angeles, 1976, p. 28.

[32] "Organized Labor in Politics," *The Independent*, 61 (1906), 175–176.

aim at government ownership, the control of legislation by selected classes in the community, and which in the long run tend toward Socialism," concluded Henry Cabot Lodge after the Maine results were recorded.[33]

During the rest of the campaign, Roosevelt sought to blunt the Democratic-labor drive by the use of cabinet officers such as Taft and Attorney General William H. Moody in hotly contested states like Massachusetts, Illinois, and Indiana. Taft also went to Idaho, where the Republican gubernatorial candidate had strong opposition from the Industrial Workers of the World, or "those dynamiters and thugs," as the president described them. Roosevelt called in his debts from others in the labor community not directly tied to the American Federation of Labor, and urged the congressional campaign leaders to "Put all the emphasis on what we have done for labor; not on attacking certain labor men, who are then identified by a large number of slovenly thinkers with the whole labor body." Despite Roosevelt's attempts at evenhandedness, his direct intervention against labor in the campaign, the attacks of other GOP speakers on the unions, and the generally negative response of the Republicans toward labor's program moved the A.F. of L. closer to the Democrats. The 1906 election was an important early step in creating the later alliance between organized labor and the Democratic party.[34]

Bryan also hurt Democratic chances in 1906 when he returned from his world travels in September and advocated, in a long speech in New York, government ownership of the interstate railroads. Although he distinguished between federal operation of the interstate lines and state control of intrastate companies, the protest within his own party, and the assaults of the Republicans, caused him to back away quickly. "Within six hours after he landed at the Battery," said the New York *World*, Bryan "had split his party wide open again." Nonetheless, the party continued its campaign as friends of labor and better supporters of Roosevelt than his own party.[35]

---

[33] Lodge to W. S. Bigelow, September 18, 1906, Lodge Papers.

[34] Roosevelt to Gifford Pinchot, September 15, 1906, Roosevelt to Cannon, September 17, 1906, Morison, *Letters*, V, pp. 413, 414.

[35] New York *World*, September 7, 1906, quoted in Sarasohn, "The Democratic Surge," pp. 43–44.

The Republicans entered the campaign with the tariff issue once again threatening their cohesion. Party members asked why the Congress and the president could not supply "a rational revision of tariff schedules, along protection lines." Speaker Cannon and his House colleagues on the Republican congressional campaign committee solicited and obtained a letter from Roosevelt that endorsed the work of the preceding session and declared against an immediate revision of the Dingley law. More sensitive to the public mood than Cannon, Roosevelt avoided the label or language of a "stand-pat" position on the tariff, and secured the deferral of the question "simply by not saying 'stand pat' in an offensive way." He was quite willing that his successor "be nominated on a platform which shall promise immediate action in the direction of a revision" and have to grapple with the difficulties he had so assiduously dodged.[36]

The turmoil over protection did not abate during the contest. Secretary of War William Howard Taft expressed his own sympathy for revision in a Maine speech in September, and Senator Beveridge told a Des Moines audience in October that "no tariff schedule is immortal. When conditions change the tariff schedule that was adjusted to that condition ought also to change." Speaker Cannon did not agree. For him the Dingley law was "all things considered, the most perfect and just customs law ever enacted." Cannon's position, although acceptable to staunch protectionists and party regulars, drew fire in the Midwest and from the growing number of supporters of revision. "If the Republican party does not adjust itself to changing conditions from time to time, but stands pat forever on schedules made ten years ago," wrote a Connecticut congressman, "the time is not far distant when I am afraid some of us will have to take seats at the foot of the committee room tables, even if we are allowed to represent our Districts at all."[37]

Unlike previous Republican canvasses, the campaign of 1906 also encountered nagging organizational and factional obstacles. Contributions came in slowly, especially from the business commu-

---

[36] E. D. Crumpacker to Roosevelt, July 28, 1906, Roosevelt Papers (first quotation); Roosevelt to John A. Sleicher, August 11, 1906 (third quotation), Roosevelt to Leslie M. Shaw, September 11, 1906 (second quotation), Morison, *Letters*, V, pp. 354, 405.

[37] *Des Moines Register Leader*, August 17, October 4, 1906; E. J. Hill to William Loeb, September 13, 1906, Roosevelt Papers.

nity, and a halfhearted attempt to solicit funds from individual
GOP voters fizzled. Criticism of Speaker Cannon was so prevalent
some candidates asked that he not speak on their behalf. Democratic complaints about the high cost of living, intraparty quarrels
over reform, the Roosevelt program, vexing ethnocultural issues
such as prohibition, and an absence of the usual cohesion and high
morale crippled the Republican cause.

As the campaign proceeded, however, opposition mistakes and
the threat of an enemy victory offset some of these weaknesses. In
addition to Bryan's railroad speech, the gubernatorial candidacies
of William Randolph Hearst in New York and James B. Moran in
Massachusetts aroused GOP fears about what radical Democrats
might do. These considerations, combined with Roosevelt's active
participation as campaign manager and his endorsement of the Republican Congress, limited the party's off-year losses.[38]

The president was delighted with the results. "It is very gratifying," he told his daughter, "to have ridden iron-shod over
Gompers and the labor agitators, and at the same time to have won
the striking victory while the big financiers either stood sullenly
aloof or gave furtive aid to the enemy." The election of Charles
Evans Hughes over Hearst in New York and the success of the party
in Ohio represented "a victory for civilization." Republicans held
on to the control of Congress, though a loss of 28 seats in the House
trimmed its majority there by half, to 56 seats. Party strength in the
Senate increased slightly. Those close to Roosevelt gave him the
credit for the election's outcome and told the White House that
"not one of our men would have pulled through had it not been for
the appeal to 'stand by Roosevelt.' " Enemies of the president were
less certain, and they attributed Democratic gains and Republican
troubles to a spreading discontent with the Roosevelt program.[39]

Whatever the merit of these two explanations, and the Roosevelt side commanded a greater following in the press, the elections
did disclose serious problems for the GOP. Actually, Hearst's race

[38] Sarasohn, "The Democratic Surge," pp. 39–50, looks at 1906 from the Demo-
cratic side; for Republican comments, see Lodge to Roosevelt, August 1, 1906,
H. C. Loudenslager to Roosevelt, November 3, 1906, Roosevelt Papers. Mortimer
Durand to Edward Grey, September 21, 1906, FO371/158, Public Record Office,
London, offers a British perspective.

[39] Roosevelt to Alice Roosevelt Longworth, November 7, 1906, Roosevelt to Taft,
November 8, 1906, Morison, *Letters,* V, pp. 488–489, 491; Beveridge to William
Loeb, November 9, 1906, Beveridge Papers.

Charles Evans Hughes, 1906. *American Monthly Review of Reviews*, November 1906.

in New York had come very close to success, while the Democrats had won the statehouse in Rhode Island, had run strongly in Massachusetts, and had picked up a number of congressional seats in the Northeast. This pattern of Democratic strength in Congress would persist and grow in the next three elections. Furthermore, likelihood of a labor-Democratic coalition had been increased, with all that it portended for the future. In states such as Kansas, Iowa, and Indiana, the Republican vote fell off from its 1904 high, beginning a process of erosion that continued through 1912. The Democrats would go into the presidential election of 1908 in a better position than might have seemed likely in 1904, while the Republicans faced the next race for the White House in a less harmonious and stable condition than had been the case four years earlier. Within both parties, the issue of the reach and extent of governmental regulatory power was as yet unresolved.

CHAPTER 5

Taft and Bryan in 1908

As the Republicans looked ahead to the election of 1908, Theodore Roosevelt's program of government regulation was the most tangible source of intraparty friction. In October 1906 the president went to Harrisburg, Pennsylvania, to dedicate the new state capitol. His speech called for "adequate supervision and control over the business use of the swollen fortunes of to-day," and alluded to the need for an inheritance tax on great wealth. He asserted that the national government "has and is to exercise the power of supervision and control over the business use of this wealth." Although much had been accomplished, Roosevelt promised: "we shall not halt; we shall steadily follow the path we have marked out, executing the laws we have succeeded in putting upon the statute books with absolute impartiality as between man and man, and unresting in our endeavor to strengthen and supplement these by further laws which shall enable us in more efficient and more summary fashion to achieve the ends we have in view."[1]

During the last years of his second term, Roosevelt supported many new areas in which regulatory power should operate. His annual messages in 1906 and 1907 endorsed the income tax, federal incorporation of interstate business, national marriage and divorce laws, regulation of campaign expenses, postal savings laws, and a wide array of other proposals. "We hold," he contended in December 1906, "that the government should not conduct the business of the nation, but that it should exercise such supervision as will insure its being conducted in the interest of the nation." In his most innovative and comprehensive statement, sent to Congress on January 31, 1908, the president advocated passage of an employers lia-

---

[1] *The Works of Theodore Roosevelt: American Problems*, XVI, pp. 71, 72, 74.

bility law, a workmen's compensation measure, regulation of injunctions in labor disputes, and greater supervision of the railroads and large corporations. "We seek to control law-defying wealth," he wrote, "in the first place to prevent its doing dire evil to the Republic, and in the next place to avoid the vindictive and dreadful radicalism which, if left uncontrolled, it is certain in the end to arouse."[2]

In Roosevelt's mind, a large amount of strong presidential leadership and discretion in the execution of policy was needed to make business behave correctly through increased government regulation. By use of agencies like the Bureau of Corporations and the Justice Department, erring companies would be made to improve themselves and thereby avert "schemes of wild, would-be remedy which would work infinitely more harm than the disease itself."[3]

In the second Roosevelt term, the actual agents of bureaucratic regulation became much more visible to the public. James R. Garfield of the Bureau of Corporations conducted probes of Standard Oil, United States Steel, and International Harvester, among others. Gifford Pinchot of the Forest Service spoke out for conservation and a larger government voice in the management of forest reserves, grazing lands, and water resources. Roosevelt appointed the Keep Commission in 1905 to consider how the federal government might be made more efficient and better organized. The use of academic experts, the reliance on presidential commissions, and the widening scope of social questions with which Washington was concerned conveyed between 1905 and 1909 a powerful sense of an assertive government that differed in kind from the modest federal establishment of even the 1890s.

Persuaded that he knew best which businessmen and industries conformed to the highest standards of corporate morality, the president entered willingly into private understandings with key companies such as United States Steel and International Harvester. Against those companies, such as Standard Oil, or those corporate leaders, like E. H. Harriman, whose activities he disliked, he applied the full force of national power in court suits and prolonged investigations. During the president's second term, the Roosevelt administration filed more than 35 antitrust actions against consoli-

[2] *State Papers as Governor and President*, XV, p. 366 (first quotation); Morison, *Letters*, VI, p. 1582 (second quotation).

[3] *American Problems*, XVI, p. 73.

dation in the oil, tobacco, meatpacking, and other industries. This cluster of regulatory ideas and executive actions became known as the "Roosevelt policies," and potential Republican presidential hopefuls were measured against the criterion of fidelity to the administration's program.

Roosevelt's approval of a broadened campaign of regulation and government intervention coincided with, encouraged, and drew strength from the growing power of the progressive wing of his party. In Iowa, Cummins won a third gubernatorial race in 1906, and prepared to challenge Senator William Boyd Allison's bid for reelection in 1908. Joseph L. Bristow launched a similar assault against incumbent Senator Chester I. Long, excoriating Long for his alleged lack of sympathy with Roosevelt's program. Other insurgent efforts gained momentum in California under Hiram Johnson and the Lincoln-Roosevelt League, in South Dakota behind Coe Crawford, and in Oregon in the persons of Jonathan Bourne and William S. U'Ren. The main centers of GOP progressivism were west of the Mississippi, but leaders like Governor Charles Evans Hughes of New York, Winston Churchill in New Hampshire, and George L. Record in New Jersey gave eastern representation to the spirit of party reform and change after 1906. As the most celebrated embodiment of this new party spirit in the Middle West, Senator La Follette prepared to make a race for the presidential nomination in 1908.

The goals of the progressive faction now included both procedural and substantive issues. Tariff reform remained a large concern for Cummins and other midwesterners, who believed that the policy was "brought into disrepute when it is used to shield extortionate profit, instead of giving fair and adequate protection." Railroad regulation that went beyond the Hepburn Act seemed imperative, including measures that would enable the Interstate Commerce Commission to initiate proceedings against railroad rates and that would use the physical value of railroad property as a basis for rate making. In a larger sense, argued Cummins, "if the Government did not take on new functions and protect the weak against the strong in the struggle for wealth and commercial liberty, our vaunted equalities and liberties would be but meaningless phrases."[4]

[4] Albert B. Cummins, "A Western Republican's View of the Issues of 1908," *Appleton's Magazine*, 10 (1907), 531, 534.

Equally important to progressive Republicans were alterations in the way that public policy was made and political affairs conducted. The direct primary, the direct election of senators, and the initiative and referendum represented changes that could enable government better "to carry out and express the well formulated judgment and the will of the people."[5] In these same years, local governments in the Midwest, like their counterparts in the South, adopted first the commission form of city administration and later the city manager plan. These innovations in such municipalities as Des Moines, Houston, Galveston, and hundreds of other moderate-sized cities, reflected the same skepticism about partisanship that animated Republican reformers.[6]

In the House of Representatives, the dominance of Speaker Cannon and his use of the power of that office to guide favored legislation and block reform proposals earned the animosity of an ever-larger number of Republican members, particularly from the upper Midwest. Restiveness about the leadership of Senator Aldrich and his conservative colleagues also surfaced in the Senate as La Follette, and then Jonathan P. Dolliver, found allies and converts. Sharp battles in the spring of 1908 over naval appropriations and currency legislation foreshadowed the more celebrated struggles of Taft's term.

As the progressives gained in power and influence, they also stimulated the resentment of the conservatives, who regarded the tactics and rhetoric of the reformers as distasteful. When La Follette took to the stump and read the record of roll call votes to show how the Old Guard in the Senate blocked progress, he accurately predicted that other senators "will think I am the meanest fellow ever to 'go and tell.'" One of the victims of La Follette's technique responded that he did not believe "that one of the duties of a senator is to engage in agitation."[7] Friction between prominent progressives and their stand-pat counterparts also involved personalities. Senator Beveridge's conceit and posturing repelled many in the Senate, and the records of La Follette in Wisconsin and Cum-

[5] Torelle, *Political Philosophy of Robert M. La Follette*, p. 182.

[6] Bradley Robert Rice, *Progressive Cities: The Commission Government Movement in America, 1901–1920* (Austin: University of Texas Press, 1977).

[7] Belle Case La Follette and Fola La Follette, *Robert M. La Follette, 1855–1925*, 2 vols. (New York: Macmillan, 1953), I, p. 212; Chester I. Long to S. A. Monger, March 25, 1908, Long Papers.

mins in Iowa revealed to their enemies as much opportunism as principle.

The men around Roosevelt, his Tennis Cabinet of Gifford Pinchot, James R. Garfield, and other young officials and reporters, seemed to the president's critics a coterie of yes-men or Incense-Swingers who built up Roosevelt at the expense of his adversaries. Most of all, the right wing of the Republicans thought that the progressives were potential or actual party-wreckers. While ignoring their own willingness to cross partisan lines when it suited the situation, the regulars scorned "radical Republicans who do not differ in any essential respect from Mr. Bryan and his followers."[8]

Faced with a shift from older party doctrine that advocated national power to encourage economic activity and expansion, Republican conservatives displayed obvious unhappiness about policies that brought more government interference and supervision of previously private economic decisions. Roosevelt and his "progressive" friends, decided a railroad president, were "consciously or unconsciously ... trying to concentrate all power in Washington, to practically wipe out state lines, and to govern the people by commissions and bureaus."[9]

Where Democrats had had almost exclusive custody of the concept of state rights for half a century, anti-Roosevelt Republicans now discovered more appeal in "the dual form of government for which our Constitution provided." Of course, many conservatives also regarded regulatory ideas as a threat to their private property and a harbinger of collectivism. "I happen to know that many of our leading spirits are becoming tired of the present fire works administration," wrote a journalist privately in mid-1907, "because it squints too much in the direction of Socialism, that is, paternalism from which may easily follow various encroachments upon property rights and the rights of the individual states."[10]

Elements in the business community, predominantly those in

[8] Long to S. W. Fitzpatrick, February 9, 1908, Long Papers.

[9] Charles E. Perkins to Henry L. Higginson, June 17, 1907, Henry L. Higginson Papers, Baker Library, Harvard Business School, Boston.

[10] Foraker to George Gray, September 9, 1907, Foraker Papers; E. L. Scharf to William Boyd Allison, July 25, 1907, Box 366, Allison Papers.

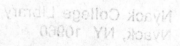

the Northeast, became more critical of Roosevelt's work as 1907 proceeded. A British diplomat attended a dinner with "several very well known and influential business men, all of whom were staunch Republicans hitherto," and reported them "so incensed at the President's actions" that they intended to vote against Roosevelt at the next election even if Bryan ran against him. "The great trouble with the President is that he is not a business man and does not understand commercial affairs," decided an Ohio banker, who was "inclined to think that the only way he will ever learn is to have everything take a bad tumble, and then study business and commerce as it arises from the ruins." The Panic of 1907, with its bank failures and recessionary impact in the autumn, provided the "bad tumble" that confirmed for these Roosevelt critics the danger of his program. "Congress must stand between the country and his ill-considered recommendations and hasty policies," announced an angry New York stockbroker.[11]

During the last two years of Roosevelt's second term, Congress became more and more inclined to come between the president and his policy goals. The Senate in February 1907 responded to western unhappiness with the administration's conservation policies by adding a rider to an appropriation bill that limited the executive's power to create forest reserves. Before he signed the measure, Roosevelt set aside or increased more than thirty national forests, much to the displeasure of the lawmakers.

In the same short session of 1906–1907, Roosevelt asked Congress to approve a measure that would have subsidized the American shipping industry through a system of payments for the movement of mail across the oceans. Direct subsidies to the merchant marine was an issue that since 1900 had divided eastern and West Coast Republicans, who favored the idea, from their midwestern colleagues, who opposed such payments. The alternative approach of ocean mail subsidies, backed with a presidential message, cleared the House later in the session and then expired in the Senate. Midwestern Republicans voted overwhelmingly against the bill in the House, and the debate in both bodies revealed the sec-

[11] C. Clive Bagley to James Bryce, May 2, 1907, Bryce Papers; Myron T. Herrick to Higginson, October 2, 1907, Higginson Papers; George F. Dominick to Herbert Parsons, November 9, 1907, Box 6, Herbert Parsons Papers, Columbia University Library.

tional strains within the party that further complicated Roosevelt's problems with Capitol Hill.[12]

Quarreling between the president and the legislative branch continued into 1908. On the currency, funding for the navy, and amendment of the antitrust laws, the differences were sharp. "The feeling at the Capitol against anything and everything the President wants, is very bitter," wrote an associate of J. P. Morgan's in March 1908. Roosevelt reciprocated these sentiments. "The ruling clique in the Senate, the House, and the National Committee," he remarked in May 1908, "seem to regard every concession to decency as merely a matter of bargain and sale with *me,* which *I* must pay for in some way or fashion."[13]

The worsening relations between the White House and the Hill, however, did not stem solely from differences over policy. The lawmakers had grown weary of the flood of presidential messages, and resented Roosevelt's public and private scorn of them and their work. "That fellow at the other end of the Avenue," said Speaker Cannon in an angry mood, "wants everything, from the birth of Christ to the death of the devil."[14] The president further contributed to his problems with Congress when he indulged more frequently in personal attacks on legislators and used the investigative machinery of the government, particularly the Secret Service, to probe alleged wrongdoing among congressmen and senators. All these developments increased Roosevelt's national popularity, as the voters applauded presidential chastisement of Capitol Hill. But this acclaim was purchased at the price of intensified legislative-executive friction, which reached its nadir after the 1908 election.

Republican discord brightened the prospects of the Democrats in 1908. Following the 1906 elections, Bryan shifted his emphasis to procedural issues like the direct election of senators, the initiative, and the referendum, subsumed under the general inquiry "Shall the People Rule?" He struck out at the Republicans regarding campaign contributions, and told a friend in March 1908: "Until we can

[12] "Vote of Mississippi Valley Republicans in National House on Ocean Mail Bill, March 1, 1907," table in Roosevelt Papers.

[13] George W. Perkins to J. P. Morgan, March 16, 1908, George W. Perkins Papers, Columbia University Library; Roosevelt to Albert Shaw, May 22, 1908, Morison, *Letters,* VI, p. 1033.

[14] J. Hampton Moore, *Roosevelt and the Old Guard* (Philadelphia: Macrae Smith Co., 1925), p. 219.

"How Can He Fail?" Bryan tries to launch the Democratic campaign. *Harper's Weekly,* April 4, 1908.

get the United States Senate elected by the people, it is impossible to do anything in the way of national reforms."[15] By this change of focus he was able to hit at points where the Republicans were vulnerable, to stress areas of general Democratic agreement, and to capitalize on the growing popular suspicion of the devices and practices of older political methods. Party divisions over the reach of governmental power were not discussed. After the Panic of 1907, Bryan also called for government guarantees of bank deposits.

Bryan had now achieved an ascendancy among Democrats that approached possession of a personal machine within the party. In the first half of 1908, he and his supporters easily dominated the delegate selection process in state conventions and repulsed the conservative challenges of Governor John A. Johnson of Minnesota and Judge George Gray. The Nebraskan had reassured the South of his sympathy for its racial policies, telling a New York audience "that the white men in the South are giving the negroes better laws than the negroes would give to the white men if they were making the laws."[16] He made similar gestures to the Pacific Coast on Oriental immigration. With the progressives in the party behind him, the conservatives in disarray, and the South and West solidly for him,

[15] Bryan to Walter Clark, March 13, 1908, in Aubrey Lee Brooks and Hugh Talmage Lefler, eds., *The Papers of Walter Clark,* 2 vols. (Chapel Hill: University of North Carolina Press, 1950), II, p. 96.

[16] *The Independent,* 64 (1908), 940.

Bryan had no real contest to secure the party's nomination in Denver in July 1908.

The national platform, written under Bryan's supervision, was more reformist than its Republican counterpart, calling as it did for lower tariffs, increased railroad regulation, and federal licensing of corporations that controlled more than 25 percent of a single product. But the document also sought to strike a more conservative posture than in Bryan's previous races. Controversial matters such as government ownership of interstate railroads, the initiative, and the referendum were omitted. The Democrats advocated economy in government, the preservation of state rights and home rule, and pledged "to combat with unceasing vigilance the efforts of those who are striving by usurpation to seize the powers of the people of the states for exploitation by the federal government."[17]

Bryan stressed caution and harmony in 1908 because he believed that a united party had a good chance of electing him president. The Panic of 1907 took away the force of Republican claims about prosperity, and the prospective GOP nominees were all less popular figures than Roosevelt. Furthermore, there seemed to be the possibility of black voters defecting from the Republicans over Roosevelt's attitude toward them. In midwestern states, the issue of alcohol control divided Republicans into wet and dry factions, to the benefit of the more culturally tolerant Democrats.

An even greater asset, Bryan believed, was the support of organized labor in the person of Gompers and the American Federation of Labor. Following its failure in the 1906 election, the union decided to work with the Democrats to defeat Republicans who were unreceptive to limiting the judicial power to grant injunctions in strikes. To Gompers' appeals, the Republicans made no favorable response in Congress or in their 1908 national convention, while the Democrats incorporated three-quarters of the union's requests, albeit in cautious language, in their platform. Whether labor could deliver the vote remained to be seen, but the precedent of active union participation on the Democratic side in 1908 was another step toward the alliance of the Woodrow Wilson and Franklin D. Roosevelt years.

As the Republicans prepared to select their presidential nomi-

---

[17] Mark H. Salt, ed., *Candidates and the Issues: An Official History of the Campaign of 1908* (Charles B. Ayer, 1908), p. 86.

nee in 1908, the divisions within the party between friends and enemies of Roosevelt, between progressives and stand-patters, and between president and Congress presented the party with a situation it had not faced for more than a decade. "There is pretty wide dissatisfaction and more factions and division than I have ever known in the Republican party in years gone by," remarked a Kansas party member in April 1908.[18]

A number of candidates came forward from the conservative camp who were in implicit opposition to the direction of the party under Roosevelt. Speaker Cannon had support in his home state of Illinois and among his congressional cohorts, but his advanced age, uncouth manner, and reactionary record disqualified him. Senator Philander Knox of Pennsylvania had been Roosevelt's attorney general and sometime trust-buster. Unfortunately his state was certain for the GOP, and his corporation connections and conservative voting performance hurt him nationally. Senator Foraker of Ohio sought to control his state delegation and to combine those votes with support from southern Republicans. But since he had become the most celebrated anti-Roosevelt senator in the party after 1904, Foraker had no serious chance. Vice-President Fairbanks was probably the most earnest conservative hopeful, and he had a grip on the Indiana delegation. Against these assets, however, were his uninspiring platform style, an aloof personality, and his support of stand-pat policies. The most fatal obstacle to all these candidates, moreover, was Roosevelt's resistance to a nominee who would not "carry out the governmental principles in which I believe with all my heart and soul."[19]

On the progressive side, two candidates had varying degrees of backing. Senator La Follette hoped to build on his Wisconsin base and emerge as a compromise candidate in event of a deadlock. Despite some optimistic claims, his campaign never gained much force and by the convention was moribund. More substantial was the candidacy of Charles Evans Hughes. His defeat of Hearst propelled the forty-four-year-old Hughes into the national limelight. When the new governor pushed a reform program through the state legislature in 1907, his political fortunes further prospered. Perceived as the champion of honesty in politics against corrupt in-

---

[18] Bernard Kelly to Chester Long, April 24, 1908, Long Papers.

[19] Roosevelt to William Allen White, July 30, 1907, Morison, *Letters*, V, p. 735.

fluences, Hughes was, according to a New York congressman, "wonderfully strong with the people" in the summer of 1907.[20] Since New York State always figured largely in Republican electoral calculations, Hughes's ability to carry it added to his appeal. The Hughes candidacy had two serious weaknesses, the second of which proved fatal. As governor, he had irritated and alienated party leaders in the state with his brusque manner and insensitivity to partisan considerations. He had failed, wrote a Taft supporter, "to recognize the great need of a Party organization in the State if victories are to be won and the service it has rendered in the past, and even in his election." Roosevelt's adamant opposition represented the most dangerous drawback to the New Yorker's hopes. After Hughes's election, the president had attempted to serve as an adviser to the new governor. Two such strong-minded men could not cooperate for long, and personality differences soon emerged over New York patronage in April 1907. Roosevelt became convinced that Hughes had embarrassed him. Thereafter the president rapidly persuaded himself that Hughes was not a progressive candidate at all but, instead, the choice of reactionaries.[21]

Happily for Roosevelt, he could see alternatives to Hughes within his own cabinet. Elihu Root, now secretary of state, would have gained the presidential blessing had he been receptive. His age, poor health, and background in corporation law reinforced his personal inclination against running. Secretary of War William Howard Taft became after 1905 the logical heir of Roosevelt's support. Because their friendship eroded once Taft became president, and because of the consequences of that rupture, the development of Taft's presidential race merits close examination. Roosevelt's fulsome praise of his successor's qualifications, a tendency to overdramatize the extent of their personal closeness, and a failure to sort out the subtleties of Taft's nomination campaign have led to much confusion about the crisis of succession through which the Republican party passed from 1907 to 1909.

William Howard Taft was fifty in 1907. He had been nationally prominent since 1900, when McKinley had named him to head the Second Philippine Commission. From that post he had become

[20] James S. Sherman to D. S. Alexander, July 19, 1907, James S. Sherman Papers, New York Public Library.

[21] Herbert Parsons to Charles D. Hilles, July 24, 1907, Charles D. Hilles Papers, Sterling Memorial Library, Yale University.

governor general of the islands, and then secretary of war early in 1904. A lawyer by profession, a judge in temperament and experience, and a government official by the appointment of others, Taft was an able, if sometimes erratic, administrator who felt more at home implementing the policies of superiors than in breaking new ground for government action. His size gave him a reputation for amiability and good humor; at the same time, he possessed an abundance of stubbornness and a well-disguised tendency to hold a grudge. Ambition moved him toward the Supreme Court and the judicial calling he loved. His wife and family envisioned him in the White House. Their influence, and the promptings of duty, led him to spurn several appointments to the Court during Roosevelt's presidency. If the position of Chief Justice had been open, Taft would have taken it in preference to a presidential race. As an Ohio associate noted in December 1906, "he shrinks from a political campaign which involves him personally."[22]

When describing his political views in late 1907, Secretary Taft wrote: "I agree heartily and earnestly in the policies which have come to be known as the Roosevelt policies." On the major issues, Taft's positions coincided with the president's. They agreed on railroad regulation, opposed socialism, and shared similar attitudes on corporate regulation. Roosevelt "takes the most conservative course," Taft told an Ohio audience in August 1907, "in insisting on adopting measures entirely consistent with the principle of private property in order to stamp out the evils which have attended its abuse." Taft was more inclined than Roosevelt had been to take up the tariff problem, and made revision of the Dingley law a recurring theme in his campaign speeches. Despite its impact on his presidential hopes among black Republican voters, Taft loyally supported Roosevelt's actions in dismissing the black soldiers who were unjustly accused of complicity in the Brownsville episode of 1906. "He and I view public questions exactly alike," Roosevelt said of Taft in June 1908.[23]

Roosevelt's perception of Taft as a man and politician reflected

[22] James R. Garfield Diary, December 8, 1906, Garfield Papers.

[23] William Howard Taft to C. M. Heald, December 25, 1907, William Howard Taft Papers, Manuscript Division, Library of Congress; Roosevelt to George O. Treveleyan, June 19, 1908, Morison, *Letters*, VI, p. 1085; William Howard Taft, *Present Day Problems* (New York: Dodd, Mead, 1908), p. 190.

the flawed and uncertain basis on which their personal friendship rested. In the years when Roosevelt was the president and Taft the cabinet officer, they did not discuss their divergent opinions concerning the methods by which public policy should be carried out. Sympathetic to the objectives of the Roosevelt program, Taft believed that the president should operate within the framework of the law and not stretch the prerogatives of his office as Roosevelt had done. The task of the next president would not be to extend and expand what Roosevelt had advocated, but to administer efficiently and thoroughly the legislation and policies already in effect. At a time when Roosevelt's progressivism was accelerating, Taft was preparing to consolidate and regroup.

The secretary of war admired and respected President Roosevelt, but he found other leading progressives a motley lot. He dabbled in the summer of 1907 in Iowa politics to block Cummins's race for the Senate, and he described the state as "full of gum-shoe statesmen that you can't tell anything about." Taft had no regard for La Follette or Beveridge, disliked Gifford Pinchot, and usually found the conservatives more amusing company. His friendship with the president, however, overshadowed these temperamental allegiances before he entered the White House. During Taft's race for the nomination, Republican regulars regarded him as "an avowed tariff ripper," and "so Rooseveltian in his notions about wealth that he is not to be trusted."[24]

Another element of fragility within the Taft-Roosevelt relationship stemmed from the familial and domestic pressures on both men. Mrs. Taft, her husband's leading booster for the presidency, viewed Roosevelt with profound suspicion, resented his slowness in identifying Taft as his successor, and provided continuing skepticism about Roosevelt's good faith. In his immediate circles, Taft received little positive reinforcement about Roosevelt. Similarly, the men close to Roosevelt eyed Taft distrustfully, a sentiment the secretary reciprocated. None of these considerations meant that the camaraderie of Taft and Roosevelt between 1904 and 1908 was false. When this delicate rapport ebbed, however, there was no

[24] "Conference Between Secretary Taft, Mr. Burton, and Mr. Vorys, June 8, 1907," Taft Papers; J. W. Blythe to John F. Lacey, January 7, 1908, John F. Lacey Papers, Iowa State Department of History and Archives.

common bond of ideological agreement or political empathy to slow the breakdown of relations. Although Taft was regarded as "Roosevelt's shadow" in his race for the nomination, the president did not make an outright endorsement of his secretary of war until the latter half of his second term. He uttered encouraging words to Taft in 1906, but these remarks were carefully hedged and stopped well short of actual support. Roosevelt told Mrs. Taft in October 1906 that her husband was "his first choice," but also suggested that Hughes might be an alternative if he beat Hearst. Taft interpreted this conversation as a presidential prod to be a more receptive candidate; Mrs. Taft found her suspicions of Roosevelt deepened. At the end of the year, the Ohioan moved reluctantly closer to a formal declaration when he said "that in the improbable event that the opportunity to run for the great office of President were to come to me," he would not decline it. Taft naively hoped that this announcement would reduce the pressure on him to run. His brother, Charles P. Taft, a Cincinnati newspaper publisher, emphasized the positive side of the release and launched the Taft drive in Ohio.[25]

None of these actions had yet made Taft the choice of the Roosevelt administration. The opposition of Senator Foraker to the president's handling of the Brownsville case caused the White House to get behind Taft. In response to a shooting episode at Brownsville, Texas, in August 1906, Roosevelt summarily discharged three companies of black troops in November. Acting hastily on inadequate evidence, Roosevelt refused to recognize that he had erred. Senator Foraker led the struggle for a congressional probe of the case. The senator acted out of honest indignation at what had happened to the black soldiers; he also thought that Taft and Roosevelt might be politically vulnerable. Tension between Roosevelt and Foraker erupted at a private banquet at the Gridiron Club in late January 1907 with senator and president exchanging barbed charges. To block Foraker's power and to vindicate the president's decision on Brownsville, Taft's race was now deemed to merit more solid support.

[25] Alfred D. Sumberg, "William Howard Taft and the Ohio Endorsement Issue, 1906–1908," in Daniel R. Beaver, ed., *Some Pathways in Twentieth Century History* (Detroit: Wayne State University Press, 1969), p. 77; Helen H. Taft to Taft, October 27, 1906, Taft Papers; Mark Sullivan, *Our Times 1900–1925*. Vol. IV: *The War Begins, 1909–1914* (New York: Scribner, 1936), p. 304.

From March 1907 onward, the president swung his office behind Taft's candidacy. Roosevelt told the postmaster general and
the secretary of the treasury of his "peculiar regard" for Taft's
judgment. The Ohioan should be consulted on all important appointments in his state. The decision to allow the secretary of
war a determining voice in Ohio patronage assured Taft of dominance in his political base. Elsewhere, Roosevelt and his private
secretary, William Loeb, were, Taft noted in June 1907, "looking after the whole of the South." In that region they quelled
third-term talk for the president and assembled delegations behind Taft's campaign. Most of all, of course, Roosevelt spread
the word that he was behind Taft and that he believed "Taft
comes nearer than anyone else to being just the man who ought to
be President."[26]

At two key points, Roosevelt intervened directly to assist Taft.
With the secretary out of the country in late 1907, his campaign
slipped because of reverses in the Ohio off-year elections and the
emergence of a small boom for Secretary of the Treasury Cortelyou
in New York after his handling of the Panic of 1907. Faced with the
potential for an embarrassing split in the cabinet, Roosevelt decided that the administration should rally behind Taft. On December 12, 1907, the White House sent out a statement reiterating
Roosevelt's 1904 pledge. It was a step, observed the secretary of
war, "which seems to have cleared the political atmosphere somewhat and given a chance to my smothered boom to rise again to respectable proportions." Taft was right. The Cortelyou boom
collapsed, talk of a third term ended, and southern Republicans
rapidly swung to Taft.[27]

After December 1907, Taft's candidacy overcame the challenges of Cannon, Fairbanks, Knox, and Foraker on his right. The
Hughes alternative on the left remained the most worrisome threat
the Taft camp had to confront. With Hughes strength growing in
New York, the Taft-Roosevelt forces there agreed to the governor's
control of the state's delegation in mid-January 1908 as a means of
keeping his boom confined to his home base. The administration

---

[26] Roosevelt to George von Lengerke Meyer, March 16, 1907 (first quotation),
Roosevelt to William Allen White, July 30, 1907 (third quotation), Morison, *Letters*, V, pp. 625, 735; "Conference . . . June 8, 1907," Taft Papers (second quotation).

[27] Taft to William R. Nelson, December 25, 1907, Taft Papers.

"Loading the Bandwagon for Taft." Spokane *Spokesman-Review*, in Shaw, *A Cartoon History*.

supporters then moved to obtain as many second-choice votes for Taft as possible—a campaign that achieved success at the Republican state convention in April. More important, when Hughes delivered an address on national issues on January 31, 1908, Roosevelt sent his most stinging message to Congress that same afternoon. The next day the president had the headlines, Hughes the inside pages, and Taft the benefit. "If Hughes is going to play the game, he must learn the tricks," a delighted Roosevelt told a reporter.[28]

With effective assistance from the White House, the Taft campaign gathered up delegates in early 1908 and rolled on toward the convention in Chicago. Whether Taft would have secured the nomination without Roosevelt's active encouragement cannot be determined. The amount of genuine enthusiasm for the secretary of war was moderate, and he gained votes from some conservatives as the only alternative to Roosevelt and from progressives as the best substitute for the president. In a direct contest with Hughes, and Roosevelt neutral, Taft would probably have been an underdog to the New Yorker. But, of course, the president was not neutral, and his support made the difference for Taft.

It was a result with lasting consequences. By appointing pro-Taft candidates to federal offices, Roosevelt limited the amount of patronage at the disposal of his successor in March 1909. Presidential endorsement of Taft also made the Ohioan seem more progres-

[28] Sullivan, *The War Begins*, p. 304.

sive than he actually was. By portraying Taft not just as the best man available, but as his chosen heir, Roosevelt created assumptions about Taft's future fidelity to the president's program that were bound to be disappointed. On a more subtle level was the ever-present reminder to Taft that his nomination and ultimately his election were gifts from another and not simply the result of his own labors. Later this obligation, once so freely assumed, would rankle and fester.

By the time the Republican national convention neared its opening session in mid-June, Taft had the nomination well in hand. The last semblance of opposition from the conservative "allies" appeared at the Republican National Committee's hearings on disputed delegates in the early part of the month. With the administration supporters on the committee deciding 200 contests in Taft's favor, the Foraker and Fairbanks campaigns had no serious chance. When the convention got under way on June 16, Taft had more than 600 pledged delegates and eventually received 702 on the first ballot.

Even with the selection of the nominee decided, the convention had ample tension behind the usual pageantry. Anxious Taft leaders stood ready to stave off a Roosevelt boom at the last minute, and Mrs. Taft did not put aside her fears that the president might yield to a third-term stampede until her husband's nomination was made unanimous. Party conservatives, who had named one of their own as keynote speaker instead of Roosevelt's choice, Senator Beveridge, consoled themselves that, at least, Taft was not Roosevelt.

When both the president and Taft kept out of the vice-presidential intrigue until the nomination was safe, the regulars scored another success. Senator Dolliver refused to have his name considered; Governor Hughes declined Taft's offer; and Beveridge and others also said no. Hughes's refusal left the way open for the New York delegation to push forward Congressman James S. "Sunny Jim" Sherman. An eastern balance to Taft's "western" nomination, Sherman was from a doubtful state, was a friend of Speaker Cannon, and was widely liked among stand-patters. Taft and Roosevelt stumbled over the vice-presidency when forethought and resolve could have found an acceptable progressive or moderate figure.

Taft drafted, and Roosevelt approved, the major planks in the

1908 platform. Its significant provisions reflected Taft's commitment to the president's policies and included planks endorsing a postal savings bank system, further amendment of the interstate commerce laws, and alterations in the Sherman Antitrust Act. The most notable pledge called "unequivocally for a revision of the tariff by a special session of Congress immediately following the inauguration of the next President."[29] By the spring of 1908, revision sentiment had gained such strength that the House Ways and Means Committee was beginning to shape a new tariff bill, and Republican state conventions supported revision in their spring platforms. The plank did not specify the direction of revision, but few expected upward changes whenever Congress acted.

Efforts to include a statement in favor of limitations on the issuance of judicial injunctions in labor disputes ran afoul of the organized protest from the National Association of Manufacturers and the opposition of Cannon and other conservatives. The overtures from organized labor were dismissed, and the convention accepted a very watered-down plank that pledged to "uphold at all times the authority and integrity of the Courts," and asked only for improvements in the procedures for issuing injunctions. The delegates also voted down overwhelmingly planks from Wisconsin's delegates (expressing La Follette's views) that advocated direct election of senators, physical valuation in railroad rate making, a stronger stance on tariff revision, and restrictions on campaign contributions. The anti-injunction struggle and the repulse of the progressive amendments made the platform seem more reactionary than it actually was and contributed to the convention's stand-pat reputation.[30]

In the two months after Taft's selection, the Republican campaign appeared dormant. The manager of the campaign, Frank H. Hitchcock, built his organization slowly, concentrated on the last month of the contest, and ruffled some feathers in the party over his seeming inactivity during the summer. There was cause for Republican concern. Bryan's nomination put the best Democratic campaigner in the field with a united party at his back. Taft also faced restiveness from labor voters about his decisions on unions made

[29] Milton W. Blumenberg, comp., *Official Report of the Proceedings of the Fourteenth Republican National Convention* (Columbus, Ohio: Press of F. J. Heer, 1908), p. 117.

[30] Ibid., p. 119.

while he was a federal judge in the 1890s. The black community was unhappy over Brownsville. Among Republican Protestants, whispering persisted about the candidate's Unitarian faith and his tolerant attitude toward Catholics in the Philippines. Fundraising went slowly before September as Taft backed a limited public disclosure of the origins of contributions. Opposition to the renomination of Hughes added to worries about carrying New York. "This election is not going to be an open-and-shut affair," said a Republican journalist in late August.[31]

Factionalism intensified the party's problems. In the Middle West Republican congressional candidates ran as hard against Cannon as they did against the Democrats. The liquor issue, with Republicans still marked as the champions of prohibition and local option to make districts dry, divided the party bitterly in Maine, Ohio, and most of all, Indiana. When reports circulated that the national committee would send Senator La Follette on a tour of the Far West, a Montana senator complained that "To put him on the stump seems to be like going on the hunt with a kicking gun." A Kansas progressive, Joseph L. Bristow, took a contrary view. "Our party has got to keep abreast of the times—to consider the interests of the country and free itself from the domination of the Aldrich and Cannon regime." The task of the party's candidate, as the summer ended, was to promote at least a truce in this intramural combat in the interest of the national ticket.[32]

Taft's managers had advised him to stay at home and avoid extended touring following the convention. By mid-August, as Republicans called for his presence on the campaign trail, the nominee decided that "if the candidate does not go out and work himself, the subordinates in the ranks are not liable to tear their shirts." Republican headquarters announced a western swing in early September, and Taft visited the Middle West, New York, and parts of the South in the last month and a half of the contest. He proved a solid performer on the hustings, and drew large, friendly crowds. He responded vigorously to assaults on his labor record. Playing down his true suspicions of union activity, he informed Ohio voters that "it would be a sorry day for this country if labor

[31] Judson C. Welliver to James C. Keely, August 21, 1908, Cummins Papers.
[32] Thomas H. Carter to Knute Nelson, July 30, 1908, Nelson Papers; Joseph L. Bristow to Samuel Judson Roberts, August 13, 1908, Bristow Papers.

organizations were not encouraged." The tariff revision promised in the platform should be downward, and he pledged that "the plighted faith of the party on this subject" would be observed "in letter and in spirit."[33]

To his receptive audiences Taft laid out the direction of the next administration. At St. Louis he remarked in October that the need of government in the succeeding four years was "not to be spectacular in the enactment of great statutes laying down new codes of morals, or asserting a new standard of business integrity," but to supply the executive with the "men and machinery" to assist the president in the process of regulation along the lines Roosevelt had begun. Promising tariff revision, defending his labor record, and coming across as an administrative extension of Roosevelt, Taft campaigned "to strengthen the impression that the Republican party is a more trustworthy instrument of government than the Democratic." Few commentators asked what the implications of Taft's themes might be when he became president.[34]

An equally important force in the Republican effort was Roosevelt. He persuaded New York Republicans that they had to renominate Hughes in September. Wishing that Taft "would put more energy and fight into the matter," the president decided to inject "a little vim into the campaign by making a publication of my own." As Taft began to travel, Roosevelt released the first of a series of public statements in which he praised the nominee and endorsed, somewhat less strongly, the election of a Republican Congress. By the middle of October, Roosevelt had converted his office into a publicity bureau for Taft, and was serving as an informal cheerleader and manager for the campaign.[35]

On the other side, the Democratic campaign in 1908 made the most of the party's electoral assets. Bryan was the basic resource and, after some discussion of staying home, made his usual far-flung and exhausting canvass before large, appreciative crowds. "Our contention is that Democratic success will restore prosperity," he

[33] Taft to Roosevelt, September 11, 1908, Roosevelt Papers; *Chicago Tribune*, October 4, 14, 1908.

[34] Blumenberg, *Fourteenth Republican National Convention*, p. 205; *Chicago Tribune*, October 7, 1908; *American Monthly Review of Reviews*, 38 (1908), 517.

[35] Roosevelt to Conrad Kohrs, September 9, 1908, Roosevelt to Nicholas Longworth, September 21, 1908, Roosevelt to P. H. Grace, October 19, 1908, Morison, *Letters*, VI, pp. 1218, 1245, 1302.

said in Lincoln, Nebraska; "How can the Republicans threaten us with a panic when a panic came under the present President and still threatens us?" No one issue dominated his speeches, though he gave the greatest stress to why labor should support him and reject Taft. At the end of the race, speaking in New York, he summarized the Democratic posture on regulation and government authority. His party was "the champion of the Constitution in all its power." It believed "that all powers delegated to the Federal Government must be exercised to the full," but also "the powers reserved to the States must remain in the States, and cannot be taken away by judicial interpretation or by the encroachment of any department."[36]

Short of funds in a year when both parties spent less than in previous elections, the Democratic National Committee sent out the customary corps of supporting speakers, including the running mate, John Worth Kern of Indiana. But it also relied primarily on an abundance of "bureaus, sub-committees, and auxiliary committees" that sought "to reach the American people . . . in their lives and daily occupations." By now both parties had committed themselves to the advertising style of reaching the voters. The campaign clubs of an earlier day had virtually disappeared.[37]

There was a modest Democratic drive to court the black vote and a more elaborate appeal to Protestants based on Taft's religion and sympathy for Catholics. Still the Democrats did not yet match their opponents in wooing ethnic voters as such. Concerned about Catholic support, Bryan named a New Yorker, Norman E. Mack, to manage the canvass, but did not determine that while Mack's family was Catholic, he was not. The basic electoral strategy did not differ all that much from Parker's with, of course, a more progressive cast. Bryan hoped to add Kentucky and Oklahoma to the South for 140 electoral votes, and then find 100 more votes in New York, Indiana, Illinois, Missouri, and Nebraska. In the early stages of the contest, the Democrats seemed ahead. "Things are looking well," Bryan wrote in early October, "and I see no reason why they should not improve."[38]

Instead of improving, the Democratic situation had actually

[36] *New York Times*, October 3, 27, 1908.

[37] Josephus Daniels, "Mr. Bryan's Third Campaign," *American Monthly Review of Reviews*, 38 (1908), 424.

[38] Bryan to House, October 7, 1908, House Papers.

begun to deteriorate in September and it worsened in October. Bryan's ability to exploit the issue of Taft's campaign contributions diminished when his own treasurer, Governor Charles N. Haskell of Oklahoma, came under attack first from Hearst and then from Roosevelt for questionable financial practices in his own affairs. When Roosevelt became active in the race and Taft took to the stump, the Republicans rebounded. Bryan never found a continuing theme for his campaign as he moved back and forth among antitrust, tariff, campaign contributions, and procedural reforms. Older, heavier, and more respectable, Bryan was a man whom Americans admired, for whom they cheered, but in whose leadership capacity they lacked confidence.

In the last month the Republican campaign overcame its initial problems and rolled toward victory. Party orators, particularly Hughes and Beveridge, made a strong case for the national ticket. The party treasury, though smaller than in years past, had enough resources to fund a strong publicity drive. Hitchcock's structure, which built on the advertising techniques of Cortelyou in 1904, added to it the extensive polling of individual voters by the formal party organizations in key states. He timed the high point of the oratorical phase of the campaign for the last four weeks. The expected large defections from labor did not appear, and the black community stayed with the ticket. Combined with Taft's effectiveness as a campaigner and Roosevelt's dramatic intervention, the persistence of Republican electoral strength dispelled the earlier apprehension and gave positive indications of solid victory in the closing days.

On November 3, 1908, Taft received 7,675,320 popular votes to Bryan's 6,412,294. The winner's total in the electoral college was 321 to the loser's 162. Approximately 1,367,000 more Americans voted in this election than had cast ballots in 1904, though the percentage of eligible voters who turned out remained in the 65 percent range, with perhaps a slight increase in the northern states. Taft accumulated almost 50,000 more votes than Roosevelt four years before, but the increase in Bryan's total over Parker's of nearly 1,400,000 trimmed the Republican plurality in 1908 to half of Roosevelt's in 1904.

In its broad results, this election duplicated the outcomes of the McKinley-Bryan contests in 1896 and 1900. The Democrats carried 16 states in 1908. Bryan had won 13 of them, 11 southern states,

Colorado, and Nevada, twice before. He recaptured voters who had deserted Parker, but the electoral pattern established in 1896 remained in place. Taft continued and expanded Republican strength in the cities. He won Chicago, Jersey City, and New York City, and lost narrowly in Boston. The candidate's appeal to Catholic voters, as compared with Bryan's evangelical moralism, more than offset Protestant defections over his Unitarianism. Roosevelt's endorsement helped Taft substantially, but the winner in 1908 was a vote getter of solid ability in his own right.[39]

Bryan's resounding defeat shocked him, because he believed that he had a genuine hope of victory. The black vote remained Republican, labor did not turn out the rank and file, and Catholics went for Taft in large numbers. The Nebraskan was now eliminated as a presidential hopeful, and the Democrats came out of the campaign with no lasting bitterness and much cohesion. Its internal division remained unresolved, but the Democrats by 1908 had given both their major factions a fair chance to make a case in a presidential contest. If the Democrats had not between 1901 and 1909 offered much of a political challenge, they had survived. They could also take comfort in their electoral resurgence since the low point of 1904. The task of the party, as Taft's presidency began, was to maintain its fragile unity and hope for Republican discord.

The election returns offered warnings of that possibility. Taft ran ahead of his party in many states. In five, including Minnesota, Ohio, and Indiana, the Democrats elected governors while the Republican presidential ticket was winning. This ticket-splitting, more prevalent than in 1904, offered evidence that "the day of absolute partisan control is gone." Seeking an explanation for the state of popular unhappiness with partisanship, Elihu Root told Roosevelt that it was "a growing irritation & resentment caused by the failure of party machinery to register popular wishes correctly & that conventions & legislatures give their allegiances first to the managers and second only to the voters." Root correctly noted that in both the short and long run, "discontent hurts only the party in

---

[39] Taft to Chester I. Long, November 21, 1908, Taft Papers; *The Statistical History of the United States from Colonial Times to the Present* (Stamford, Conn.: Fairfield, 1965), p. 690; Allen and Clubb, "Progressive Reform and the Political System," p. 140; David, *Party Strength in the United States, 1872–1970*, pp. 33–38.

power," and the popular suspicion of partisanship, expressed in the campaigns for changes in political rules, crippled the Republicans most after 1908.[40]

The continuation of factional and ideological quarrels within the party represented an even more ominous menace. A California senator told a colleague that he was having difficulty writing a campaign speech in September 1908. "I am unable to subscribe," he said, "to a great many of the doctrines of the radicals like La Follette and his followers," but he was "not as conservative as a great many members of our party who carry their conservatism so far that they are really reactionaries."[41]

Even before he was nominated, and throughout the campaign, Taft became the focus for the divergent conceptions about the direction the party would follow under his leadership. "He will be a very wise, conservative and cautious president, and will give us a period of comparative rest after the agitation of which we have been subjected during the last four years," commented a conservative in early June. After the voting, William Allen White of Kansas told a friend that he had "felt all along that Mr. Taft's administration would not be a continuation of the battle," but "since the election I have had a strong intimation that Taft is going to fight as well as work." Other progressives were less certain. In view of the influence of the conservatives at the convention, Mark Sullivan of *Collier's* asked Roosevelt: "Are we to hope that Taft will be a bigger man than the party?—and that is the hope in which most progressive men are supporting him."[42]

On March 3, 1909, the day before Taft's inauguration, Theodore Roosevelt and his wife visited the home of his closest friend Henry Cabot Lodge. Lodge recalled years later that there was an "abundance of emotion near the surface" when the Roosevelts left. As they departed, Mrs. Lodge said: "The great and joyous days are

[40] Fay N. Seaton to Bristow, November 6, 1908, Bristow Papers; *American Monthly Review of Reviews*, 38 (1908), 655; Root to Roosevelt, September 12, 1908, Roosevelt Papers.

[41] Frank P. Flint to Beveridge, September 7, 1908, Beveridge Papers.

[42] Joseph Hodges Choate to Henry White, June 9, 1908, Joseph Hodges Choate Papers, Manuscript Division, Library of Congress; William Allen White to Irvine L. Dungan, November 25, 1908, William Allen White Papers, Manuscript Division, Library of Congress; Mark Sullivan to Roosevelt, September 11, 1908, Roosevelt Papers.

over, we shall never have anything like them again—There is no one like Theodore."[43] For the Republican party the great and joyous days were over. Already divided over the question of regulation, weary and less cohesive as a result of Roosevelt's presidency, and expecting more from Taft than he could deliver, the GOP entered its thirteenth consecutive year of national power with Congress and the president at odds, with Taft and Roosevelt already suspicious of each other, and with revision of the tariff requiring immediate attention. The next two years would take the party beyond division to rupture and defeat.

[43] Henry Cabot Lodge to Corinne Roosevelt Robinson, September 18, 1921, Corinne Roosevelt Robinson Papers, Houghton Library, Harvard, quoted by permission of the Houghton Library.

CHAPTER 6

The Republicans Divide

Following the 1908 election, William Howard Taft left for Hot Springs, Virginia, to recover from the campaign and to begin constructing his cabinet. On November 7, 1908, he informed Roosevelt, "the chief agent in working out the present status of affairs," that "you and my brother Charlie made that possible which in all probability would not have occurred otherwise."[1] This bracketing of the president with Taft's brother irritated Roosevelt then and later, but the need to acknowledge help from such diverse quarters underscored the divided obligations that soon troubled the president-elect.

The problem of "Cannonism" flared up immediately. In public statements the Speaker cast doubt on the prospects for serious tariff revision, and dissident House members came out against his re-election when the new Congress convened. Committed to change in the tariff, Taft looked to the possibility of joining the anti-Cannon fight. Surveys of the House membership revealed that the insurgents could count on fewer than 50 of the 219 Republicans. Taft doubted the wisdom of intervening in congressional affairs, and Roosevelt and Elihu Root advised conciliation, since there was no credible alternative to Cannon.

Taft and Cannon met in early December in what the former characterized as "a most satisfactory talk." Discussion of the Speaker's leadership in the press persuaded Taft that he and the anti-Cannon men had facilitated a change in the House rules to restrict Cannon's power. More important, they had made possible, he believed, "such a thorough and genuine revision" of the tariff "that the people will believe that the Republican party is complying

[1] Taft to Roosevelt, November 7, 1908, Taft Papers.

121

with its promise."[2] The Cannon issue subsided temporarily, but Taft's difficulties with it were not over. He would soon have to decide whether to work with the Republican congressional majority at the risk of alienating the progressives, or to capitalize on the antipartisan mood of the day by supporting a revolt against Cannon's dominance at the cost of angering party regulars.

The main task of the working vacation was picking a cabinet, and Taft faced hazards in reconciling the sectional and ideological pressures within the party. He consulted widely and acted carefully, but the process of cabinet making began the troubles he never surmounted. He wished to have lawyers around him who would assist in the detailed implementation of the Roosevelt legacy. Philander Knox as secretary of state, George W. Wickersham as attorney general, Richard A. Ballinger in the Interior Department, as well as other appointees, provided a legal flavor that struck some progressives as too heavily tilted toward corporate law practice. The selection of Jacob M. Dickinson for the War Department and Franklin MacVeagh for the Treasury, both of them Democrats, embodied Taft's desire to have a bipartisan tinge, a gesture regular Republicans disliked. It was a panel that promised competence and continuity, qualities Taft missed in some of his colleagues under Roosevelt, but it also lacked excitement, innovation, and progressives.

In choosing the cabinet, Taft also opened the first perceptible fissures in his friendship with Roosevelt. As he assembled his administration, Taft received advice from his family "to be his own king," to minimize Roosevelt's influence in his presidency.[3] By doing so, the president-elect complicated a process that went back to the time when he was nominated in June 1908. After his selection as the candidate, Taft told Roosevelt, in an offhand manner, that he wished the members of the cabinet "to stay just as they are." Taft apparently then "thought nothing more about it."[4]

Meanwhile, Roosevelt informed Secretary of the Interior James R. Garfield, Secretary of Commerce Oscar S. Straus, and several

[2] Taft to Joseph L. Bristow, December 5, 1908, Taft to Horace Taft, June 27, 1909, Taft Papers.

[3] George von Lengerke Meyer Diary, January 4, 1909.

[4] Henry L. Stoddard, *As I Knew Them: Presidents and Politics from Grant to Coolidge* (New York: Harper & Bros., 1927), p. 386; *Taft and Roosevelt: The Intimate Letters of Archie Butt*, 2 vols. (Garden City, N.Y.: Doubleday, Doran & Co., 1930), II, p. 551.

others that they would be kept on. Coming from the president, these remarks became, in the minds of those who heard them, firm commitments. When Taft in early 1909 selected other men and excluded Garfield, Straus, and others, bitterness grew in the Roosevelt circle. The retention of Roosevelt's secretary of agriculture, James Wilson, and the appointment of his postmaster general, George von Lengerke Meyer, as secretary of the navy, was not enough continuity. Oscar Straus told Roosevelt that "through influence or surroundings Taft did not wish to take those who distinguished themselves under him (Roosevelt)." The outgoing president agreed with these judgments, and said to his secretary of war, whom Taft had replaced, "unfortunately you have been too close to me, I fear."[5]

Other episodes strained feelings between Taft and Roosevelt. When Charles P. Taft ran for Foraker's Senate seat in Ohio in late 1908, Roosevelt took part in a way that ensured Foraker's defeat, but did not help the president-elect's brother. Mrs. Taft's pre-inaugural attempts to supervise the White House staff brought on additional recriminations between the presidential families. Roosevelt sought to obtain a brief cabinet appointment for his personal secretary, William Loeb, in a manner that Taft found unwise, and Loeb had to settle for collector of the port of New York.

In the last months of his presidency, Roosevelt quarreled with Congress over his use and defense of the Secret Service. During this controversy, Taft did not defend Roosevelt in public. To those in the White House circle, it was not the first time that the future president missed an opportunity to endorse his predecessor. But now, wrote James R. Garfield, "Taft's silence [is] more puzzling than ever—his failure to say a single word in favor of the President now when Congress is attacking him is simply astounding."[6]

These rifts remained private as the transition of power occurred on March 4, 1909. Roosevelt left on the African expedition that kept him away for more than a year after mid-March, and Taft settled down to governing. The political tasks before him were imposing, and the weakened condition of the Republican party limited the choices open to the new president. Taft had to take up the tar-

---

[5] Oscar Straus Diary, January 23, 1909, Oscar Straus Papers, Manuscript Division, Library of Congress; Lawrence F. Abbott, ed., *The Letters of Archie Butt* (Garden City, N.Y.: Doubleday, Page & Co., 1924), p. 338.

[6] Garfield Diary, January 23, 1909, Garfield Papers.

Stepping Out of the White House

"Well Begun and Well Done."
Roosevelt passes responsibility
to Taft. *New York Evening
Mail,* 1909, in Shaw, *A Cartoon
History.*

iff, with all its dangers, in an atmosphere of friction between the White House and Congress, with factionalism straining the party, and with the basic philosophical differences of the Republicans unresolved.

Taft failed as a political leader, but the usual picture of him as an indecisive, indolent executive gives a misleading impression of his problems. Although he did not possess as mercurial and as stimulating a mind as Roosevelt's, the president's intelligence was solid and perceptive. He worked harder than the public realized and could, when his emotions were uninvolved, be a shrewd judge of character. What Taft lacked was a sense of public relations. He snubbed the press, played too much golf, and traveled too often without a clear purpose. Slow to decide, he could be persuaded to alter a decision once made, a process that left him open to charges of irresolution. A mean and petty streak confirmed Roosevelt's opinion that the president "was one of the best haters he had ever known."[7] With a weak White House staff, a family that indulged in social feuds, and a propensity for procrastination that produced hasty and sometimes inept speeches, Taft had a presidential style

[7] *Taft and Roosevelt,* I, p. 38.

that alienated many, without the compensating assets of Roosevelt's glamour and fun.

On a more basic level, Taft perceived his political role as that of a party leader who must restore Republican unity and assist in the enactment of a legislative program. To minimize strife and obtain laws, Taft moved naturally toward the existing Republican leadership in Congress. As he became more identified with Senator Aldrich and Speaker Cannon, however, he angered those progressives who saw opposition to the party hierarchy as an essential reform. Taft reacted bitterly to their tactics and thought critics did the work of Democrats. In defending party procedures and leaders during a time of increasing suspicion of partisan devices, Taft swam against the tide of change in ways that stamped him as conservative and obstructive.

During the internal debate among Republicans after 1908, Taft found himself, somewhat to his own surprise, more and more aligned with the regulars. Presidential complaints against reformers mounted as his term unfolded. When insurgent senators did not attend a bill-signing ceremony in June 1910, the president said: "I don't give a damn. If they can get along without me, I presume I can do the same without them."[8] Pushed into closer association with Aldrich, Senator Winthrop Murray Crane of Massachusetts, and others in the conservative camp, Taft came to have greater respect for their opinions and abilities.

Taft's campaign for downward revision of the tariff was carried on within the context of his desire to maintain party unity, but the controversy over the Payne-Aldrich Tariff rocked the GOP in 1909. To obtain rapid House action on the tariff, Taft supported Cannon's bid for reelection as Speaker in March 1909, much to the unhappiness of the rebels. The message summoning Congress to act on the tariff was general and vague, as the legislative leaders requested. The passive strategy appeared to work when the Ways and Means Committee reported and the House passed in early April a bill, named after Sereno B. Payne of New York, that reduced rates on lumber, sugar, and iron, and put cattle hides and coal on the free list.

Presidential success in the House phase of tariff making masked problems in the Senate. By 1909, the writing of a tariff had become

---

[8] Ibid., I, p. 414.

a familiar scenario. The Senate constructed its own version, with some rates designed for maximum effect with constituents, and a conference committee then produced a version that ostensibly reconciled the House and Senate bills, but that often represented a whole new measure. The Republicans controlled the Senate by a margin of 61 to 31, and the party leader, Senator Aldrich, had a reputation for imperious dominance. In 1909, however, Aldrich's position had serious weaknesses. Prolonged tariff debate was divisive, and failure to pass a bill in accordance with its platform promises would make the party look ridiculous. The Senate leadership wanted speedy action, but lacked the means to obtain it.

By the spring of 1909, between 7 and 10 midwestern Republicans had become irritated with Aldrich's rule in the Senate. The tariff offered them an opportunity to assault an enemy, make points with their constituents, and express their unhappiness about high rates and excessive protectionism. Eastern Republicans also wanted to safeguard duties on industrial products, while far western senators wished to protect wool and hides. Aldrich needed a secure majority to pass a bill, something he found difficult to assemble in the tariff fight of May and June. To retain the votes of the preponderance of Republicans, the Senate bill that came out of Aldrich's Finance Committee contained more than 800 amendments to the Payne bill, over half of which raised rates back toward the levels of the Dingley Tariff. With this action, Aldrich put together the beginnings of an enduring but tenuous majority. But the bill, and the parliamentary methods Aldrich used in its behalf, outraged La Follette, Beveridge, and especially Jonathan P. Dolliver.

Beginning in late April and with rising intensity in May and June, these progressives launched an orchestrated attack on the Aldrich bill. They divided the controversial schedules, wool, cotton, sugar, and others, among themselves and prepared elaborate criticisms of the Finance Committee's proposals. "The American people expect us, if it can be done, to reduce the schedules of the Dingley tariff act somewhat,"[9] Dolliver said on April 22, and his associates, Cummins, La Follette, Beveridge, and other midwesterners, joined him during the following weeks. The attacks did not produce significant changes in the Aldrich bill, and their own votes

---

[9] *Congressional Record*, 61st Cong., 1st Sess. (April 22, 1909), p. 1460.

ensured that protection remained on the products of their states. Nonetheless, the airing of differences over the tariff, and the bitter critiques of the rebels, ate away at Republican unity, and left the congressional party demoralized by the time the Senate passed the bill on July 8 by a vote of 45 to 34, with 10 Republicans in opposition.

William Howard Taft faced the most perplexing choices as the struggle between regulars and insurgents went on. Knowing that the key decisions would come in the conference deliberations, Taft remained publicly aloof from the battle. To advice that he use the patronage to gain support for lower rates, the president correctly responded that most officeholders were Roosevelt appointees and were already friends of the administration. That position made good legislative sense, but the midwesterners complained that they "received no support whatever in this tremendous fight we have made, from the White House." When the president maneuvered to stave off an amendment that would have added an income tax, progressive senators did not share Taft's view that a corporation tax provision and a resolution supporting an income tax amendment to the Constitution were substantial victories.[10]

The conference committee, on which Taft expected to use his presidential influence, began its work in mid-July 1909. The goals of the White House were reductions in the rates for oil, coal, wood pulp, lumber, scrap iron, and especially cattle hides. If these decreases could be achieved in protected raw materials, Taft wrote, "the adoption of the lower rates will be taken by the public as a victory for the downward revisionists and as a substantial step in the performance of the promises made by the party when it agreed to revise the tariff."[11] For the next two weeks the president stood firm against western senators who wanted a duty on hides, held out when Cannon sought higher rates on gloves and lumber, and used his authority to compel a consensus among the conferees on the final bill.

Taft secured these concessions because he had the support of the public, the House, and eastern Republicans. If he had endeavored, as the insurgents suggested, to deal with the schedules on wool, cotton, or industrial products, the coalition of eastern and far

[10] Bristow to Harold T. Chase, May 27, 1909, Bristow Papers.
[11] Taft to Helen Taft, July 11, 1909, Taft Papers.

western senators, representing the Republican majority, would have defeated him. Convinced that the Payne-Aldrich Tariff was the best he could get and unwilling to keep the Dingley law in force, the president also rejected progressive recommendations of a veto. The tariff passed in early August, and Taft signed it into law. Seven insurgents voted against it in the Senate, and the House vote on whether to recommit the bill produced an uncomfortably close margin of five votes in favor of the measure.

The struggle over the Payne-Aldrich Tariff laid bare the divisions within the Republican party. As they discussed the merits of particular schedules, the GOP senators also examined their divergent perceptions of the direction their party should take. "To be a protectionist," said Senator Beveridge, "does not mean that we are to be extortionists." But conservatives believed "that the President and all the rest of the republican party, ought to stand by the tariff, their own legislative child. If we are to have any kind of a party at all, we must let the majority determine its policies."[12]

Despite the displeasure of the progressives with the tariff, public reaction to the long battle was relatively mild. The demands of party regularity, however, soon led Taft to adopt a stance praising the law and those who voted for it. When called on by regular Republicans to endorse it "with a strong forceful statement" during a junket in the fall, Taft responded at Winona, Minnesota, on September 17. He described the Payne-Aldrich law as "the best tariff bill that the Republican party ever passed" and defended the legislators who supported it. The speech made "all good Republicans feel that the party once more has a leader," said a conservative representative from Minnesota. Progressive senators told each other that Taft "seems to have surrendered absolutely to Aldrich," and that "we might as well get ready to make our fight without him."[13]

Public quarrels over the proper duty of Republicans drove the midwestern insurgents and the president apart in late 1909. Secure in their home states and in touch with opinion there, progressives

---

[12] J. L. Waite to John F. Lacey, September 9, 1909, John F. Lacey Papers; *Springfield Republican*, July 14, 1909, quotes Beveridge.

[13] Taft to Horace Taft, August 11, 1909, James A. Tawney to Taft, August 18, 1909, Taft Papers; Tawney to John J. Esch, September 22, 1909, John J. Esch Papers, Wisconsin State Historical Society; Bristow to Albert J. Beveridge, September 20, 1909, Albert B. Cummins to Bristow, September 25, 1909, Bristow Papers; William Howard Taft, *Presidential Addresses and State Papers* (New York: Doubleday, Page & Co., 1910), p. 222.

such as La Follette, Cummins, and Dolliver believed that they were defending the party's true creed and working to keep Taft faithful to GOP orthodoxy as they embodied it. Criticism of their actions, reprisals on patronage, or encouragement of their local enemies were tactics that put Taft on the side of Cannon, Aldrich, and reaction in an effort "to annihilate politically the progressive republicans." In the president's mind, internal opposition to his legislative program came from "a cooperative knockers association against my administration."[14]

The regular congressional session that began in December 1909 and continued until June 1910 failed to bring the discordant factions within the party any closer or to prepare for the imminent elections. Popular anxiety about the rising cost of living was expressed in the protests of angry consumers in several cities. The climb in the cost of living index from a level of 100 in 1898 to nearly 130 by 1910 struck with special force against the protective tariff and the higher prices associated with it. A congressional probe of the dispute between Secretary of the Interior Richard A. Ballinger and Gifford Pinchot embarrassed the administration in the winter and spring, and Speaker Cannon persisted as a focus of internal bitterness. In March the Republicans lost a special election in a normally safe Massachusetts congressional district, a result that left a conservative senator "more fully persuaded than ever that we are to get a tremendous trouncing next fall so far as the National House of Representatives is concerned."[15]

The feuding between the White House and the congressional insurgents that had marked the latter months of 1909 also continued unabated into the new year. In January Taft told the progressives on Capitol Hill that they could not expect patronage if they opposed the administration, and he then fostered Republican factions favorable to him in states of progressive strength. When the president defended his actions in a Lincoln's Birthday address, Senator Joseph L. Bristow of Kansas called him a "reactionary" who "will not do anything in the curbing of trusts, the regulation of railroads, the enactment of progressive legislation of any kind, that

[14] Bristow to Oscar King Davis, November 1, 1909, Bristow Papers; Taft to Lafayette Young, November 15, 1909, Taft to Otto Bannard, December 20, 1909, Taft Papers.

[15] J. H. Gallinger to James O. Lyford, March 24, 1910, Lyford Papers.

Uncle Sam tells President Taft to "Do It Now," and write his annual message before he travels. E. W. Kemble cartoon, circa 1909, author's collection.

is not in absolute accord with the purposes of Aldrich, Cannon, Root and Sherman." Aware that Cannon was a campaign liability, House Republicans stripped him of some of his power in March, but Taft gained little because of his earlier support for the Speaker. The president's insistence on the need for partisan loyalty to the administration only provoked additional anger. In April, the attorney general told a Chicago audience: "The time of running with the hare and hunting with the hounds is over, and everyone must choose whether he is for the president and the party. He that 'hath no stomach to the fight,' let him depart." The speech, wrote Senator Beveridge, expressed "the real sentiments of the administration," and "made things much worse than ever."[16]

During the last two months of the congressional session, however, the White House backed away from this stringent position, and relations with the progressives improved mildly. Out of this relative abatement of public hostilities came the Mann-Elkins Act,

[16] Bristow to F. S. Jackson, February 18, 1910, Bristow Papers; "Are the Insurgents Traitors?" *Literary Digest*, 40 (1910), 793; Beveridge to Albert Shaw, April 11, 1910, Shaw Papers.

which amended and broadened the regulatory power of the Inter-state Commerce Commission. Also passed were a postal savings measure, conservation legislation, and action on campaign contributions, a tariff board, and naval appropriations. Both the president and the progressives continued to be suspicious and distrustful of each other, but Taft could say, as the session neared its end: "I think things are coming our way a little more than heretofore." Some administration supporters even described "the situation" as "very roseate for the fall campaign."[17]

Such a judgment was too optimistic. Despite the party's legislative record, the condition of the Republicans in Washington and around the nation was extremely poor. Although Taft had dropped his patronage offensive against some of the insurgents in their own states, he did not abandon all his efforts. Believing that he faced an organized movement to repudiate his leadership, the president encouraged anti-progressive campaigns in citadels of insurgency like Iowa, Wisconsin, and Washington. Such a strategy had obvious risks. Dolliver and Cummins had strong support within Iowa, for example, and could easily rally sentiment against the pro-Taft side. The progressives viewed themselves as confronting the coherent, well-financed conspiracy of an increasingly conservative national administration, whereas Taft regarded them as ungrateful Republicans who did the work of Democrats and denied him the support his record deserved. "Unless something unforeseen occurs or Roosevelt shall come and prove the peacemaker, we are sure to lose the House this year and almost as sure to lose the Presidency in 1912—unless, as General Grant always said, the Democrats act the fool in our favor at the right time," observed a long-time party stalwart in April 1910.[18]

The reliance on Democratic mistakes, so long a part of Republican thinking, was misplaced in 1910, because the opposition had positioned themselves to exploit GOP troubles in the fall elections. In 1908 they selected Champ Clark of Missouri as their leader in the House, and he built upon the efforts of his predecessor, John Sharp Williams of Mississippi, for party unity between 1903 and 1908. Democrats in both houses continued their support of

---

[17] Taft to Otto Bannard, June 11, 1910, Taft Papers; Chauncey M. Depew to Elihu Root, June 23, 1910, Chauncey M. Depew Papers, Sterling Memorial Library, Yale.

[18] James S. Clarkson to Grenville M. Dodge, April 11, 1910, Grenville M. Dodge Papers, Iowa State Department of History and Archives.

progressive legislation, though a significant number still rejected
child labor laws or pure food and drug bills that would increase national power or work against the South's drive for more industry.

Currents of parochialism, localism, and simple selfishness battled with the emerging impulses toward Democratic coherence
and purpose in 1909. During the Congress that met in the spring,
these pressures prevailed to the detriment of the party's cause.
When Republican insurgents opposed the election of Speaker Cannon in March 1909, nearly two dozen of the minority voted with
regular Republicans against amendments to limit the Speaker's
power. In the debate over the Payne-Aldrich Tariff that followed,
House and Senate Democrats, particularly the latter, demonstrated
that on individual tariff schedules, the desire for reform and lower
rates yielded to the need to bring home "our share of the booty."
On lumber, cotton, hides, coal, pineapples, and iron, a sizable number of Democratic senators voted with Nelson Aldrich. Even after
the bill passed, Bryan and Senator Joseph Weldon Bailey of Texas,
a leader of those Democrats who sought "incidental" protection for
the raw materials of their states, debated whether party tariff policy required duties "for revenue only" or allowed some higher rates
on nonindustrial products.[19]

The opportunity that Republican quarreling presented was too
tempting for the Democrats in Congress, however, and they succeeded in 1910 in restraining their internal battles. Instead, they
drew together and harassed the embattled enemy. In the Ballinger-
Pinchot controversy, during the struggle over Speaker Cannon in
March 1910 that curbed his power, and throughout the session of
Congress, Champ Clark and his colleagues hammered away at the
tariff, the high cost of living, and Republican extravagance. "The
high cost of living," said a New York congressman, "is directly
chargeable to the unnecessarily high duties on the commodities of
life, such as building material, food, and clothing." Clark proclaimed that the Democrats were now "a courageous, vigilant,
hopeful, militant band, not only ready but eager for the fray."[20]

[19] Claude E. Barfield, " 'Our Share of the Booty': The Democratic Party, Cannonism, and the Payne-Aldrich Tariff," *Journal of American History*, 57 (1970),
318.

[20] *Democratic Campaign Book for 1910* (Baltimore: National Democratic Congressional Committee, 1910), p. 92; Geoffrey F. Morrison, "A Political Biography
of Champ Clark," Ph.D. dissertation, St. Louis University, 1972, p. 203.

Cautioning each other against reopening party wounds, Democrats moved into the campaign with events rolling in their direction. Everywhere the Republicans battled, while the opposition observed candidates such as Judson Harmon in the Ohio governor's race, John Worth Kern in a Senate fight against Albert J. Beveridge in Indiana, and other gubernatorial aspirants such as Eugene Foss in Massachusetts, John A. Dix in New York, and Woodrow Wilson in New Jersey open large leads over their foes. The Democratic party, said one journal, "seemed to have learned the lesson that for success . . . they must put the very best men at the head of their tickets."[21]

Any Republican hope that Theodore Roosevelt might return from his travels and prove a party peacemaker was illusory. The collapse of the Roosevelt-Taft relationship made the former president an improbable conciliator as he approached the end of his safari and European speaking tour in the spring. The fragile bonds of the presidential friendship had been subjected to intense pressure during Taft's first year. Because of a social slight he and his wife had received a quarter of a century earlier, the new president relieved one of Roosevelt's closest friends, Henry White, as ambassador to France. Within Washington's narrow social circle, the Taft family made clear its supremacy over its predecessor and, remarked an observer of Capitol society, "The war on the Roosevelt section has gone to a point of scandal."[22] A frank correspondence might have alleviated the misunderstandings between the two men somewhat, but each believing the other should write first, they communicated only through third parties. Roosevelt got predominantly negative reports about Taft from those who wrote him; the president, for his part, expected reassurance and counsel and obtained only silence.

A policy dispute about conservation, the program closest to Roosevelt's heart, brought the philosophical and political differences to the surface. When he left office, Roosevelt looked back with the greatest pride at the millions of acres added to national forests, the wildlife preserves created, and the public interest that

---

[21] *Independent,* September 22, 1910, quoted in Sarasohn, "The Democratic Surge," p. 177.

[22] Worthington Chauncey Ford, ed., *Letters of Henry Adams (1892–1918)* (Boston: Houghton Mifflin, 1938), p. 520.

the National Conservation Commission (1908) and Country Life Commission (1909), among other initiatives, had generated. The decision-making machinery that he and aides such as Chief Forester Gifford Pinchot had devised to resolve issues of resource development was for Roosevelt an equally important innovation.

Although he raised the national consciousness about the environment, Roosevelt also provoked questions about the manner in which he sought to safeguard the natural heritage. As secretary of war, Taft agreed with the goals of the administration's conservation actions, but had reservations about Pinchot's bureaucratic independence and Roosevelt's indulgent attitude toward legal restraints on executive action. Soon after Taft's term began, Secretary of the Interior Ballinger and Pinchot found themselves at odds. The chief forester saw his influence ebb and came to believe that Taft and Ballinger were enemies of conservation. The president and the secretary, on the other hand, sought what they deemed to be more orderly and legal methods, and watched Pinchot with skepticism and caution.

This bureaucratic struggle became explosive when Ballinger was charged with favoritism toward anticonservation interests and with misconduct in office relating to coal lands in Alaska. Pinchot endorsed the allegations; Taft rejected them. In late 1909, Pinchot helped to make the controversy public in the muckraking press, and in January 1910 he attacked both Ballinger and the president in an open letter to Senator Dolliver. His resulting dismissal led to a congressional inquiry that convicted Ballinger in the public mind, left an unwarranted impression of extensive wrongdoing by the administration, and ultimately brought Ballinger's resignation in the spring of 1911.

Given Roosevelt's closeness to Pinchot, and his belief that in conservation he had used the power of the presidency in the public interest, it did not take great perception to grasp the dangers the controversy posed for Taft. The affair, wrote Root in November 1909, "is pregnant with immense evil for the Administration and the republican party." To Roosevelt's admirers, Taft's position on the Ballinger-Pinchot crisis offered additional evidence that his election had been a mistake. "Taft goes deeper into trouble each week—he is proving a weak man—yielding to those who are really opposed to the great policies upon & for which Taft was elected," concluded Garfield on the day Pinchot was fired. In the press and on the political circuit, talk of "Back From Elba" clubs to support Roosevelt's nomination in 1912 intensified.[23]

Throughout most of his hunting excursion, Roosevelt gave no outward sign of unhappiness with Taft. "It looks to me as if the Administration were getting on admirably in every way," he told the secretary of the navy in September 1909. By the early months of 1910, however, negative evaluations of Taft's performance reached him. Henry Cabot Lodge wrote at length to say that the president "fails now to interest the country" and that the party was "in great danger of losing the House." Pinchot asserted that "the general tendency" of Taft's term was "away from the Roosevelt policies and the people, and in favor of the special interests and the few."[24]

Before these letters arrived, Roosevelt had learned of Pinchot's dismissal. "I cannot believe it," he wrote his friend, "it seems to me absolutely impossible that there can be any truth in this statement." Six weeks later his fears were confirmed, and his relationship with Taft entered a new, delicate phase. During the three and a half months that remained before he returned home in June 1910, Roosevelt received a barrage of advice about his future political course. In the battle for his favor, Pinchot and the insurgents gained a perceptible advantage over Root, Lodge, and implicitly Taft. The president became part of "the Taft-Aldrich-Cannon regime," and after giving Taft the benefit of the doubt for a year, Roosevelt "finally had to admit that he had gone wrong on certain points; and then I also had to admit to myself that deep down underneath I had known all along he was wrong, on points as to which I had tried to deceive myself, by loudly proclaiming to myself, that he was right."[25]

Having decided that Taft was unsatisfactory, that he had "not proved a good leader, in spite of his having been a good first lieutenant," Roosevelt confronted a complex situation in the spring of

---

[23] Root to Henry L. Stimson, November 18, 1909, Henry L. Stimson Papers, Sterling Memorial Library, Yale; Garfield Diary, January 7, 1910, Garfield Papers.

[24] Roosevelt to George von Lengerke Meyer, September 10, 1909, George von Lengerke Meyer Papers, Massachusetts Historical Society; Lodge to Roosevelt, December 27, 1909, Lodge Papers; Gifford Pinchot, *Breaking New Ground* (New York: Harcourt Brace, 1947), p. 500.

[25] Roosevelt to Pinchot, January 17, 1910, Roosevelt to Lodge, April 11, 1910, May 5, 1910, Morison, *Letters*, VII, pp. 45, 73, 80.

1910. An endorsement of the administration, which Taft expected, became impossible, because the progressives would be alienated. But Taft could not be openly repudiated. The task was to locate "a common ground upon which Insurgents and Regulars can stand." In plotting his actions, Roosevelt did not ask himself whether he was acting like "a good first lieutenant" within the GOP, but assumed that if a vacuum of leadership existed, he had a duty to fill it. That such a strategy meant inevitably a challenge to Taft's position as party chief seemed less compelling than the need to restore unity to the Republicans on terms that Roosevelt defined. In his mind, he had left the party in excellent condition on March 4, 1909, Taft had split it, and now the Republicans required his healing touch. Roosevelt might even have to run for president in 1912, although that eventuality remained in the background in 1910, to be considered only if "it was practically universally demanded."[26]

When Mark Hanna and Roosevelt differed between 1901 and 1904, a senator observed that there were "two Executive Mansions" in Washington.[27] In 1910 Roosevelt embarked on a course that logically led to the creation of an informal government-in-exile within the Republican party. By meeting with the insurgents at his home, by withholding his approval of the administration, by his very presence, Roosevelt attracted the anti-Taft forces and bathed them in the glow of his popularity and celebrity status. But to keep his appeal alive, to maintain his influence, he had to preserve the option of becoming a candidate in 1912. Lacking power, Roosevelt had to rely on the politics of possibility. As he kept the option open, he increased the probability that it would be exercised. He honestly believed he sought only unity for his party, but his future rested on the ultimate lure of disunity and a repudiation of Taft.

The difficulties of Roosevelt's position emerged clearly in the months after he returned home. Reminded by conservative friends of the biblical passage, "Discretion shall preserve thee, understanding shall keep thee," he first announced that he had nothing to say about politics.[28] Within a week, however, he entered the New York State contest between Governor Hughes and the Old Guard

[26] Roosevelt to Pinchot, June 28, 1910, Roosevelt to Nicholas Longworth, July 11, 1910, Morison, *Letters*, VII, pp. 95, 99; Lucius B. Swift to Mrs. Swift, July 8, 1910, Lucius B. Swift Papers, Indiana State Library, Indianapolis.

[27] Thomas Beer, *Hanna* (New York: Knopf, 1929), p. 279.

[28] Nicholas Murray Butler, Paul Morton, and Ogden Mills to Roosevelt, June 11, 1910, Nicholas Murray Butler Papers, Columbia University Library.

on behalf of a direct primary bill. Since Taft was on the side of reform in this state, unlike the situation elsewhere, it appeared to
offer a chance to pursue the harmony Roosevelt sought. Unhappily,
his intervention could not stop the defeat of the reform measure,
and the former president now felt compelled to reassert his influence in the state.

On Roosevelt's arrival in London in early June, he had received
a letter from Taft detailing the administration's troubles and inviting him to visit the White House. But, once back in the United
States, Roosevelt declined the offer in a cool note, and the two met
at the summer White House in Beverly, Massachusetts, on June 30,
1910, in a correct, nonpolitical talk that Taft called "a social personal visit." While keeping his distance from the president, Roosevelt entertained a stream of visitors at Oyster Bay who had a
predominantly progressive flavor. Privately Roosevelt told the
party reformers that Taft's remark about owing his election to
Roosevelt and his brother equally was like saying that "Abraham
Lincoln and the bond seller Jay Cooke saved the Union." The public statements that followed these meetings did not endorse individual progressives, but indicated a sympathetic feeling for the
insurgents. All this made the Taft camp nervous. "Our position is,"
the president's secretary told newsmen, "that we don't know what
Oyster Bay is going to do and we don't give a damn."[29]

In fact, Taft cared a great deal, and watched what a cabinet officer called "the pilgrimage of insurgents to the shrine on Sagamore
Hill" with intense interest. "I do not see how I am going to get out
of having a fight with President Roosevelt," he told an aide in early
July. With the threat of a Roosevelt challenge in his mind, the president continued to mix in Republican factional warfare. Schemes to
oust Ballinger, to nominate conservatives in progressive states, and
to wield the patronage against reformers flitted in and out of view
from administration headquarters. The outcome of these initiatives
was a series of late summer defeats for Taft in Kansas, Iowa, Wisconsin, Washington, California, Michigan, and New Hampshire. In
Ohio the regulars prevailed, but with bleak prospects for the general election.[30]

[29] *Taft and Roosevelt*, I, p. 431 (first quotation); Swift to Mrs. Swift, July 8, 1910 ,
Swift Papers (second quotation); H. J. Haskell to William Allen White, July 21,
1910, White Papers.
[30] George Wickersham to Charles Nagel, July 3, 1910, Charles Nagel Papers,
Sterling Memorial Library, Yale; *Taft and Roosevelt*, I, p. 434.

Amid these political setbacks, the attempt at cooperation between the two Republican leaders in New York came unraveled. In
the contest for control of the state convention in September, Taft's
anxiety to secure the New York delegation in 1912 caused him first
to appear to bargain for Roosevelt's assistance, then to oppose him
for temporary chairman in favor of Vice-President Sherman, and finally and belatedly to disavow participation in the anti-Roosevelt
movement. Taft's statement cleared the air temporarily, though for
Roosevelt "it came a little slow," but the rift between the two had
measurably widened.[31] An arranged meeting in late September
passed amicably enough, only to have the White House assert that
Roosevelt had asked for the conference to obtain Taft's help in
New York. This blunder renewed Roosevelt's anger, and the possibility of a genuine rapprochement disappeared.

Shortly after the August flareup with Taft in New York, Roosevelt went on a three-week speaking tour of the West "to announce
myself on the vital questions of the day, to set the standard so that
it can be seen, and take a position that cannot be misunderstood."
To the degree that he hoped to bring the Republicans closer together, Roosevelt failed, but his remarks emphasized how dif-
ferently he and Taft viewed the issues. In Denver on August 29 he
charged that the courts had "tended by a series of negative decisions to create a sphere in which neither nation nor state has effective control; and where the great business interests that can call to
their aid the ability of the greatest corporation lawyers escape all
control whatsoever." These decisions, he asserted, were "funda-
mentally hostile to every species of real popular government," and
he believed that the people, whether in Congress or state legislatures, should "have complete power of control in all matters that
affect the public interest."[32]

Two days later at Osawatomie, Kansas, he delivered an address
called "The New Nationalism" before an estimated 30,000 listen-
ers. Before getting to the meat of his message, Roosevelt commented that "No man is worth his salt in public life who makes on
the stump a pledge which he does not keep after election," a reference that many interpreted as a slap at Taft. He then went on to

[31] J. Kent Hamilton to William Howard Taft, August 30, 1910, Charles D. Hilles
Papers.

[32] Roosevelt to Fremont Older, August 18, 1910, Morison, *Letters*, VII, pp.
118–119; Theodore Roosevelt, *The New Nationalism* (New York: The Outlook
Co., 1910), pp. 38–39, 41, 42.

praise progressive reforms such as limiting corporate influence in politics, extensive regulation of industry, nonpartisan and expert revision of the tariff, graduated income and inheritance taxes on large fortunes, and laws on workmen's compensation and child labor. The "New Nationalism regards the executive power as the steward of the public welfare," he said, and the broadened governmental power should operate beyond the earlier principles of the Square Deal. "When I say that I am for the square deal, I mean not merely that I stand for fair play under the present rules of the game, but that I stand for having those rules changed so as to work for a more substantial equality of opportunity and of reward for equally good service."[33]

Roosevelt's programs combined the themes of strong executive authority, more active regulation, and the pursuit of social welfare programs that he had been moving toward since 1904. In the program's stress on justice, equality, and the powerful broker state, it anticipated many of the goals of modern liberalism. In its dependence on the strength of the presidency, its preference for nonpartisan experts in a bureaucratic setting, and its assumption that progressive tools would always serve progressive aims, it also foreshadowed later difficulties of liberal doctrine.

For the Republican progressives, the speech was a delight. Attacks on a stand-pat congressman in Minnesota and his refusal to appear at a dinner for a senator whose election was being contested as corrupt added to Roosevelt's reform appeal in September 1910. Reaction among party conservatives, however, was negative and vehement. The remarks in Kansas, said a New York regular, "had startled all thoughtful men and impressed them with the frightful danger which lies in his political ascendancy." So strong was the response from the right that Roosevelt toned down his endorsement of the New Nationalism on his way home. It was, a Syracuse audience learned, "nothing but an application to new conditions of certain old and fundamental moralities," and in an article Roosevelt identified his criticism of the courts with Lincoln's comments on the Dred Scott decision in the 1850s. These concessions did not mollify the suspicions among regular Republicans at the implications of the New Nationalism for traditional party doctrine.[34]

[33] Roosevelt, *The New Nationalism*, pp. 5, 11–12, 28.

[34] Robert S. La Forte, "Theodore Roosevelt's Osawatomie Speech," *Kansas Historical Quarterly*, 32 (1966), 199; Roosevelt, *The New Nationalism*, p. 231.

On his return from the West, Roosevelt resumed the fight for control of the New York situation. A strenuous battle brought victory at the state convention in late September, and the nomination of a friend, Henry L. Stimson, as the gubernatorial choice. The platform carried favorable language about Taft's record as president and spoke approvingly of the Payne-Aldrich Tariff. There was no statement on behalf of Taft's hopes for 1912, but the platform disappointed the reformers. "T.R. fell down sadly in his platform making in N.Y. *He doesn't see,*" wrote the prominent muckraker Ray Stannard Baker.[35] By speaking for Lodge in Massachusetts and Beveridge in Indiana, against the tariff in the West and for it in the East, and by becoming involved in unseemly controversies while campaigning for Stimson, Roosevelt left many elements in the party discontented with his course in 1910.

In the two months of campaigning before the voting in 1910, the Republicans attempted unsuccessfully to find a semblance of their old cohesion. The White House drew back from its campaign against progressives and promised to end the use of patronage against rebellious Republican officeholders. But it was all too late. Added to factionalism, philosophical disagreement, and adroit Democratic exploitation of the issues was general voter unhappiness with the Republicans. The country, said Elihu Root, was like a "man in bed. He wants to roll over. He doesn't know why he wants to roll over, but he just does; and he'll do it."[36]

Meanwhile, the resurgent Democrats effectively capitalized on Republican division in New York, New Jersey, Ohio, and Indiana. The high cost of living provided one cutting issue, and they used the temperance question with equal impact in the Midwest, where the Republicans appeared to favor regulation of personal behavior toward alcohol. To these matters, Theodore Roosevelt's New Nationalism added the prospect of enhanced federal power and presidential dictation. The Democratic convention in New York deplored "this exaltation of Federal centralization power" and "the destruction of home rule," and predicted that "whatever advance its adoption would bring is advance toward socialism."[37]

[35] Ray Stannard Baker to Robert M. La Follette, September 30, 1910, La Follette Family Papers, Manuscript Division, Library of Congress.

[36] "Personal Recollections of the Convention and Campaign of 1910," Stimson Papers.

[37] *The World Almanac and Encyclopedia* (New York: The Press Publishing Co., 1910), p. 212.

Table 6.1 Party Strength in Congress, 1894–1916

Congress and Year Elected		Republicans	Democrats	Other
		Senate		
Fifty-fourth	(1894)	43	39	6
Fifty-fifth	(1896)	47	34	7
Fifty-sixth	(1898)	53	26	8
Fifty-seventh	(1900)	55	31	4
Fifty-eighth	(1902)	57	33	
Fifty-ninth	(1904)	57	33	
Sixtieth	(1906)	61	31	
Sixty-first	(1908)	61	31	
Sixty-second	(1910)	51	41	
Sixty-third	(1912)	44	51	1
Sixty-fourth	(1914)	40	56	
Sixty-fifth	(1916)	42	53	
		House		
Fifty-fourth	(1894)	244	105	7
Fifty-fifth	(1896)	204	113	40
Fifty-sixth	(1898)	185	163	9
Fifty-seventh	(1900)	197	151	9
Fifty-eighth	(1902)	208	178	
Fifty-ninth	(1904)	250	136	
Sixtieth	(1906)	222	164	
Sixty-first	(1908)	219	172	
Sixty-second	(1910)	161	228	
Sixty-third	(1912)	127	291	17
Sixty-fourth	(1914)	196	230	9
Sixty-fifth	(1916)	210	216	6

Source: The information in this table is derived from *The Statistical History of the United States* (Stamford, Conn.: Fairfield Publishers, 1965).

Events had positioned the Democrats between the conservatism of the Taft Republicans and the New Nationalism of Roosevelt. From this fortuitous posture, they could draw moderate voters from the Republicans and avoid unseemly quarrels about where they stood on how strong and innovative government should be.

On November 8, 1910, the Republicans suffered substantial defeats and lost control of the House of Representatives for the first time since 1894. The party dropped 58 congressional seats to the opposition, and the Democrats had a majority of 67 members in the next Congress. The most extensive reverses for the GOP came in the East; 26 seats changed hands in New York, New Jersey, Penn-

sylvania, and West Virginia. In the Senate the Republicans lost 10
seats, and their majority of 51 to 41 was even narrower because of
the independence of the bloc of insurgent senators.

Inspecting the ruins of their campaign, Republicans debated
the meaning for the next White House contest. "Where the administration was a factor in the campaign, as in Ohio and New York,
the Democrats won," said Gifford Pinchot. "Where the Republicans did not support the administration, as in California, Kansas,
and Wisconsin, the Republicans won."[38] The progressive wing had
fared better than its counterparts, to a degree because its strength
lay where Democrats remained weak. The party survived factionalism in California, Washington, North Dakota, and Kansas in
1910, albeit with diminished margins in some areas, but division
proved too heavy a burden in the contested Northeast. It remained
to be seen whether the reform wing of the GOP could prevail outside securely Republican states, or whether its appeal was a limited
and inherently divisive one.

The Democrats had reason for delight in November 1910. They
controlled the House, and had almost an effective majority in the
Senate. Their success in electing Woodrow Wilson as governor of
New Jersey, reelecting Judson Harmon to the statehouse in Ohio,
and installing party candidates as governors in New York, Massachusetts, Maine, and Connecticut gave them fresh faces for the
presidential race in 1912. Beyond the election of governors, the
Democrats obtained partial or complete supremacy in the legislatures of New York, Ohio, Indiana, Maine, and New Jersey, a development with important long-range consequences. Republican
division in the Northeast and Middle West enabled the Democrats
to elect state lawmakers from immigrant, "new stock" back-
grounds. More disposed to support social welfare measures such as
workmen's compensation, pro-labor legislation, and regulation of
public utilities, politicians like Alfred E. Smith and Robert F.
Wagner of New York, Edward F. Dunne of Illinois, and David I.
Walsh of Massachusetts relied on urban machines for electoral victories, but added a leaven of humanitarian sympathy and governmental activism that looked forward to the New Deal coalition.

In the decade after 1910, however, the urban new stock members of the party became one element in an evolving cultural battle

[38] *New York Tribune,* November 10, 1910.

that split the Democrats for more than fifteen years. Even as the Republican fissures were promoting the fortunes of Democrats in the North and East, state parties in the South and West were adding the emotionally charged issue of prohibition to their political agenda. The rising tide of dry sentiment among Nebraska, Texas, Alabama, and Tennessee Democrats between 1905 and 1915, for example, compelled candidates and leaders to take positions on such heated topics as local option, prohibition on a statewide basis, or even, as time passed, a national prohibition amendment.

When the Republicans were viewed as the party of Protestant moralism in the late nineteenth century, Democrats had found a ready link between limited government and cultural tolerance. This traditional posture had been advantageous in Ohio, Indiana, and Maine as Republicans pushed temperance in those states before 1910. But when southerners and westerners spoke of "the slum civilization of the great cities" and even Bryan proclaimed in Nebraska that prohibition was "a moral question" with only one side, the Democrats embarked on an agony over alcohol that was to trouble them for two decades.[39]

The result of the 1910 elections also fixed the attention of Republicans on the presidential race to come. President Taft put his political affairs in order during the first half of 1911 and made a strong beginning on a renomination effort. The progressives sought to unify themselves behind an alternative to the incumbent. With varying degrees of enthusiasm and accord they promoted Senator La Follette in his bid for the nomination. Meanwhile, in the early stages of the 1912 race, the shadow of Roosevelt hung over the deliberations of the reformers. His attitude toward an anti-Taft race lingered as a tantalizing and worrying imponderable to the various elements within the party.

After his party's defeat in 1910, Taft regained his composure and balance as a chief executive. He sought a rapprochement with Roosevelt and made conciliatory gestures toward the congressional progressives. In his annual message in 1910 and in the last session of the Sixty-first Congress, the president pushed hard for tariff revision on his own terms through adoption of reciprocity with Canada. The executive agreement for which Taft sought legislative

[39] Paolo E. Coletta, *William Jennings Bryan.* Vol II: *Progressive Politician and Moral Statesman 1909–1915* (Lincoln: University of Nebraska Press, 1969), p. 14; Dallas *Baptist Standard*, July 30, 1914.

approval in January 1911 grew out of the strained economic relations between the two countries that the Payne-Aldrich Tariff produced. Negotiations over many months ended in an arrangement that would, if the legislatures of the two nations concurred, admit agricultural products freely to both, place reciprocal duties on some manufactured items, and make selective reductions on rates for other products in Canada and the United States. Taft supported the agreement because it was "right" and to demonstrate that "there are other things besides high protection for which the party stands."[40]

Canadian reciprocity managed, however, to alienate some conservatives and most of the progressives. Removing protection from the agricultural products of their constituents and leaving higher rates on manufactured goods was not what La Follette, Cummins, and the others meant by tariff revision. The agreement, wrote Senator Bristow, "is a queer thing" that usually "protects the monopolized articles and puts on the free list the things on which there is no monopoly." A Pennsylvania manufacturer, speaking for the protectionists, called a vote for the legislation "a vote to aid the democrats to disrupt the Republican party by alienating the farmers."[41]

Despite this opposition, Taft lobbied hard for passage. Although the House approved the bill in mid-February, it failed to emerge from the Senate before the end of the session. Taft called the new, partially Democratic Congress into special session in April and once again obtained House passage in late April and Senate concurrence at the end of July. Unhappily for the president, Canadian voters, apprehensive about American intentions toward their nation, rejected the government that made the agreement, and Canadian reciprocity died in September 1911. Beyond the ultimate failure of the idea, Taft came out of the fight with mixed losses and gains. The opposition of the insurgents to reductions on the goods of their own states cast doubt on their sincerity as tariff revisionists, but the administration also lost support along the Canadian border, an area that the president's foes exploited for votes in 1912.

[40] *Taft and Roosevelt*, II, p. 599; Taft to Horace Taft, January 25, 1911, Taft Papers.

[41] Bristow to H. J. Allen, February 14, 1911, Bristow Papers; J. R. Grundy to J. Hampton Moore, February 13, 1911, J. Hampton Moore Papers, Pennsylvania Historical Society, Philadelphia.

Emerging in a stronger position with regard to Congress in the spring of 1911, Taft also took a series of steps that opened his renomination campaign. In public the chief executive adopted positions that sought voters from both wings of his party. He replaced Ballinger with a conservationist and named Roosevelt's friend Stimson as secretary of war. He stood for reciprocity with Canada and a tariff commission to recommend rate changes, but he opposed Democratic and insurgent moves to lower individual schedules in advance of a report from his tariff experts. He advocated international arbitration of disputes among nations, signed treaties with France and Great Britain in August, and worked hard for Senate ratification of what he hoped would be "the great jewel of my administration."[42]

More quietly, an inept presidential secretary, the source of so much trouble in 1910, went out, and the shrewd and capable Charles D. Hilles took over. In early June Hilles wrote Republicans "to ascertain the attitude of all sections of the country toward the president," and the skeleton of an organization emerged. At the end of August, Taft left on a month-long national tour while Hilles consulted with party leaders in various states. He told Taft's brother Charles on October 28 that the president should have close to a thousand delegates at the Republican National Convention.[43]

As a candidate, Taft sought to preempt possible rivals and sew up the maximum number of delegates informally before the 1912 campaign opened. Such a strategy required that party regulars control the Republican machinery and oppose efforts to select delegates in primaries. This plan achieved a great measure of success by the end of the year and, if the president faced only Senator La Follette, victory seemed assured. At no point did Taft or his advisers ask whether victory at the convention promised success in the election. He never considered not running in 1912 because he believed that he deserved a second term, that conservative principles needed a champion, and most of all that control of the party must not pass to the progressives. An unwillingness to accept a victory that brought reformers supremacy within the GOP would be a significant cause of the disasters that lay ahead.

Progressive Republicans came through 1911 in less satisfactory

[42] *Taft and Roosevelt*, II, p. 635.

[43] Hilles to R. I. Gammill, June 6, 1911, Hilles to Charles P. Taft, October 28, 1911, Hilles Papers.

condition than the president. Late in 1910 they told each other "that it is time that those of us who are making the progressive fight in the ranks of the Republican party should begin to draw closer together with a view to preparing for the contest of 1912." Out of these discussions came a plan for a National Progressive Republican League that was officially organized at Senator La Follette's home on January 21, 1911. Some sponsors of the league, believing that "There is a loss of moral force in party action," wished to have a nonpartisan movement, but it proved impossible to obtain the support of progressive Republican senators and congressmen without the party label. The league put forward the program of legislation that it hoped to achieve through state branches and vigorous lobbying. Its goals were the direct election of senators; direct primaries; direct election of delegates to the national convention; adoption by the states of the initiative, referendum, and recall; and enactment of laws to curb corrupt practices.[44]

The league did not secure the influence its sponsors sought. Its internal management was inept, and it was widely, and to a degree correctly, regarded as a vehicle for La Follette's presidential ambitions. The fight over Canadian reciprocity also hurt the reputation of the reformers. As a body in Congress, the insurgents had some impact in 1911. When the special session met in April, they sought committee representation from the Republican leadership in proportion to their numbers, but these demands were refused and the divisions in the party continued. Cooperation with the Democrats on the tariff bills that lowered rates on a single schedule illustrated the harassing effect the progressives could have on the administration. It was less apparent that the insurgents, relying on their own political resources, could deny the nomination to Taft and gain supremacy in the party.

The travails of Senator La Follette's candidacy in 1911 demonstrated this dilemma very well. With Roosevelt seemingly on the sidelines and no other strong contender available, La Follette became "the only man in sight." Over the next several months, the Wisconsin senator assembled funds for a presidential race from wealthy supporters, and took the lead in the Senate in fights over conservation, the tariff, and the contested seating of Senator Wil-

---

[44] Fredric C. Howe to La Follette, December 4, 1910, La Follette Family Papers; George L. Record to William Allen White, December 3, 1910, White Papers.

liam Lorimer of Illinois. In June, La Follette eased into the race with an informal announcement of his candidacy, and by August the National Progressive Republican League had openly emerged as his campaign organization. In late September, La Follette's campaign manager reported confidently that "The movement for the nomination of a Progressive Republican" was "gathering strength daily."[45]

Actually the La Follette campaign never got off the ground. Congressional duties tied the candidate to Washington through the first eight months of 1911, and a commitment to write his autobiography brought in needed cash but kept him off the hustings until late in the year. More vigorous campaigning could not have surmounted La Follette's political weaknesses. Except within his base in the upper Midwest, La Follette was regarded as a dangerous radical whose French name and extreme opinions placed him outside the Republican mainstream. After his campaign had run for six months, an informed journalist predicted that the senator "could not get one delegate from East of Ohio."[46]

As La Follette faltered and Taft moved ahead, the question for Republicans became what Roosevelt would do. The 1910 elections, especially the defeat of Stimson in New York, left the former president's political fortunes at a low point. During the first half of 1911, he and Taft, at the president's initiation, resumed a friendly correspondence in which Roosevelt, among other things, wrote warmly of Canadian reciprocity. He informed friends that "as things are now it would be a serious mistake from the public standpoint, and a cruel wrong to me, to nominate me."[47] The process by which Theodore Roosevelt moved from that posture to an open challenge of Taft in early 1912 was a complex one. It resulted in a split Republican party, opened the way to the presidency for Woodrow Wilson and the Democrats, and made the 1912 presidential election a decisive contest in the history of both major political parties.

[45] Pinchot to George C. Pardee, February 24, 1911, George C. Pardee Papers, Bancroft Library, University of California, Berkeley; Walter L. Houser to John D. Fackler, September 26, 1911, La Follette Papers.

[46] Mark Sullivan to George S. Loftus, December 27, 1911, James Manahan Papers, Minnesota Historical Society.

[47] Roosevelt to William Allen White, January 24, 1911, Morison, *Letters*, VII, pp. 213–214.

CHAPTER 7

Decision in 1912

Theodore Roosevelt spent the first half of 1911 in what passed for him as a political eclipse. The American people, he told one of his sons after the 1910 elections, were "a little tired of me."[1] Roosevelt professed to enjoy being out of the limelight, but he kept a careful watch on the presidential race and his two potential rivals. While his friendship with Taft was warming slightly, he fended off Senator La Follette's attempts to secure an endorsement of his candidacy. The Wisconsin senator thoroughly mistrusted Roosevelt by this time, but he could not express his real feelings without destroying his presidential chances. Instead he wooed Roosevelt, and said that he would run as the progressive candidate only if a better choice could not be found. To La Follette's overtures Roosevelt responded with friendly but noncommittal replies. The former president indicated repeatedly that he was neutral toward candidates for the nomination, but that he expected Taft would be named. If that occurred, Taft would have Roosevelt's support once he was nominated. Believing that La Follette would lose the nomination and Taft would lose the election, Roosevelt was following a course that left the road to the 1916 race open.

Roosevelt's fragile relationships with La Follette and Taft both collapsed in the latter half of 1911. The new harmony with the president went first. The two men met in Baltimore in early June, and newspapers announced that Roosevelt would endorse Taft. The incident reminded the ex-president of the similar episode after their September 1910 meeting, and the old suspicions reappeared. Roosevelt differed publicly and bitterly with his successor through-

[1] Theodore Roosevelt to Theodore Roosevelt, Jr., November 11, 1910, Morison, *Letters*, VII, p. 160.

out the summer on conservation in Alaska and on the president's
advocacy of international arbitration treaties. In August the tone of
contempt toward Taft resurfaced. The president was, Roosevelt
told his oldest son, "a flubdub with a streak of the second-rate and
the common in him, and he has not the slightest idea of what is necessary if this country is to make social and industrial progress."[2]

Meanwhile, the failures of La Follette's campaign and the
emergence of Taft-Roosevelt tension fed the resentments of the
Wisconsin hopeful. He became convinced that Roosevelt's friends,
especially Gifford Pinchot, Amos Pinchot, and Garfield, as well as
others, were sabotaging his campaign. Accordingly, he resisted attempts to work out a joint strategy with Roosevelt supporters or to
share delegates in states such as Ohio. La Follette believed that he
had earned the right to be the progressive candidate, and Roosevelt's entry into the race, should it occur, would not drive him out.
"This game of stampede by lots of old liners and some of the very
new liners," he told a friend, would be "a bit hard to sustain"
through the convention. Despite his campaign's lack of success, despite the popular sentiment for Roosevelt in the progressive camp,
La Follette allowed his deep ambition for the White House to determine his actions as 1912 neared. His resolve to maintain his candidacy added to the complex situation Roosevelt faced as he
pondered his options in late 1911.[3]

The final break with Taft began on October 26, 1911, when the
Justice Department brought an antitrust suit against the United
States Steel Company. The indictment contained language which
created the impression that Roosevelt had been deceived in 1907
when, during the Panic, he approved the purchase by United States
Steel of a competing firm. The statement was accurate but politically dangerous. Roosevelt had recently denied similar allegations
before a congressional committee. To have the government, a Republican administration, make the same charge was insupportable.
In treating this sensitive matter in the same manner it handled
other legal briefs, for the president did not see it before its release,
the Justice Department had, as Elihu Root put it, made "a sin of

[2] Roosevelt to Theodore Roosevelt, Jr., August 22, 1911, Morison, *Letters*, VII, p. 336.

[3] La Follette to S. H. Clark, January 27, 1912, Belle Case La Follette and Fola La Follette, *Robert M. La Follette, 1855–1925*, I, p. 392.

omission, rather than of commission." Whatever its background, the blunder proved disastrous for Taft and the party.[4]

Roosevelt told friends that the president and his attorney general were "playing small, mean and foolish politics in this matter." He attacked the administration's antitrust policy in mid-November, urging a course "of attacking, not the mere fact of combination but the evils and wrong-doing which so frequently accompany combination." The national attention his article gained inspired a revival of calls for Roosevelt's candidacy. From early December 1911 onward he listened more sympathetically to these entreaties. The third-term pledge of 1904 did not apply, he contended, to a former president "who is out of office." He did not want to run "unless it could be made as clear as day that the nomination came not through intrigue or political work, not in the least to gratify any kind of wish or ambition on my part, but simply and solely because the bulk of the people wanted a given job done, and for their own sakes, and not mine, wanted me to do that job." Roosevelt had many friends who were eager to attest to, create, and foster a public sentiment that met these requirements, and they worked hard in the weeks that followed.[5]

By early 1912 Roosevelt was willing to take a nomination that was "the result of a honest widespread desire of the people," and events proceeded rapidly. Negotiations began within the Roosevelt circle about the best way to announce his candidacy. He decided that he should respond to a letter from a group of progressive governors by stating that he would accept the Republican nomination. While plans went forward to put together a campaign organization, to raise money, and to draft the speech that Roosevelt was to give at the Ohio Constitutional Convention, the threat of La Follette as a competitor eased dramatically. At a banquet on February 2 before newspaper publishers in Philadelphia, the senator, overworked, beset with family crises, and aware of Roosevelt's surge, gave a rambling, disconnected address that provided the Pinchots, Garfield, and other reformers with an excuse to switch sides. For a time, it seemed that La Follette might withdraw altogether. The

---

[4] James C. German, Jr., "Taft, Roosevelt, and United States Steel," *The Historian*, 34 (1972), 610.

[5] Roosevelt to Garfield, October 31, 1911, Roosevelt to Benjamin B. Lindsey, December 5, 1911, Morison, *Letters*, VII, pp. 431, 451; Theodore Roosevelt, "The Trusts, The People, and the Square Deal," *The Outlook*, 99 (1911), 655.

political situation thus looked reasonably promising on February 21, 1912, when Roosevelt told reporters: "My hat is in the ring, the fight is on and I am stripped to the buff."[6]

Why did Roosevelt run in 1912? Policy differences with Taft played their part, as did his belief in the New Nationalism. The Republican progressives had no other national leader, and wealthy contributors stood ready to underwrite the anti-Taft campaign. But in the end the dominant motives were personal. Taft's slights demanded revenge. Moreover, rhapsodies about the joys of Roosevelt's private life could not mask his boredom, and a presidential race would bring the reporters and the spotlight back to Oyster Bay. Roosevelt liked being a celebrity, and for a former president only a return to the White House matched the expectations his public had for him. Conservative friends like Root and Lodge found Roosevelt's entry into the race a source of anguish, but the candidate relished the joys of battle, which outweighed the prospect of probable defeat or second thoughts about the wisdom of his action.

In taking the line of least resistance, however, Roosevelt had failed to consider or answer satisfactorily a number of hard questions. Was not a split party a likely result of a fight between Taft and Roosevelt, and what would the nomination be worth after such a struggle? If Roosevelt could not support the president before the two men battled for the prize, was there any real chance of backing Taft if the convention selected him? Was not a bolt and a third party an inevitable consequence of an unsuccessful Roosevelt candidacy? He doubtless believed that he had some chance to win, and his personal ambition received a higher value than his loyalty to his party. By 1912 the Republicans had forfeited some claims to Roosevelt's allegiance, and Taft and his allies acted no more in the interest of party success than Roosevelt did. Yet Roosevelt held the future of the Republican party and its progressive wing in his grasp. In pursuit of his own goals, he administered a devastating blow to the political organization that had made his career and prominence possible.

The nomination contest that followed Roosevelt's actual declaration on February 26, 1912, fell into two distinct phases. For the first six weeks, the tide flowed in Taft's direction. Roosevelt's initial

[6] Roosevelt to William L. Ward, January 9, 1912, Morison, *Letters*, VII, p. 474; *New York Times*, February 23, 1912.

"All Hail." *Harper's Weekly*,
May 4, 1912.

speech to the Ohio Constitutional Convention advocated, in addition to his customary program of social welfare proposals, the
recall, through popular elections, of state judicial decisions.
Roosevelt's willingness to subject judicial acts to a popular election
seemed to Republican conservatives further evidence of his radicalism and disrespect for institutions that stood against the rising
tide of progressive ideas. To the degree that moderate or conservative Republicans looked favorably on the challenger as a potential
winner in November, this speech, which "turned Taft from a man
into a principle," moved them back toward the president. The insistence of La Follette on staying in the race meant a competition
for progressive votes. As a result, precious time was spent on disputes over the events of late 1911 and early 1912. The Roosevelt
campaign had to raise money, construct an organization from the
incongruous assortment of bosses, reformers, and ambitious politi-

cians supporting the candidate, and fight to overcome the lead Taft had compiled.[7]

To offset the president's strength in the South, where Hilles' strategy of early dominance was paying off, the Roosevelt men contested formally the delegates chosen at district and state conventions in Dixie. This response reduced Taft's public total of committed votes until Roosevelt could make a showing, but it left a legacy of trouble for the national convention. In other states the challenger sought presidential preference primaries to enable the Republican rank and file to "declare against both political and financial privilege."[8] Six states decided to hold these primaries, and this development gave the Roosevelt side hope that it might prevail in April and May. The month of March was less rewarding. La Follette carried North Dakota on March 19 over Roosevelt and Taft, ensuring that the senator would remain in the chase to the end. A week later, delegates favorable to Taft prevailed in New York. By the end of April, Hilles predicted, the president would have 500 of the 540 votes needed for nomination.[9]

Roosevelt abandoned his original strategy of not making an extended personal campaign and took to the stump at the end of March. In Illinois, where a primary had been secured, he won 56 delegates on April 9 and, with the help of a strong machine organization in Pennsylvania, gained 67 delegates in that state from the election held on April 13. Roosevelt added victories in Maine, Nebraska, and Oregon to his April total, while Taft prevailed in Vermont, New Hampshire, Kentucky, Michigan, and Indiana. "The situation is critical," wrote Taft a week before the Massachusetts primary on April 30, 1912.[10]

As it became evident that every delegate would count, both sides resorted to more ruthless methods. Roosevelt lumped Taft with the political bosses, assaulted him on Canadian reciprocity, and accused the administration of abusing the patronage. "Outside of the delegates that represent either the unscrupulous use of patronage or else sheer fraud," he said in Omaha on April 17, "Mr.

[7] Lodge to Brooks Adams, March 5, 1912, Lodge Papers.

[8] Roosevelt to Joseph M. Dixon, March 8, 1912, Morison, *Letters*, VII, p. 523.

[9] Hilles to J. A. O. Preus, April 6, 1912, J. A. O. Preus Papers, Minnesota Historical Society.

[10] Taft to William A. Barnes, Jr., April 22, 1912, Hilles Papers.

Taft's strength would be trivial and indeed negligible in the present contest." The Taft men criticized the financial support Roosevelt received from wealthy donors such as newspaper publisher Frank A. Munsey and former Morgan partner George W. Perkins. They used government records to suggest that, as president, Roosevelt had postponed the prosecution of the International Harvester Company. Finally, the question of a third term gained constant emphasis. "From a chief magistracy of more than two terms the nation would be insensibly carried," declared the president of Cornell University, "by the machinations of able and unscrupulous leaders, to a chief magistracy of several terms or to a life office."[11]

The opposing sides in 1912 cast their conflict in ideological terms. "In the long run, this country will not be a good place for any of us to live in unless it is a reasonably good place for all of us to live in," Roosevelt remarked, and he advocated "social and industrial justice, achieved through the genuine rule of the people." Nicholas Murray Butler told the New York Republican state convention that "This contest within the party, and this presidential election, may decide whether our government is to be Republican or Cossack." Progressives like William Allen White countered that "our party must be definitely either liberal or else definitely reactionary," but a Taft supporter believed that "Roosevelt doctrines and still more himself, spell out the complete overturn of our institutions, revolution and the establishment of a one-man autocracy for life."[12]

Roosevelt had the better of the verbal combat with the Taft forces throughout the early weeks of the campaign, and especially when he took to the hustings. Taft wished to avoid "a personal controversy" with his opponent, but many of his phrases, including a reference to "extremists" who "are not progressives; they are political emotionalists or neurotics," were interpreted as slaps at Roosevelt. As the Taft campaign stumbled in mid-April, the president concluded that "The reckless abandon of Mr. Roosevelt in the campaign will make it necessary for me to speak in self-defense."

[11] *New York Tribune*, April 18, 1912; Jacob Gould Schurman, "The Republican Presidential Nomination," *The Independent*, 72 (1912), 601.

[12] *Tribune*, April 11, 1912; *The Works of Theodore Roosevelt: Social Justice and Popular Rule*, XVII, p. 170; White to C. L. Davidson, May 15, 1912, White Papers; Nicholas M. Butler, *The Supreme Issue of 1912* (New York, 1912), p. 7; Marjorie Phillips, *Duncan Phillips and His Collection* (Boston: Little, Brown, 1971), p. 45.

On April 26, Taft traveled through Massachusetts speaking to large crowds of Roosevelt's failure to accord him "a square deal." In Lowell, he said: "I was a man of straw; but I have been a man of straw long enough; every man who has blood in his body and who has been misrepresented as I have is forced to fight."[13]

To Taft's assault, Roosevelt responded with a denunciation of his rival's "policy of flabby indecision and helpless acquiescence in the wrong doing of the crooked boss and the crooked financier." For Roosevelt's partisans, their leader had all the best of the exchange. "Taft certainly made a great mistake when he began to 'fight back.' He has too big a paunch to have much of a punch, while a free-for-all, slap-bang, kick-him-in-the-belly, is just nuts for the chief." In Massachusetts, however, Taft managed a narrow victory that kept his campaign alive. If Roosevelt had won in that eastern state, his momentum might have been irresistible. As it was, he swept through the remaining contests in Ohio, New Jersey, and Maryland. In Ohio the vituperative tone of the contest reached its peak, and at the end of the delegate selection process, the Republicans were hopelessly split and the nomination still was in doubt.[14]

In the states where primaries had been held, Roosevelt won 1,157,397 popular votes and 278 delegates, Taft gained 761,716 votes and 48 delegates, and La Follette won 351,043 votes and 36 delegates. These results, in Roosevelt's estimation, made him the people's choice; his enemies countered that Democrats and independents had cast ballots that clouded the issue. After all the delegates had been chosen in all states, Roosevelt had 411 committed votes, Taft had 201, La Follette had 36, Cummins had 10, 166 were uninstructed, and 254 were contested. The bulk of the uninstructed votes, especially the large New York slate, were really in the Taft column, and the disposition of the contests would give one of the two major candidates the 540 votes needed for nomination.

The Republican National Committee sat in Chicago in early June to decide the disputed seats. Dominated by Taft supporters, it awarded 235 delegates to the president and 19 to Roosevelt. In the

[13] Henry F. Pringle, *The Life and Times of William Howard Taft*, 2 vols. (New York: Farrar and Rinehart, 1939), II, p. 767 (first and second quotations); Taft to Louis E. Payn, April 23, 1912, Hilles Papers (third quotation); *Tribune*, April 26 (fourth quotation), 30 (fifth quotation), 1912.

[14] *Tribune*, April 30, 1912; Dan Casement to Garfield, May 10, 1912, Garfield Papers.

great majority of cases, at least 200 in all, the national committee's decision was correct. Roosevelt probably deserved about 30 more delegates than he received. That would not have been enough, even with all the La Follette and Cummins delegates, to have given him a majority, but it would have challenged Taft's precarious hold on the organization of the convention. In these 30 cases, the Taft men on the national committee acted on the basis of political expediency, a standard the Roosevelt supporters would have employed had the situation been reversed.

Roosevelt apparently believed he was entitled to enough of the seats to provide him with a majority. Whether he remembered that many of the contests in the South were first made to hold down the public total of Taft delegates is not clear, nor did he recall that the national committee had performed similarly on Taft's behalf in 1908, with Roosevelt's approval. When the committee seated Taft delegates from Arizona, California, Texas, and Washington, states where Roosevelt's case was stronger, he decided that Taft was engaged in the theft and that he must go to Chicago and run separately on a third-party ticket if necessary. "I have absolutely no affiliations with any party," he wrote a week before the convention opened.[15] Three days later he left for Chicago, defying the precedent that candidates did not appear at the party's convention.

A Democratic visitor to the Republican conclave remembered the scene as "a flat, flat lake, sizzling asphalt pavements, bands circling and zigzagging along Michigan Avenue, tooting and booming, 'Everybody's saying it, Roosevelt, Roosevelt.'" The candidate arrived on June 15 and, the night before the first session, addressed supporters in the Chicago Auditorium. The nation confronted "a great moral issue," and he insisted that "sixty to eighty lawfully elected delegates" had been stolen from him. Within a few days that number became eighty to ninety, and after the convention Roosevelt suggested that the figure might be even higher. He asked that only those delegates "whose seats have not been contested" be allowed to vote, an action that would have given his forces control of the convention. He insisted that "no action of the convention which is based on the votes of these fraudulently seated delegates binds the Republican party or imposes any obligation upon any Republican." After attacking Taft in the harshest terms, he con-

---

[15] Roosevelt to James Bronson Reynolds, June 11, 1912, Morison, *Letters,* VII, p. 561.

cluded his oration with the affirmation that "fearless of the future, unheeding of our individual fates; with unflinching hearts and undimmed eyes; we stand at Armageddon, and we battle for the Lord."[16]

When the convention began the next day, the Roosevelt men lost in an effort to select their choice, Governor Francis E. McGovern of Wisconsin, as temporary chairman. Instead, with the indispensable support of La Follette's cadre of loyal delegates from the same state and North Dakota, Elihu Root was chosen by a vote of 558 to 501. For La Follette, the prospect of progressive dominance of the proceedings, and the consequent nomination of Roosevelt, was an intolerable affront to his own ambition. On June 19 the Roosevelt attempt to substitute 72 delegates for the ones that the Republican National Committee had placed on the temporary roll of the convention went down 567 to 507. The Taft forces were in the saddle, especially with their firm hand on the credentials committee, and now Roosevelt had to make his next move. Despite the president's ascendancy, Roosevelt still could have won the nomination. There was enough daily slippage in Taft's support to indicate that, if a first-ballot victory did not occur, the incumbent would lose. As the convention proceeded, talk of a compromise candidate, possibly Governor Herbert S. Hadley of Missouri, also surfaced. To such talk, Roosevelt responded as he had before the convention: "I'll name the compromise candidate. He'll be me. I'll name the compromise platform. It will be our platform."[17]

A bolt remained as a final option. The question of whether Roosevelt would support Taft after the convention had come up early in the campaign. At the outset of the struggle, the challenger assured reporters that he would back Taft if he were selected. By mid-April, Roosevelt was telling the governor of Michigan that "a new party" would have to be considered "if the political thugs" in the GOP, using corrupt tactics in the South and Midwest, brought about Taft's nomination, "against the will of the States where the people really are represented, as in Pennsylvania and Illinois." In the early days of June the prospect of a third party was widely discussed in the Roosevelt camp. The candidate wrote an English

[16] Daisy Borden Harriman, *From Pinafores to Politics* (New York: Henry Holt and Co., 1923), p. 99; *Social Justice and Popular Rule*, pp. 204, 211, 212, 213, 231.

[17] Pringle, *Taft*, II, p. 795.

friend that his opponents "will have to steal the delegates outright
in order to prevent my nomination, and if the stealing is flagrant no
one can tell what the result will be." When he departed for Chicago, Roosevelt knew that he would win the nomination or, if he
lost, lay claim to the Republican label or run under the banner of a
new party.[18]

After the results in the temporary chairman contest and the
disputed delegate fight solidified Taft's position, the Roosevelt high
command turned to arrangements for a defection from the party.
Negotiations over organization and campaign finance fell into
place during June 20 to 21, when sufficient funds were pledged
from Perkins and Munsey. The next day, Republican delegates
heard Roosevelt's statement. Because of the seating of "fraudulent
delegates," the gathering was "in no proper sense any longer a Republican convention," and delegates pledged to him should take no
further part in the proceedings. With 344 of the Roosevelt delegates sitting mute, Taft won renomination on the first ballot with
561 votes to Roosevelt's 107 and 41 votes for La Follette. That evening Roosevelt told a crowd of delegates and supporters at Orches-
tra Hall that they should convene, after consulting opinion at
home, "to nominate for the presidency a Progressive on a Progressive platform."[19]

The outcome of the Republican convention meant almost certain defeat for the party in November 1912. Only if the Democrats,
meeting a week later, blundered badly could victory become possible. Roosevelt's departure made Taft's selection almost worthless.
For the conservatives, it was not their triumph but Roosevelt's defeat that mattered. His nomination, thought Taft, "would be a
great danger and menace to the country," and Vice-President
Sherman believed "it was essential, both for the life of our party
and the continuance of our Government" that Roosevelt be "sidetracked." If defeat left the regulars in control and ousted "those
d—— insurgents," the loss would be worth it.[20]

All the factions within the party shared the blame for the disas-

[18] Roosevelt to Chase S. Osborn, April 16, 1912, Roosevelt to Sydney Brooks,
June 4, 1912, Morison, *Letters*, VII, pp. 534, 553.

[19] To the Republican National Convention, June 22, 1912, Morison, *Letters*, VII,
p. 562; Bishop, *Theodore Roosevelt and His Time*, II, p. 334.

[20] Bishop, *Roosevelt*, II, p. 326; Sherman to Frank S. Black, July 5, 1912, Sherman
Papers; Taft to Hilles, June 18, 1912, Hilles Papers.

ter in Chicago in 1912. Senator La Follette allowed pique with Roosevelt and an obsession with his own chances to block progressive hopes of dominating the convention and nominating the only reformer with a chance to win. President Taft insisted on his own nomination for ideological reasons and rebuffed attempts to select a compromise candidate. His willingness to cooperate with the most sordid representatives in the conservative camp and to use harsh political methods underlined his commitment to victory no matter what the cost to the party.

In the end, however, Roosevelt's position was central to the debacle. He entered the race willing to play by the rules if he won, expecting his opponents to support him if he was nominated, but unwilling to accept the possibility that he could lose. In a campaign where both sides relied on tough political tactics, Roosevelt accepted his triumphs as the will of the people and labeled Taft's victories as theft. The nomination was not stolen from Roosevelt, because he never possessed a majority of the votes. In the hunt for delegates, Taft outstole his adversary, but it would never do for Roosevelt to admit that the president, despite his primary losses and lack of popularity with the electorate, proved the better party politician in 1912. Never a good loser, Roosevelt cried foul, picked up his support and his cause, and began anew outside the existing structure of the two-party system.

Despite the melange of bitterness, ambition, and principle that comprised Roosevelt's motives in 1912, his departure was a serious blow to the long-range health of the Republican party. He represented a commitment to moderate progress, a toleration for innovation, and a receptivity to fresh ideas and new voters that the party could not afford to lose. When he left, he removed much of the stimulus that had kept the Republicans alert to the problems of regulating an industrial society. With Roosevelt and his supporters gone, and despite the constructive presence of those insurgents who did not bolt in 1912, the Republicans emphasized conservatism, unity, and caution. In a short time the ascendancy of reactionary principles would cause stagnation and rigidity, and foreshadow the GOP's decline in the first half of the twentieth century.

After Chicago, there remained one consoling hope. "Our Democratic friends, as a rule," a conservative had written late in 1911, "have always had a faculty of blundering at the right time to save us from the consequences of our own mistakes."[21] Would the Democrats now stumble, and avert a Republican disaster? In fact, the prospect of victory had revived the Democrats, and they nominated their strongest candidate in 1912.

The congressional elections in 1910 thrust several Democrats forward as presidential contenders, and Governor Woodrow Wilson of New Jersey emerged as a frontrunner for the nomination in 1911. President of Princeton University since 1902, the fifty-four-year-old Wilson had been identified with the eastern wing of the party. He had called Bryan "foolish and dangerous in his theoretical beliefs," and had said in 1908 that "it would be fatal to our political vitality really to strip the States of their powers and transfer them to the Federal Government." Since 1906 conservatives such as George Harvey, editor of *Harper's Weekly*, had dropped Wilson's name as a potential aspirant for the White House. There was a moment of mild interest in him as an alternative to Bryan in 1908, but nothing came of it. As Wilson encountered controversy and opposition within Princeton over the university's social clubs and academic future, he moved away from the earlier avowal of conservatism and adopted language that, in tone and emphasis, echoed the progressive critique of American society. At the same time, his ambition for public life quickened. "This is what I was meant for, anyhow," he remarked in 1909 of an article he had written attacking the Payne-Aldrich Tariff, "the rough and tumble of the political arena."[22]

George Harvey and his conservative friends in New York and New Jersey hoped to place Wilson in the arena by securing his election as governor of New Jersey. It was, in Wilson's words, "the mere preliminary of a plan to nominate me in 1912 for the presidency." The boss of the regular Democratic machine, James Smith, Jr., was quite ready to further Harvey's plan and to use Wilson to avert a more reformist candidate. Securing Wilson's selection proved to be a difficult matter, but the state convention nominated

[21] Charles W. Fairbanks to Foraker, November 23, 1911, Foraker Papers.

[22] Arthur S. Link, *Wilson: The Road to the White House* (Princeton, N.J.: Princeton University Press, 1947), p. 118, for Wilson's view of Bryan; Ray Stannard Baker and William E. Dodd, eds., *The Public Papers of Woodrow Wilson: College and State*, 2 vols. (New York: Harper & Bros., 1925), II, p. 48; Wilson to Mary Allen Hulbert Peck, September 5, 1909, in Arthur S. Link, ed., *The Papers of Woodrow Wilson: Volume 19, 1909–1910* (Princeton, N.J.: Princeton University Press, 1975), p. 358.

him in mid-September 1910. He told the delegates that, if elected, there would be "absolutely no pledges of any kind to prevent me from serving the people of the state with singleness of purpose."[23] During the campaign, Wilson set out the themes that marked his later presidential race. He attacked Republican leaders, not the party's voters, condemned boss rule and crude partisanship, and labeled the GOP as divided, conservative, and incapable of governing. Simultaneously, in his language he moved away from the machine in his own party and aligned himself with the goals of New Jersey progressives of both parties. An attractive campaigner and a fresh personality, Wilson won a decisive victory that immediately made him a national figure and presidential contender.

Even before he became governor and in the early months of his term, Wilson added to his appeal as a progressive Democrat. When Smith sought to have the state legislature elect him to the Senate, Wilson defeated his one-time sponsor. Describing the contest as "part of the age-long struggle for human liberty," the governor threw his influence behind the candidate who had won the senatorial primary. The repudiation of the boss led newspapers in other states to call Wilson "the exponent of new political ideas" and to discuss his chances for the White House. Wilson further increased his national reputation when the state legislature, under his guidance and partial direction, enacted direct primary, corrupt practices, utility regulation, and workmen's compensation laws. By the spring of 1911 "the scholar turned statesman" was "the toast of every decent citizen of his adopted state and the man toward whom millions of his countrymen are turning for National leadership."[24]

Because of the worldwide impact of his life, and the tragic, pathetic end of his presidency, Woodrow Wilson has become one of the most intensely analyzed historical figures of the United States in this century. To a greater degree even than Theodore Roosevelt,

[23] Wilson to David Benton Jones, June 27, 1910, in Link, ed., *The Papers of Woodrow Wilson: Volume 20, 1910* (Princeton, N.J.: Princeton University Press, 1976), p. 543; Charles Reade Bacon, *A People Awakened: The Story of Woodrow Wilson's First Campaign* (Garden City, N.Y.: Doubleday, Page & Co., 1912), p. 21.
[24] Link, *Wilson: The Road to the White House*, p. 232; *Dallas Morning News*, December 22, 1910; *San Antonio Express*, April 24, 1911.

Wilson seemed to embody the moral aspirations, lofty ideals, and human failings of an era of reform. A president, statesman, and world leader, Wilson was also, for the last decade of his active life, a Democratic politician of notable strengths and striking weaknesses. In the half dozen years from his candidacy for governor through the presidential election of 1916, he rode a wave of success that won him the presidency twice and began the evolution of the modern Democratic party.

Wilson achieved these results because he was, though he came to politics late in life, a party leader with impressive skills. A compelling speaker, his mastery of the language allowed him to articulate policies and sway opinion with uncanny effectiveness. His mind, although not intellectual or brilliant, was swift, adroit, and opportunistic. He inspired loyalty without granting intimacy, had a shrewd sense of the fluctuations of public attitudes, and conducted partisan warfare with relish and success. Where Roosevelt added the grating tones of brashness and bellicosity to his moral preaching, Wilson advanced the same themes in a clear, astringent manner that, if it lacked the excitement of the Rough Rider, was equally useful as a political weapon. Most of all, Wilson had the tide of events to carry along his career. Washington gossip in 1916 contended that if the president "was to fall out of a sixteen story building . . . he would hit on a feather bed."[25]

Throughout the years of his political ascendancy, Wilson also gave evidence of a darker side to his character that led him into extreme difficulties during his second term. Health problems, including a possible stroke in 1906, probably accentuated his tendency toward rigid opinions and intolerance of opposition. A congressman remarked in 1915 that the president "always impresses me that he feels cocksure about everything and does not need help or advice."[26] From the campaign trail Wilson called for open government and "common counsel"; in the White House he was one of the most isolated presidents of this century. In a partisan fight Wilson was not always scrupulous about fair play. With the press he practiced what a friend called "grazing the truth" to gain an advantage. Because of his facility with words, his statements required

---

[25] S. E. High to Claude Kitchin, September 23, 1916, Claude Kitchin Papers, Southern Historical Collection, University of North Carolina, Chapel Hill.
[26] Joe Eagle to Kitchin, April 24, 1915, Kitchin Papers.

more careful examination than most for the hidden overtones they might contain. A cold, aloof, often ruthless public figure, Wilson strengthened the Democratic party for a season. In the end, however, he left it weaker and less united than when he first became its leader.

By the late winter of 1911, the sentiment for Wilson across the country led to a campaign on his behalf for the Democratic nomination. The candidate enjoyed a good press from the start. Approving articles appeared in reform journals where friends had influence or controlled editorial policy. Wealthy associates and admirers provided ample financing. From the beginning, he was the Democratic contender with a national campaign and at least the rudiments of a national organization. Grassroots movements for him appeared in states such as Texas, South Carolina, North Carolina, Kansas, and Pennsylvania that were not equaled for his opponents. Southern birth gave him strength in Dixie; power in New Jersey made him also likely to carry votes in the Northeast; progressive sentiments in the West attracted support for him. Although the breadth of the Wilson campaign did not result in committed delegates before the national convention in June 1912, it laid the basis for the second-choice votes that brought him victory.

The primary asset of the Wilson effort, of course, was the candidate himself. During 1911 he perfected the standard political themes that, with occasional refinements, carried him to the convention. He told his audiences that "The present trend of the people on matters of public interest is strong toward the abolition of party lines," but, while Republicans were unresponsive to this movement, the "free forces" of the Democratic party "are the forces of progress and popular reform." Having linked himself with antiparty sentiment and made it an argument for his own political organization, he also carefully distinguished Republican voters from the party leaders who were "unenlightened, uninformed, absolutely blind and stubborn." In policy terms Wilson pointed to the growth of industrial combinations as the main social problem, and noted that "No corporation can ever get big enough to make the Government of the United States afraid, but all of them combined might in some sinister and fateful day make the Government of the United States subserve them." To counteract the dire effect of these developments, Wilson concluded, "The business of government is to organize the common interests against the special interests."[27]

The indictment Wilson framed of American politics went much farther than the remedies he proposed to solve the problems. His answer for most of society's difficulties was tariff revision downward, coupled with an expanded export trade. "It is in the tariff schedules," he said in July 1911, "that half the monopolies of the country have found cover and protection and opportunity." Wilson did not, however, contemplate rapid changes in the schedules. "We have got to approach" a tariff for revenue only, he remarked in January 1912, "by such avenues, by such stages, and at such a pace as will be consistent with stability and safety of the business of the country."[28]

On corporate regulation, Wilson showed comparable caution. He advocated dealing "not with corporations but with individuals." Once the offending businessman was in jail, "the thing will be stopped, and business relieved of the embarrassment of breaking up its organization in order to stop these practices."[29] Proposals of this kind avoided a commitment to regulation of the structure of American business, left the question of state rights against national power alone, and sounded more stringent than they could be in practice. Wilson had compiled an attractive mix of tough, antipartisan, antimachine rhetoric, and mild cautious measures. It seemed, as 1911 ended, that the formula would bring him the nomination.

Republican troubles made the Democratic nomination more attractive in early 1912, and Wilson soon faced effective and nearly fatal challenges. As a Democrat from outside the existing party hierarchy, and because of his flirtation with the initiative and referendum, as well as his growing progressive reputation, Wilson attracted more intense conservative opposition. The initial candidate of the right wing, Judson Harmon of Ohio, had faded badly because of his drab record, but still had backers in his home state and scattered support elsewhere. The leadership of Congressman Oscar W. Underwood of Alabama in the special session of 1911,

---

[27] Baker and Dodd, eds., *The Public Papers of Woodrow Wilson*, II, pp. 285, 333, 414, 422; Denver *Daily News*, May 8, 1911.

[28] *Public Papers*, II, p. 306; Link, ed., *The Papers of Woodrow Wilson: Volume 23, 1911–1912* (Princeton, N.J.: Princeton University Press, 1977), p. 649.

[29] Link, ed., *The Papers of Woodrow Wilson: Volume 24, 1912* (Princeton, N.J.: Princeton University Press, 1977), p. 198.

particularly over Canadian reciprocity and the Democratic attempts to revise individual tariff schedules, made him a serious aspirant from the South. His well-heeled campaign spread out from
his home base to challenge Wilson's hold on Dixie. The delegates
Underwood won from southeastern states such as Florida and Mississippi usually looked to Wilson as a second choice, and the im-
probability of a southerner's being nominated placed limits on the
credibility of the congressman's campaign.

James Beauchamp (Champ) Clark presented the most serious
threat to Wilson. His long party service and regularity gave him
friendships and political debts that Wilson could not match. The
success of the Democrats in Congress in 1911—their unexpected
cohesion on reciprocity and the tariff—boosted the Speaker's stock.
Under his direction, said a Democratic newspaper, the Speakership
"has become the post of national party leadership." He had a solidly progressive record on the tariff and trusts, drew on Bryan support in the West, and had the resources of Hearst's newspapers
behind him. His backers spoke of his "firm, dignified course" that
caused the people to "turn to him as a rock of safety." The Wilson
men had underestimated Clark, and his rapid rise in early 1912
shocked them.[30]

Although Clark enjoyed a potent appeal to the midsection of
the party, his limitations hobbled his long-range chances. His safety
and dependability made him also seem boring. More important, he
had a penchant for indiscreet statements, of which his remark in
the midst of the reciprocity struggle that he wished to annex "every
foot of the British North American possessions, no matter how far
north they extend," was the most notorious. Bland and colorless,
Clark was vulnerable to being painted as less reformist and more
inept than he in fact was. The Wilson men who portrayed him in
the popular journals described him, with nice condescension and a
sure eye for antiparty attitudes, as "a fine example of the old-fashioned partisan politician."[31] Although he gathered delegates in the
first five months of 1912, Clark did nothing to offset his reputation
as a conservative alternative to Wilson.

As 1912 began, however, the momentum of the Wilson cam-

---

[30] *Washington Post,* July 17, 1911, June 9, 1912.

[31] *Congressional Record,* 61st Cong., 3rd Sess. (February 14, 1911), p. 2520; Ray
Stannard Baker, "Our Next President and Some Others," *American Magazine,* 74
(1912), 132.

paign had slowed. Clark experienced a rise in popularity within the party that carried him to the edge of the nomination. The main element in stopping Wilson was public criticism from both extremes of the party. Conservatives exploited controversies over a request for a pension that Wilson had made to the Carnegie Foundation, an anti-Bryan letter he had written in 1907, and, the most sensational episode, his break with George Harvey and subsequent public fight with Harvey's friends. From the radicals came charges that Wilson's historical writings attacked labor and immigrants. Some of these assaults had merit; most were trivial or scurrilous. Their combined impact was to destroy any sense that Wilson's candidacy was inevitable, or that he was likely to go into the convention with a lead in delegates toward the two-thirds majority needed to nominate.

The delegate-hunting season opened solidly enough for Wilson with a partial victory in Oklahoma, a mixed result in Kansas, and a strong showing in Wisconsin on April 2. Then the tide turned toward Clark. He won overwhelmingly in Illinois on April 9, had abundant strength in the New York delegation selected on April 11, and added Nebraska, Colorado, and Massachusetts during the rest of the month. Wilson's success in Delaware and Oregon, and good performances in Michigan and Ohio, were only partial consolation for the wave of Clark triumphs. May was even worse. Clark carried more than fifteen states, including California, Iowa, and New Hampshire. By June 1, he had between 400 and 500 committed or leaning delegates in his total.

While Clark rose, Wilson declined. The campaign organization was a shambles in mid-May, out of money and leaderless. Some close advisers, including Colonel Edward M. House of Texas, talked privately of other candidates. Yet Clark was not as strong as he seemed and Wilson was not as weak. In early May the Wilson men carried Texas and put 40 firm votes in his total at the state convention on May 28. New Jersey delivered 24 delegates the same day, and North Dakota, South Dakota, North Carolina, and Minnesota fell to Wilson. As the convention approached, he had 248 instructed votes and might control, with other delegates, close to one-third of the meeting. Optimistic supporters, including William G. McAdoo of New York, realized that their man had ample second-choice strength. If the convention became a contest between Democratic progressivism and reaction, Wilson would benefit.

The Baltimore convention, where Wilson was nominated on the forty-sixth ballot, was no easy victory. In the end, Wilson was the nominee with the best claim to support from the progressive majority of the party, and the candidate best able to capitalize on the opportunities in the convention to dramatize his standing as a reform choice. The key figure in the early stages was William Jennings Bryan. Courted by Wilson and feared by Clark, he remained publicly neutral because the difference between the two was not "sufficient to justify me in taking sides."[32] When conservatives named Alton B. Parker to be temporary chairman, Bryan first wired all candidates to join him in blocking Parker. After hesitating on the advice of one campaign manager, Wilson agreed with Bryan, the only aspirant to do so. Bryan's personal challenge to Parker lost on the convention floor, but helped to make Wilson seem the progressive option as reactionaries appeared to square off against reformers. Clark blundered badly here, and the Wilson men exploited fully the ostensible ideological difference.

If the Democrats had required only a simple majority for the nomination, Clark would have been the candidate when he obtained 556 votes on the tenth ballot. With two-thirds needed, the Wilson delegates held firm, as did the Underwood contingent, on the next several ballots. Clark had nowhere to go but down. As ballot succeeded ballot, the well-organized Wilson forces, spearheaded by the Pennsylvania and Texas delegations, drew in the delegates who wanted Wilson as a second choice. On the fourteenth ballot, Bryan threw his support to Wilson, a gesture that swayed few votes in the hall. Outside, it reinforced Wilson's progressive claims. Underwood's strength peaked on the nineteenth ballot, and his delegates were then open to wooing from the Wilson camp. Meanwhile the Wilson leaders negotiated with the party bosses of Indiana and Illinois. By the thirtieth ballot Wilson passed Clark, but it took the addition of 58 votes from Illinois on the forty-third ballot and intensive pleading with the Underwood men to produce victory on the forty-sixth ballot. Many people— Bryan, the Underwood delegates, the leaders of the party in large industrial states, and the loyal Wilson following—received and deserved some credit for the outcome. More fundamental was the

[32] William Jennings Bryan to Thomas B. Love, May 29, 1912, Thomas B. Love Papers, Dallas Historical Society.

candidate's standing as a progressive, his national following, and his potential as a winner.

The result of the Democratic convention completed the major party field in 1912. On the Republican side, President Taft did not, in accordance with tradition, campaign personally, but neither did he retire to the sidelines. The Republicans would have made a stronger race if Vice-President Sherman had not also been fatally ill, if it had had more prominent politicians willing to take to the stump, and if it had not had severe money problems that brought in less than a million dollars. Charles D. Hilles, the presidential secretary, directed the Republican campaign as chairman of the national committee, and he grappled energetically with the challenge of the Progressive party, raised what funds he could, and served as virtually a one-man party organization. It was not enough. Attorney General George Wickersham asked in mid-September: "Is there any campaign except that which the Colonel and Wilson are conducting?" Many Republicans concluded, as one told a conservative senator, "We can't elect Taft and we must do anything to elect Wilson so as to defeat Roosevelt."[33]

Following the Chicago convention, Roosevelt and his supporters waited to see who the Democrats would nominate. Their selection of a progressive, instead of Champ Clark, made victory unlikely for the new party that was in the process of creation. Taft and Roosevelt would be competing for the Republican vote against a united enemy. Nonetheless, Roosevelt threw himself into organization of the Progressive party from late June until its national convention in early August. Should the party cooperate with sympathetic Republicans in setting up ballots, presidential electors, and tickets, or run its own candidates at all levels? In most states, with Wisconsin a notable exception, Roosevelt took the latter course. Should the party be lily-white in the South to appeal to potential Democratic converts? Roosevelt thought that it should. In the largest sense, could the party be more than the sum of Roosevelt's personal appeal? This was a question only the campaign could answer.

Out of the Progressive convention came a ticket of Roosevelt and the governor of California, Hiram Johnson. In an emotional conclave the delegates displayed the evangelical fervor and moral-

---

[33] George W. Wickersham to Charles D. Nagel, September 19, 1912, Nagel Papers.

A membership certificate for the Progressive party in 1912, showing the candidates and the effort to raise money from the public. Author's collection.

ism that marked the party in its early months. "Our cause is based on the eternal principle of righteousness," Roosevelt told them, "and even though we who now lead may for the time fail, in the end the cause itself shall triumph." The party platform argued that the other two organizations "have become the tools of corrupt interests, which use them impartially to serve their selfish purposes." Taking as their symbol the Bull Moose, the Progressives embarked on a movement that Roosevelt believed "may be able to give the right trend to our democracy, a trend which will take it away from mere short-sighted greedy materialism."[34]

Despite their espousal of newer political methods, the Progressive party and its candidates employed traditional arguments and practices in 1912. To win the votes of Republicans, Roosevelt made much of how the Chicago convention had defrauded him. His campaign strategy was as much anti-Taft as anti-Wilson. On the tariff, the third party stood for protection in principle, a tariff commission that would be investigatory and nonpartisan, and

[34] *Social Justice and Popular Rule*, p. 298; Roosevelt to Arthur H. Lee, August 14, 1912, Morison, *Letters*, VII, p. 598; *The Democratic Text-Book, 1912* (New York: Isaac Goldman, 1912), p. 31.

against Canadian reciprocity. The latter position broadened Roosevelt's following in the states that bordered Canada. Roosevelt
thus sought a defensible posture on the tariff from which he could
attack Taft as the advocate of exorbitant rates and chastise Wilson
as a free trader and enemy of prosperity. There was also some con-
tradiction between the Progressive commitment to fresh and open
campaign practices and the large role wealthy contributors such as
Perkins and Munsey played in keeping the party alive.

How new then was the Progressive party? In its advancement
of social justice measures, it expanded the public agenda of political action. The Chicago platform of August 1912 endorsed woman
suffrage, the restriction of judicial power, a minimum wage for
women, prohibition of child labor, health and safety standards for
workers, a system of "social insurance," and ratification of the income tax amendment. "The supreme duty of the nation is the conservation of human resources through an enlarged measure of social
and industrial justice,"[35] said the party, a commitment that drew to
it social workers, academics, and proponents of an active, efficient
government. Purposely left vague was the distribution of power
between the nation and the states, and there was probably more
emphasis on state action within the party than the hindsight of the
New Deal era and beyond suggests. Still the Progressives raised
issues in a national campaign that would not thereafter disappear.

Central to the New Nationalism of the Progressive appeal in
1912 was Roosevelt's proposal for "a strong fundamental, administrative commission" to "maintain permanent, active supervision
over industrial corporations engaged in interstate commerce."
Roosevelt's view of the nature of American business in 1912 owed
much to advisers such as George W. Perkins and others who represented what was known as the "new competition," under which
"stability, agreement, and negotiation with the blessing of government replaced the competitive ideal." They contended that a business community composed of large firms would be best served
through the kind of arrangements that Roosevelt had worked out
between socially responsible, enlightened corporations and the federal government in his second term.[36]

---

[35] *The Democratic Text-Book,* p. 25.

[36] Ibid., p. 11; Richard L. Watson, Jr., *The Development of National Power: The United States, 1900–1919* (Boston: Houghton Mifflin, 1976), p. 11.

Although critical of the antitrust law as working "more mis-
chief than benefit," Roosevelt did not call for abandonment of antitrust prosecutions as a legal weapon in deference to the opinion
within his party that wanted to restore competition.[37] He was also
more than a little unclear on how the regulatory commission would
function in practice. Nevertheless, Roosevelt's regulatory program
involved an acceptance of corporate power as an accomplished
fact, the increase of national authority in the supervisory process,
and use of expanded bureaucratic machinery to manage an important sector of the economy. Within the framework of American
capitalism, which all three major party candidates accepted, Roosevelt took the most advanced position in 1912 toward the modern
welfare and regulatory state.

The Democrats enjoyed all the advantages in the presidential
campaign. They raised more than a million dollars for the party's
war chest, although a canvass of small contributors of $100 or less
produced only about one-third of the total. Despite factionalism in
New York, Illinois, and other states, reasonable unity prevailed,
and tensions between William G. McAdoo and Wilson's original
campaign manager, William F. McCombs, were successfully resolved. By late September party leaders found "hopeless division
among the Republicans" and little discord among the Democrats.[38]

Wilson at first hoped to make only a few formal appearances in
crucial states, a strategy that was soon jettisoned in favor of extensive stump tours in September and October. In his political remarks
the candidate devoted a good deal of time to the tariff, "the chief
seat of privilege in the United States," and renewed his earlier attacks on boss rule and the excesses of partisanship. Wilson also
stressed that even if Roosevelt won he would have to face a Democratic Congress. "The air would be full of clamorous voices, but the
statute book would be very empty of fulfilled promises." Only by
electing a Democratic president, he contended, could effective
government occur.[39]

The focus of the campaign was Wilson's enunciation of the
New Freedom in opposition to the New Nationalism. When con-

---

[37] *Social Justice and Popular Rule,* p. 274.

[38] Albert S. Burleson to Edward M. House, September 21, 1912, House Papers.

[39] John Wells Davidson, ed., *A Crossroads of Freedom: The 1912 Campaign
Speeches of Woodrow Wilson* (New Haven, Conn.: Yale University Press, 1956),
pp. 96, 253.

fronted with Roosevelt's political initiatives in August 1912, Wilson
evolved, in consultation with a Boston attorney and progressive
thinker Louis D. Brandeis, a position on the trust issue that exploited the political weaknesses of the New Nationalism and offered a Democratic alternative. A long-time critic of bigness in
industry as dangerous to a free society and inefficient in practice,
Brandeis rejected the arguments of the advocates of corporate size.
He believed that "the very large unit—is not as efficient as the
smaller unit," a position he rested primarily on moral grounds. The
issue, he said, was "Shall we have regulated competition or regulated monopoly?" Brandeis told Wilson to stress competition as a
means of regulating monopoly, and support a federal commission
to enforce the antitrust laws. Where Roosevelt envisioned a federal
policy that accepted consolidation and used regulatory power to
supervise corporate behavior, the Wilson-Brandeis position emphasized a restoration of competition and a reliance on government
to achieve and maintain a competitive balance.[40]

Were these concepts of the New Freedom and the New Nationalism starkly contrasting political philosophies, or inconsequential
differences of capitalistic detail? To critics and scholars seeking
change that would have moved the nation closer to the doctrines of
socialism, the debate between Wilson and Roosevelt developed
only minor variations on a theme of capitalism. Within American
liberalism, however, these doctrines represented significant differences of degree that would reappear frequently over the next several decades.

In the campaign of 1912 Brandeis's advice moved Wilson toward a response to Roosevelt that provided the Democratic candidate with effective ammunition. By endorsing competition, Wilson
could accuse Roosevelt of accepting monopoly and doing its work.
Roosevelt accordingly became a part of the system of private decision making that had corrupted politics and allowed monopoly to
flourish, and which Roosevelt would now attempt to regulate. The
Progressive candidate's proposal for an industrial commission
meant, Wilson concluded, "a government of experts," paternalism,
and "a continuation and perpetuation of the existing alliance be-

[40] Thomas K. McCraw, *Prophets of Regulation: Charles Francis Adams, Louis D. Brandeis, James M. Landis, Alfred E. Kahn* (Cambridge, Mass.: Belknap Press of the Harvard University Press, 1984), pp. 108, 110.

tween the government and big business."[41] He had found again a middle ground from which he could indict Roosevelt as the instrument of big business and simultaneously appeal to the Democratic suspicion of the stronger federal government that Roosevelt's regulatory ideas encompassed.

Similarly, Wilson spoke favorably of the aims of the social justice program of the Progressive party, but denied that the party's specific answers could achieve their goals. Thus there were rhetorical flourishes against urban overcrowding, disease, and industrial accidents, and allusions to "a great pulse of irresistible sympathy which is going to transform the process of government amongst us." Having invoked the language reformers admired, Wilson then wondered how their objectives could be accomplished when government reflected "the point of view of successful big business merely."[42] But a question also left unexplored was how far the state rights doctrine of the Democrats could stretch to handle national problems. The campaign did not define the New Freedom any more precisely than elections clarify most issues. Probably the person it most emancipated was Woodrow Wilson himself. He could, once elected, describe his positions as following one or more aspects of the New Freedom principles, confident that amid the policy of contradictions, lofty aims, and adroit language of his speeches lay a warrant for whatever course he might pursue. Master of his party, Wilson left the campaign with the flexibility to guide the Democrats along the familiar lines of party negativism or into unexplored areas of positive action once the victory was secure.

On November 5, 1912, the voters gave Wilson and the Democrats 6,293,019 popular votes and the 435 electoral votes of forty states. Roosevelt received 88 electoral votes from six states, notably Pennsylvania, Michigan, and California, and 4,119,507 popular ballots. Taft ran third with 3,484,956 votes and the 8 electoral votes of Vermont and Utah. The Democrats won control of Congress by margins of 51 to 44 seats in the Senate and 291 members to 127 Republicans and a scattering of Progressives in the House. Wilson's success aside, the results did not demonstrate any basic alteration in voting patterns.

[41] Davidson, *A Crossroads of Freedom*, pp. 83, 129.
[42] Ibid., pp. 191, 192.

Roosevelt campaigns in 1912. Reproduced with the permission of the
Theodore Roosevelt Collection, Harvard College Library.

Although the total vote rose slightly over 1908, the estimated
turnout in the North fell 12 percent, and Wilson's popular vote ran
200,000 ballots behind Bryan's in 1908. The Democrat was the
choice of only 41.9 percent of the voters, and the combined totals
of Taft and Roosevelt revealed that the Republicans, when united,
were still the majority party. In all likelihood, however, Wilson
would have been the favorite against either Taft or Roosevelt
alone, given the Democratic rebound between 1904 and 1912 and
the probability that Republican dissension would have kept some
GOP voters at home. Finally, the 900,873 votes for the Socialist
candidate, Eugene V. Debs, indicated that a significant minority of
the electorate found all three major party candidates unpalatable.
For all the exciting candidates, turbulent events, and clash of political philosophies, the election of 1912 does not appear to have interested American voters as much as the apparently colorless and
drab contest in 1908.

After the results were in, the losing parties debated their next
action. The Progressives descended almost at once into the bick-

ering and friction that crippled them for the next four years. Republicans talked of restoring unity and bringing the factions back together. But on what terms should this be done? The regulars believed that "If the Republican party is to have a future it must be on conservative lines; it must be the great conservative party of the nation."[43] The decision to take up a position as the party of the right would not be completed in the years immediately after 1912, but in response to the Roosevelt challenge the Republicans did cast their fortunes with conservatism, a limitation on government power, and a reduction in the activism of the Roosevelt years.

On the Democratic side, the euphoria of victory concealed only briefly the divergences of attitude and philosophy. Conservatives called on the new president to espouse "the old-time principles of the Democratic party," while the more innovative wing reminded party members that the voters wanted "steady but deliberate progress." Other problems remained. How was the patronage to be allocated? Could the president tame "the wilder elements" in the party?[44] Could the Democrats refute by action the Republican taunt that they were unfit to govern? The Democrats were a jumble of cultural extremes and contradictory tendencies, a weird blend of progress and reaction. Because of their enemy's errors, they now had a chance to occupy the center and left of the spectrum. It was now up to Wilson to reveal whether the party would succumb to its ancient ills or whether it might offer a positive alternative to the Republican coalition that had flowered in the 1890s and split so badly in 1912.

[43] Winthrop Murray Crane to Taft, November 12, 1912, Hilles Papers, quotes the opinion of a conservative Republican.

[44] Dallas *Morning News*, November 7, 1912; *Fort Worth Record*, November 7, 1912; James Bryce to Edward Grey, December 22, 1912, Edward Grey Papers, FO800/83, Public Record Office, London.

CHAPTER 8

The Democrats in Power

When Woodrow Wilson took office on March 4, 1913, the Democratic party regained simultaneous control of the Congress and the presidency for the first time in two decades. Wilson's inaugural address spoke eloquently of the social costs of an industrial society and the need for government to address these problems. He pointed to "the human cost, the cost of lives snuffed out, of energies overtaxed and broken, the fearful physical and spiritual cost to the men and women and children upon whom the dead weight and burden of it all has fallen pitilessly the years through." The change in the national government, he continued, meant "much more than the mere success of a party." The nation sought to use the Democrats "for a large and definite purpose." This distant echo of the antiparty appeal of Wilson's presidential campaign found other expressions in the months between his election and his inauguration. "I shall not be acting in a partisan spirit," he remarked in January 1913, "when I nominate progressives—and only progressives."[1]

Once in power, however, Wilson put aside most of his previous criticism of partisan methods and operated as a strong, imperious leader of his party through traditional techniques of management and control. If the new president wished to obtain his legislative program, he could look only to the Democrats in Congress for reliable support. Any thought of a coalition among progressives of all parties never got beyond the stage of talk. Having decided to use

[1] Arthur S. Link, ed., *The Papers of Woodrow Wilson: Volume 27, 1913* (Princeton, N.J.: Princeton University Press, 1978), p. 149; Ray Stannard Baker and William E. Dodd, eds., *The New Democracy: Presidential Messages, Addresses, and Other Papers (1913–1917) by Woodrow Wilson*, 2 vols. (New York: Harper & Bros., 1926), p. 1.

William Howard Taft and
Woodrow Wilson, inauguration
day, March 4, 1913. Reproduced
from the James H. Hare
Collection, with the permission
of the Humanities Research
Center, University of Texas at
Austin.

his own party, Wilson discovered that the Democrats, despite their
large majority in the House and much narrower hold on the Senate,
could not withstand a prolonged quarrel over principles or even
patronage. To govern, Wilson had to use the tools of partisanship,
and the regular Democrats were the only instruments at hand.
Early in his administration the president and his political advisers
agreed to recognize the regulars in the allocation of local officers,
and to give less weight to their progressive foes, many of whom had
supported Wilson's presidential cause. In time, Wilson found the
conservatives more dependable allies and valued them above the
party reformers. As a political leader, Wilson followed a course
that paralleled what Taft had tried to do in working with his
party's majority, but except for grumbles from progressive Republicans in Congress, the Democrat did not encounter the criticism
that engulfed his Republican predecessor.

Wilson did not so much work with Democrats in Congress as
through them. The president, he believed, "must be prime minister, as much concerned with the guidance of legislation as with the
just and orderly execution of law."[2] Circumstances enabled Wilson
to lead Congress with great force and effectiveness in his first term.

[2] Wilson to A. Mitchell Palmer, February 5, 1913, in Link, ed., *The Papers of
Woodrow Wilson: Volume 27*, p. 100.

More than a third of the 291 House Democrats were freshmen, on whom the White House could readily depend. In that body, where Oscar W. Underwood led, and in the Senate, under the direction of majority leader John Worth Kern, the regulars were more disposed than usual to support the legislative programs of the first Democratic president since Cleveland, to counter the gibe that the party could not govern. Through the party caucus the president was generally able before 1916 to have his way. The Democratic lawmakers did not invariably enjoy Wilson's condescending personal style and peremptory commands, but they could not easily counteract his claims as leader of the party and the nation. These conditions, more than Wilson's innovations, such as addressing Congress in person or visiting the president's room at the Capitol, laid the basis for the New Freedom's programmatic success.

In other ways, the new administration reflected more the balance of forces and attitudes within the Democratic party than it did the diverse currents of change. William Jennings Bryan became secretary of state in recognition of his past services at a time when foreign policy still seemed a secondary matter. The Great Commoner devoted some of his time to filling the diplomatic service with "Deserving Democrats" and evoked no dissent from the White House. On the civil service generally Wilson moved away from professionalism and back toward partisanship in choosing government officials.

The contributions of the South to Democratic success also received due recognition. In time, the Republicans charged, with increasing political impact, that it was more recognition than the South deserved. Wilson's cabinet included four men directly from southern states and the secretary of the treasury, William G. McAdoo, was a Georgia native. The president's closest personal associate, Colonel Edward M. House, brought his deferential manner and passion for private power from Texas. With a large southern contingent in Congress, with southerners sitting as chairmen of three-quarters of the 24 important Senate committees and all but three of 23 committees in the House, the South was indeed "in the saddle." Just how much the region influenced policy in Wilsonian Washington became apparent when the administration, under the prodding of southerners in the cabinet and Congress, agreed to racial segregation in government departments. For a president of southern descent, the color line seemed an appropriate measure. "The discrimination may not be intended against anybody, but for the benefit of both," Wilson told a black delegation to the White House in 1914. "If you take it as a humiliation, which it is not intended as, and sow the seed of that impression all over the country, why the consequences will be serious."[3]

At his inaugural, Wilson "itemized" the subjects with which the Democrats had to deal. The tariff, reform of the banking system, and regulation of corporations headed the new president's list. Tariff revision, on which there was substantial agreement within the party, came first. By now the various stages of the tariff scenario were well known, and Wilson had a draft measure to consider from Oscar Underwood and the Ways and Means Committee on March 17, 1913. Wilson then called Congress into special session on April 7 and, in the interval, had the bill rewritten to put raw wool on the free list at once and sugar on the list within three years. He also decided, breaking with a precedent of more than a century, to deliver his tariff message in person. He told Congress on April 8, 1913, that "the object of the tariff duties henceforth laid must be effective competition, the whetting of American wits by contest with the wits of the rest of the world."[4]

The bill that Underwood introduced passed the Democratic caucus easily in mid-April and rolled through the House itself by May 8. In addition to the reductions on raw wool and sugar, there were lower rates on woolen products, cotton goods, and silks; such food products as flour and wheat, meat, eggs, and milk went on the free list. In the House debate Underwood estimated that his bill, based on the principle of "a competitive tariff," would produce "a reduction below the Payne bill taxes last year of 26 per cent." It was, he continued, "an honest revision downward," but was not "so drastic as to jeopardize any legitimate industry."[5] To make up for revenue reductions from the lower rates, the Underwood bill imposed a small tax on incomes above $4,000, with modest but increasing additional surtaxes on incomes above $20,000. The Senate made the income tax more of a graduated levy on higher incomes,

[3] Link, ed., *The Papers of Woodrow Wilson: Volume 31, 1914* (Princeton, N.J.: Princeton University Press, 1979), pp. 302, 303; A. Maurice Low, "The South in the Saddle," *Harper's Weekly,* 57 (February 8, 1913), 20.

[4] Link, ed. *Papers of Woodrow Wilson: Volume 27*, p. 271.

[5] *Congressional Record*, 63rd Cong., 1st Sess. (April 23, 1913), p. 332.

but few in Congress envisioned the new tax, authorized by the ratification of the Sixteenth Amendment in February 1913, as a means to reallocate national wealth or to fund government social programs.

The Senate had been the cemetery for previous tariff measures, and the Democrats expected difficulty there. By 1913, however, the situation differed from the tariff struggles of 1894, 1897, and 1909. The hard lobbying from large-scale industries had abated; if anything, the pressure came from smaller companies for whom the tariff preserved their position relative to bigger competitors. Within the Democratic bloc, moreover, there was less discord over tariff reduction than in the past. Only two small but pivotal groups threatened Wilson's goals. The two Louisiana senators opposed the bill because of the sugar schedule. Free wool made western senators unhappy. The Louisiana votes were lost to the administration, but progressive Republican votes might offset them in the end. The focus of attention, then, was on the westerners. If they bolted the bill would lose, but they were the only other potential dissidents and could be kept loyal through the caucus, presidential pressure, and their own party allegiance.

That is essentially what happened. Although the situation was always delicate for the Senate Democrats, they hung together well. An early vote not to hold public hearings of the Senate Finance Committee indicated that the western senators could be persuaded to support the bill and would not carry their anger at free wool to extremes. President Wilson's denunciation of an "industrious" and "insidious" lobby on May 26 and his proposal to serve as a people's lobbyist did not really change the course of the bill, nor did it reveal much lobbying.[6] It did remind the westerners of their party responsibilities. By late June the caucus had approved the wool and sugar provisions, and in early July the entire measure received Democratic endorsement. The majority party in the Senate had actually reduced the House rates, in a striking departure from previous performances.

Because of Republican delaying tactics, which sought to disrupt Democratic unity and to retard work on banking legislation, there were seven more weeks of debate after the Senate bill was introduced on July 11. The bill survived progressive assaults on the in-

---

[6] Link, ed., *Papers of Woodrow Wilson: Volume 27*, p. 473.

come tax when the majority raised tax rates on large incomes. With other minor problems resolved, the bill gained passage by a vote of 44 to 37. Senator Miles Poindexter, a Washington Progressive, and Senator La Follette voted for the bill. The Senate-House conference did not cause problems like those of the Payne-Aldrich law, and the committee's report won the vote of both houses in early October. Wilson signed the Underwood Tariff into law on October 3, 1913.

Passage of the Underwood Act, said a magazine in remarks that represented the popular consensus, revealed that the Democrats "have done much to remove the grounds for the criticism which has been consistently and justly leveled against their party in the past, that it is incapable of positive action."[7] Wilson and the congressional leadership had used the caucus and favorable circumstances to succeed in fulfilling party promises where Cleveland had blundered and Taft had disappointed. In that sense, the victory in the Underwood fight was largely symbolic. The onset of World War I prevented the law from working in a peacetime setting, and the Democrats would after 1914 find themselves moving back toward protectionism.

The accomplishment of tariff reform did not complete the work of the special session. In late June 1913 Wilson told the lawmakers it was "absolutely imperative" that the Congress "supply the new banking and currency system the country needs," and recommended that "We must act now, at whatever sacrifice to ourselves."[8] The proposals the president put forward were the outcome of extensive debate within the administration and the party since the election. They also reflected the agitation for reform in the nation's banking industry that had surfaced at the end of the 1890s, sputtered along during Roosevelt's presidency, and gathered fresh impetus after the Panic of 1907.

In the wake of that crisis, Congress had passed the Aldrich-Vreeland Act of 1908, which established a National Monetary Commission under Senator Aldrich to recommend changes in the system. The weaknesses of the financial situation were apparent— lack of central control, an absence of flexibility in meeting the

---

[7] "President Wilson, The Democratic Party, and the New 'Competitive Tariff,' " *The Independent*, 76 (October 9, 1913), 62.

[8] Link, ed., *Papers of Woodrow Wilson: Volume 27*, pp. 571, 572.

monetary needs of all parts of the country, and concern for the ade-
quacy of the money supply itself—but the remedies to meet the
problem were diverse and controversial. Most of the debate cen-
tered on whether the national government or private banking
should supervise the centralized financial machinery that those of
all shades of opinion deemed imperative.

Wilson had no strong convictions about particular banking solutions, and at first he accepted ideas from conservative, eastern
Democrats that contemplated a system of reserve banks under the
control of a board of private bankers. When the substance of the
plan leaked out in the spring of 1913, the Bryan wing of the party
made clear its displeasure with anything less than federal authority
over the reserve banks and the currency they might issue. The extent of the opposition persuaded Wilson, under the tutelage of
Louis D. Brandeis, to accept the arguments of Bryan and his associates. In his June 23, 1913, message, Wilson stated that "The control
of the system of banking and of issue which our new laws are to set
up must be public, not private, must be vested in the Government
itself, so that the banks may be the instruments, not the masters, of
business and of individual enterprise and initiative."[9]

The legislative contest that ensued over the next six months was
complex. The administration had first to quell the demands of
southern and western congressmen in the Democratic caucus for
the outlawing of interlocking directorates among banks, expanded
agricultural credit, and the issuing of reserve notes based on crop
assets. As a result of a few concessions, pressure from Bryan and
Wilson, and appeals to party fidelity, the agrarian forces yielded at
the end of August, and the caucus accepted the bill. In the Senate
the Democrats withstood banker opposition until the support of
other elements of the business community could be felt. For several
Democratic senators who threw roadblocks in the way of the bill,
the president responded with conciliatory gestures on patronage
and compromise to smooth the legislative path. By mid-December
the Senate acted favorably, and within several days a conference
report cleared both houses. The Federal Reserve Act became law
on December 27, 1913. It created a structure of twelve reserve
banks, under the control of the Federal Reserve Board, and represented the most important and enduring legacy of the New Freedom and Woodrow Wilson's presidency.

[9] Ibid., pp. 572–573.

Wilson predicted, when signing the tariff bill in October, that enactment of the banking legislation "will be the final step in setting the business of this country free."[10] By the end of 1913 the Democratic administration had only antitrust remaining on the policy agenda of the New Freedom. While that issue made its way through Congress in 1914, the president provided public and private evidence of the boundaries of his commitment to progressive reform and of his allegiance to his party's principle of limited government. Until World War I and the approach of the presidential election of 1916 altered the political situation, Wilson conducted a conservative government that had not yet exploited the opportunity in the Republican turn to the right after 1912.

As the national government gathered power after 1900, it became the target of interest groups and ideological lobbyists seeking to use federal authority to accomplish economic goals or social purposes. To some of the more controversial of these new political forces, Wilson proved unsympathetic in the first two years of his presidency. He was cool to the national prohibition of alcohol, and he did not endorse rural credit bills because of a belief that the government should not extend its credit to a particular class of citizens. When Congress considered during 1914 the Burnett bill to restrict immigration, an idea that had strong support among southern and western Democrats, as well as from nativist pressure groups, the president indicated his reservations and finally vetoed the legislation in January 1915.

Advocates of woman suffrage also pressed the president for action on their cause. The Progressive era brought expanding economic opportunities for American women, especially between 1900 and 1910, when the percentage of employed females rose more than 4 percent. In the next decade, cultural change accelerated as "flappers" displayed a zest for personal freedom and beauty, notably in their sexual behavior. Reaction to the pursuit of votes for women became one aspect of how society responded to the changing role of its female members. The woman suffrage movement itself, after victories in Washington, California, and Illinois between 1910 and 1913, encountered internal differences over the proper strategy to follow in seeking congressional approval of a constitutional amendment. Discord between the older National

[10] Link, ed., *The Papers of Woodrow Wilson: Volume 28, 1913* (Princeton, N.J.: Princeton University Press, 1978), p. 351.

American Woman Suffrage Association and the more militant Congressional Union temporarily slowed the feminist cause. The proponents of suffrage found Congress not disposed to assist them in 1914–1915, and votes in both houses fell well short of the two-thirds majorities needed for passage. When a delegation of women visitors sought direct presidential support, Wilson dodged the issue, deflecting the inquiries of his callers with evasive language.

National child labor legislation was an equally sensitive topic for the president's constitutional position. The National Child Labor Committee had achieved marked success in individual states during the preceding decade. The number of states limiting employment to youths fourteen years or older had risen from 13 in 1904 to 35 by 1914. Dissatisfied with the pace of change and facing growing opposition in state legislatures where affected business wielded large power, the NCLC promoted national action in the form of the Palmer bill. Introduced in early 1914, the measure prohibited from interstate commerce goods that children under fourteen produced or materials that children under sixteen mined. Wilson believed the bill to be unconstitutional. As he remarked to backers of the reform before he took office: "It is very plain that you would have to go much further than most interpretations of the Constitution would allow if you were to give to the Government general control over child labor throughout the country."[11]

Despite the growing warmness between organized labor and the Democrats after 1906, the Wilson administration made only modest concessions to the demands of the unions in 1913 and 1914. Although he signed the Sundry Civil Appropriations Act in 1913, which contained language barring the Justice Department from prosecuting unions under the Sherman Antitrust Act, he promised publicly "that this item will neither limit nor in any way embarrass the actions of the Department of Justice." When the American Federation of Labor pressed for inclusion of this principle in the antitrust legislation of 1914, the president granted some of their requests but, along with key southern Democrats, was "absolutely set against labor's demand that the Anti-Trust law should not apply to labor organizations."[12] The Democrats and organized labor main-

[11] Link, ed., *The Papers of Woodrow Wilson: Volume 27*, p. 78.
[12] Ibid., p. 558; E. Y. Webb to T. J. Lilliard, June 5, 1914, E. Y. Webb Papers, Southern Historical Collection, University of North Carolina Library.

tained more cordial relations than the unions had with Roosevelt and Taft, but Wilson did not accept the idea that federal power should extend assistance to competing social forces in American society.

In addition to the philosophical limits of Wilson's political creed, the deteriorating economic situation, evoking memories of the Democratic debacle in the 1890s, led the administration to emphasize its affinity for the business community. "Mr. Wilson is now convinced," wrote a Republican journalist to Taft, "that the only danger that threatens his administration is from depressed business conditions." The downturn in 1913 to 1914 was probably closer to a recession than a full-scale depression, but evidence of declining production and rising unemployment gave the Republicans an issue they were eager to exploit. The president answered with optimistic statements that "the signs of a very strong business revival are becoming more and more evident from day to day." He also consulted prominent business leaders at the White House. "I have not been inviting businessmen to see me," he told a Democratic senator, "I have been welcoming them." Most indicative of Wilson's attitude were his appointments to the Federal Reserve Board. In the course of supporting an old friend and director of the International Harvester Company for the board, Wilson argued, after the nomination was withdrawn in the face of progressive opposition, that "We have breathed already too long the air of suspicion and distrust." A financial commentator in New York told business that Wilson was "suggesting an alliance between them and the Democratic Administration."[13]

These political crosscurrents helped to shape the antitrust program that completed the New Freedom in 1914. In January, Wilson told Congress that "The antagonism between business and Government is over," and predicted that "The Government and business men are ready to meet each other halfway in a common effort to square business methods with both public opinion and the law." The ensuing legislative process fell into two distinct phases. From the January message until early June, the lawmakers in the

[13] Link, ed., *The Papers of Woodrow Wilson: Volume 30, 1914* (Princeton, N.J.: Princeton University Press, 1979), pp. 210, 297; Gus Karger to Taft, January 9, 1914, Taft Papers; Wilson to Benjamin R. Tillman, July 28, 1914, and New York *American,* July 13, 1914, clipping in Series IV, Case File 1139, Woodrow Wilson Papers, Manuscript Division, Library of Congress; *New York Times,* July 24, 1914.

House put through a package of measures that included the Clayton Bill, which sought to specify and forbid business practices that
restricted competition, the creation of an Interstate Trade Commission along the lines of Roosevelt's Bureau of Corporations, and a
bill to give the Interstate Commerce Commission supervision of
railroad securities. These bills followed the implications of Wilson's
campaign in 1912 by setting out as precisely as possible what was
forbidden behavior in the business sector. "These practices, being
now abundantly disclosed," Wilson thought in January, "can be
explicitly and item by item forbidden by statute in such terms as
will practically eliminate uncertainty, the law itself and the pen-
alty being made equally plain."[14]

By the spring of 1914, however, Wilson's thoughts on this problem altered. Sentiment within the business sector preferred to rely
on the trade commission instead of specific legislation, and such a
close economic adviser as Brandeis came to believe that a federal
trade commission, operating under a general mandate, would be a
better regulatory weapon. Wilson himself never shared the skepticism of industrial businesses that animated Brandeis and permeated
the South and West. "As I talked with business men and students of
legislation," he became convinced "that these unfair practices
would be reached through the Trade Commission Law." Once
Wilson threw his weight behind this proposal, congressional
support for it grew. It weathered attacks from right and left in
the Senate. Conservative Republicans called it socialistic, and
progressives questioned the amount of power the trade commission
would have. Nonetheless the bill passed in early September, and a
much-amended, drastically weakened, and presidentially abandoned Clayton Act also emerged in mid-October. As these laws
neared final action, the president disclosed to a reporter "that he
had nearly reached the end of his economic program as outlined in
the campaign and in the Democratic platform." Such social reforms as remained, he thought, would be for the most part "the
work of the states," and he regarded improvements in "the machinery of commerce" and conservation policy as the most pressing
domestic needs.[15]

[14] Link, ed., *The Papers of Woodrow Wilson: Volume 29, 1913–1914* (Princeton,
N.J.: Princeton University Press, 1979), pp. 154, 156.

[15] Arthur S. Link, *Wilson: The New Freedom* (Princeton, N.J.: Princeton University Press, 1956), pp. 438, 440; Ray Stannard Baker, *American Chronicle* (New
York: Scribner, 1945), p. 277.

For all of Wilson's public and private signals in the first seven months of 1914 that his administration had conservative aspirations, he did not succeed in quelling anxiety in the business community. "The business men of the country know," decided an Ohio Republican, that Wilson "has put through a dangerous and destructive legislative program in which he has ignored every protest made by them and their representatives." Nor had the president been able to place the Democrats in a strong position to wage the congressional elections in the autumn. At midsummer Republicans reported a "general feeling" that their party stood "a good chance of securing the next House."

In addition to the burden of the economy, the Democrats suffered from the scars of Wilson's successful but divisive drive to repeal the exemption of American shipping from the payment of tolls in the Panama Canal. Lengthy patronage and intraparty battles in New York, Illinois, and New Jersey also hurt. Republicans criticized congressional extravagance, Wilson's policy toward the Mexican revolution, and the effect of the Underwood Tariff. Aware that the president was more popular than his party, Democrats appealed to him "to take the stump in the coming campaign" because, as a Republican newsman noted, "Reports reaching the national capital daily are far from encouraging from a Democratic point of view."[16]

Of the two opposition parties, the Republicans expected to gain the most from Democratic weakness. The Progressives had faded badly since November 1912. Theodore Roosevelt recognized that the new party had no real future without power or patronage, but he could not simply jettison those who had risked their political lives on his behalf, at least not immediately. Roosevelt kept up a public interest in the third party, but a growing distaste for Wilson's foreign policies and a sense of political reality drew him back toward his old partisan home. Out of money, divided over issues such as antitrust and the role of big business, the Bull Moosers in 1913 and 1914 quarreled among themselves and discussed whether to "amalgamate" with the Republicans.

Roosevelt's journey to Brazil in late 1913 did more than just impair his health; it removed the Progressive leader from the scene as

[16] Malcolm Jennings to Warren G. Harding, September 15, 1914, Warren G. Harding Papers, Ohio Historical Society, Columbus; Franklin Murphy to Taft, July 20, 1914, Taft Papers; *New York Tribune*, July 28, 1914.

the party's internal difficulties became acute. Meanwhile Wilson's legislative victories drained off some of the crusading spirit of a minority of the Progressives and pushed them toward the Democrats. However, opposition to the administration's actions in Mexico and on the Panama Canal tolls led many more back to the GOP. Roosevelt gave credence to the talk of a Progressive-Republican fusion when he proposed in July 1914 a joint effort behind a Republican gubernatorial candidate in New York. The party still held a balance of power between the major parties in some states and congressional districts, but its influence was clearly waning.

As the Democrats faltered, the Republicans appeared to win ground. Changes in the national convention rules eased some of the wounds of 1912, as did the actions of the Wilson administration. Although some insurgents such as La Follette supported Wilson's domestic policies, others agreed with Senator Bristow that he was "a sheep in wolf's clothing," with "a smooth and oily way of coining phrases that strike the popular ear, and make the people believe that he means what he says."[17] With the party in power seemingly succumbing to a repetition of the troubles of the 1890s, the Republicans suppressed their differences over public policy and governmental power, avoided the formulation of constructive alternatives to Wilsonian actions, and prepared to win by default.

In late July 1914 the outbreak of World War I in Europe disrupted the Republican strategy. The foreign policy crisis created a popular resolve to support the president on which he and the Democrats immediately capitalized. Wilson announced that he would not abandon his official duties to "undertake any kind of political canvass" and would rely on public letters to advance the claims of his party's candidates. The Democrats stressed the internal harmony within their ranks, and Wilson's reconciliation with antagonists from the 1912 campaign received full press attention. Candidates selected in some Democratic primaries won presidential backing despite their conservative records. While avoiding partisan activity, Wilson made partisan criteria a keynote of his statements. Unlike the Republicans, a party "utterly unserviceable as an instrument of reform," he found the Democrats with "thought . . . ambition . . . plans" that were "of the vital present and the hopeful future."[18]

[17] Joseph L. Bristow to J. R. Harrison, October 12, 1914, Bristow Papers.

[18] Link, ed., *The Papers of Woodrow Wilson: Volume 31, 1914*, p. 174; Link, ed., *The Papers of Woodrow Wilson: Volume 30, 1914*, p. 477.

But the most important Democratic theme was, as their campaign handbook put it, "War in the East! Peace in the West! Thank God for Wilson!" The cabinet officers Wilson sent out as surrogate campaigners used language that anticipated the "He Kept Us Out of War" arguments of 1916. "The President has no doubt of the patriotism of these young men," said Secretary of State Bryan in New York, "But mothers, he would rather your sons would live for their country than die on foreign soil or in an unnecessary war." At Atlantic City, New Jersey, in mid-October, Champ Clark predicted that historians might "declare that his efforts to keep the United States out of war constituted his clearest title to the gratitude of his country."[19]

As the campaign ended, it was apparent that the Democrats would suffer losses in the House. Their campaign organization had little money, the late adjournment of Congress tied down incumbents, and a conservative Republican tide was running. When the votes were counted, the Democrats did keep their majorities in both houses. In the first contest where senators were chosen by popular vote, the majority widened its lead in the upper house. Over in the House, the Democrats lost 63 seats, with the heaviest reverses in New York, New Jersey, Pennsylvania, and Connecticut.

The Progressive party was an even greater casualty of the 1914 elections. Its national vote did not quite reach 2 million, and it was left with only 9 congressmen, compared with 17 before the election. As Roosevelt wrote, "from Indiana eastward it is utterly impossible, if present conditions continue unchanged, that we shall again be able to make a serious fight."[20] Although the Moosers retained some bargaining power with the Republicans in 1916, their leader had lost the reforming thrust two years after he brought the party into existence. For the sad result of the Progressive adventure, Theodore Roosevelt was preeminently responsible. Always more interested in international questions than domestic reform, he had not sustained the commitment to social justice that had animated him while Taft was president and that had drawn so many reformers to him in 1912.

The White House put up a brave front after the election. The

[19] Ray Stannard Baker, *Woodrow Wilson: Life and Letters*, 8 vols. (Garden City, N.Y.: Doubleday, Page, and Doubleday Doran, 1927–1939), V, p. 94; *New York Times*, October 11, 14, 1914; *Washington Post*, October 29, 1914.

[20] Roosevelt to Meyer Lissner, November 16, 1914, Morison, *Letters*, VIII, p. 843.

Democrats still had a 34 vote margin in the House, and had actually picked up 5 Senate seats. But Wilson conceded privately that "People are not so stupid not to know that to vote against a Democratic ticket is to vote indirectly against me." Both the president and his political advisers took pride in the party's showing in the Dakotas, Washington, and California. Emphasis on the West would prove an important element in the next presidential election. In November 1914 Wilson still seemed persuaded that the result in the off-year contest dictated further political conservatism. He wrote a public letter to McAdoo in which he boasted that "the future is clear and bright with promise of the best things" because the Democratic legislative program had eliminated most of the nation's fundamental social problems. Critics on the left chided the president for making "extravagant claims" on behalf of his party, and charged that "he had utterly misconceived the meaning and task of American progressivism."[21]

By the early weeks of 1915, however, the impact of World War I transformed the conditions of American politics and shifted the fortunes of the 1916 presidential election toward the Democrats. This process of response to the world conflict developed during most of the two years that preceded the casting of ballots in November 1916. One early victim of the war was American foreign trade. Shipping of the belligerents left the seas, and no adequate United States merchant marine existed to make up the difference. Under the sponsorship of Secretary McAdoo, the administration asked Congress to fund the creation of government-owned and -managed shipping lines through the direct purchase of foreign vessels. Since this necessarily involved the acquisition of German ships, Republicans and some Democrats opposed the plan as likely to cause trouble with the British and the French. Moreover, Republican congressional critics described the idea as "a measure of state socialism which, if established, will inevitably destroy individual liberty."[22]

Wilson's willingness to support a bill that provided direct government promotion of foreign trade indicated that his restricted view of national power was not immutable. In 1915 the president

[21] Link, *Wilson: The New Freedom*, p. 468; Link, ed., *The Papers of Woodrow Wilson: Volume 31*, p. 327; *New Republic*, 1 (November 21, 1914), 7.

[22] Arthur S. Link, *Wilson: The Struggle for Neutrality, 1914–1915* (Princeton, N.J.: Princeton University Press, 1960), p. 147.

lost the fight over shipping in a nasty battle with Congress and, in the process, lost some of his belief in the political conciliation of conservatives as well. He was now determined "to break the control of special interests over this government and this people." As Colonel House noted while the shipping fight raged, "The Democratic party must change its historic character and become the progressive party in the future."[23]

If economic difficulties crippled the Democrats in 1914, the improvement in business conditions, fueled by Allied war orders, that began in the spring of 1915 gave the administration the opportunity to take credit for the return of good times. The Democratic National Committee began in late 1914 clipping newspaper accounts "showing the wonderful prosperity that has come to this nation under this Democratic administration," and as 1916 opened they boasted of the effect their "prosperity clippings" were having. Worried Republicans forecast that "the Democrats will make an appeal to the stomach of the nation."[24]

While the war revived the sluggish American economy, it also confronted the major parties with momentous issues in foreign policy that subjected Republicans, Democrats, and Progressives to severe strains. In May 1915 a German submarine sank the *Lusitania*, a British liner, and 124 American passengers died. The *Lusitania* was, of course, not the only example of submarine warfare that affected diplomacy between 1914 and 1917, nor was the submarine problem a single element in the difficulties that challenged President Wilson. But, more than any other individual event, this maritime disaster brought home to the nation that the war was going to have an impact few foresaw in August 1914. For politicians, it brought hard choices about how to reconcile national rights with the actions of belligerent powers, and whether and to what extent the United States should prepare for possible military involvement in the conflict.

The Democrats had to endure an uncomfortable and faction-ridden year between the torpedoing of the *Lusitania* and their na-

[23] Ibid., pp. 151, 152; Charles Seymour, ed., *The Intimate Papers of Colonel House*, 4 vols. (Boston: Houghton Mifflin, 1926–1928), II, p. 344.

[24] Thomas J. Pence to Fred B. Lynch, December 7, 1914, Josiah Bailey Papers, Duke University Library; Pence to Claude Kitchin, January 6, 1916, Kitchin Papers; James T. Williams to William E. Brigham, January 21, 1916, James T. Williams Papers, Duke University Library.

tional convention in 1916, but they found a workable answer in Wilson's program of very moderate military preparedness, a restrained and controlled assertion of American rights against Germany and Great Britain, and an emphasis on the administration's desire to keep the nation out of war. The Republicans were less fortunate, as their foreign policy differences compounded the difficulties that existed after 1912.

The crisis that occurred over the *Lusitania* convinced Wilson in the summer of 1915 that the armed forces had to be improved. Republican critics had called for such action for many months, but the president, aware of the staunch opposition to military spending among southern and western Democrats, received these proposals coolly. By November 1915, however, the administration put forward preparedness legislation, to the dismay of an influential bloc of Democrats in Congress, progressives outside the Northeast generally, and a substantial proportion of American workers and farmers. The result was an extended congressional battle in which Wilson made a speaking tour to rally public support in January and February 1916. He finally had to settle for a watered-down bill in May 1916 that increased the size of the army, but did not commit the country to a preparedness policy for an anticipated war. Wilson had more success with securing additional money for the navy. Despite their quarrels over preparedness, the Democrats were not driven apart by it because Wilson declined to go beyond the existing party consensus against a greater military establishment.

The best course to preserve peace had troubled the Democrats in the months after the *Lusitania* went down, but the party came through the hazards of 1915 to 1916 with reasonable unity. When the administration sent a diplomatic response to Germany about the sinking that Bryan feared would risk war, the secretary of state resigned in June 1915. Although he spoke against preparedness and for strict neutrality to enthusiastic audiences, Bryan did not attack Wilson's leadership directly. In early 1916 a diplomatic tangle led to a congressional challenge to the president's control of foreign affairs over the Gore-McLemore resolutions that would have kept Americans off belligerent ships. By using all his patronage power Wilson repulsed the assault and the resolutions, and the Democrats remained cohesive.

Having weathered these internal difficulties, the Democrats benefitted when the foreign policy situation improved in the spring and summer of 1916. The Wilson administration came very close to war with Mexico over the army's expedition south of the border in pursuit of Pancho Villa. Last-minute peace initiatives and American popular revulsion against hostilities pulled the government back from the brink. Relations with Germany had followed a tortuous course after the *Lusitania* sinking, ending in the president's ultimatum of April 1916 to the German Empire that demanded abandonment of that nation's unrestricted submarine warfare against belligerents and neutrals. When the Germans appeared to accept Wilson's demand several weeks later in what became known as the *Sussex* Pledge after the ship that occasioned the crisis, the United States seemed to have escaped involvement in overseas quarrels. The Democrats were the obvious beneficiaries of the peace sentiment, and they soon exploited the issue as a major element in their three-pronged appeal of prosperity, peace, and progressivism.

The foreign policy issues that vexed the Democrats compounded the predicament of the Republicans. To win, they had to reunite with the Progressives on domestic questions, where the differences of 1912 lingered. As the neutrality and preparedness issues gained in intensity, the party discovered new splits in its ranks. Eastern Republicans were inclined to favor intervention on the Allied side or, at the very least, a more vigorous defense of national rights toward Germany and in Mexico. West of the Alleghenies, progressive Republicans bitterly opposed the prospect of risking war through a more bellicose foreign policy. German-Americans, who formed a large bloc of usually dependable Republican supporters in the Midwest, made clear their resolve to attack any candidate who adopted a pro-Allied stance. The Republicans had to find a candidate who was progressive enough to placate the reformers, conservative enough to reassure the right wing, firm enough on neutral rights to keep the East happy, and pacific enough to retain the allegiance of midwestern and western peace advocates, German-Americans, and progressives.

Few Republicans even came close to fitting this set of criteria. Campaigns for Myron T. Herrick and former senator Theodore E. Burton of Ohio stalled; La Follette had Wisconsin, North Dakota, and nothing else; and Senator William E. Borah of Idaho took soundings in 1915 and then dropped out in favor of Albert B. Cummins. The Iowa senator picked up delegates in his own region, and then lost badly to Charles Evans Hughes in Oregon and was through. Support for the industrialist Henry Ford measured only the intensity of peace feelings on the Great Plains. Elihu Root, the favorite of the eastern internationalists, was too strongly identified with that policy to win.

Although he met only a part of the demands of the party at best, Theodore Roosevelt hoped and worked for the Republican nomination to defeat the president he had come to despise. In March 1916 he told the nation that he could be selected only if "the country has in its mood something of the heroic,"[25] and he assailed the German-Americans in a series of midwestern speeches. By now Roosevelt was so much the advocate of a policy that would lead to war that his nomination would have meant suicide for the Republicans. But once again Roosevelt believed he was right, and he planned to use the Progressive party and his own popularity to secure either his own nomination or the selection of a candidate with foreign policy views he found acceptable. In laying down progressive opinions he had once held, criticizing hyphenated Americans' disloyalty, and blasting Wilson for cowardice in the face of German actions, Roosevelt displayed his characteristic audacity, but took little account of Republican reality.

As an alternative to Roosevelt and the lesser candidates, in early 1916 the Republicans turned, with varying degrees of longing, to Supreme Court Justice Charles Evans Hughes. Appointed to the federal bench in 1910, Hughes had spurned offers to be a compromise choice in 1912. His assets were now compelling enough to outweigh the suspicions that Republican professionals had of his stubbornness, independence, and austere public image. He had been a progressive governor of New York, had provided strong campaigning in 1906 and 1908, and had no clear public record on the party's divisive issues. Since he was perceived as a foe of political bosses and a moderate on economic questions, Hughes came into the national convention as the frontrunner. Of course, once he was chosen, Hughes would have to declare himself on all the controversial topics about which Republicans disagreed. Although a far bigger man than Alton B. Parker in 1904, Hughes gained ground as the inscrutable savior of a split party much as his fellow jurist had done twelve years before with the Democrats.

The Republicans held their convention in Chicago in early

---

[25] Morison, *Letters*, VIII, p. 1024.

June, at the same time as the Progressives. In one sense the meeting brought about desirable results. Hughes was selected on the third ballot, with Charles W. Fairbanks as his running mate, and Roosevelt's hopes were turned back. The platform made some concessions on reform issues such as child labor and woman suffrage, and carefully straddled the preparedness, neutrality, and loyalty questions. Meanwhile, Roosevelt and his operatives kept the Progressives in check until Hughes was nominated, and then declined the presidential nomination that the third party thrust on him in the frustration and anger of its death throes.

Actually, the selection of Hughes solved only the problem of who the Republican nominee would be. On domestic issues, the party's evasive strategy provided a progressive look that expediency dictated in 1916. Behind the façade of reform, the GOP's heart remained as conservative as it had become in 1912. Was Hughes to please the right with an overt repudiation of the Wilsonian record, or should he court the left by accepting reform goals and criticizing the president's methods of achieving them? The choice of either option meant lost votes. The foreign policy dilemmas were more acute still. If the candidate endorsed Roosevelt's aggressive program, he would risk losing the German-American vote while handing the Democrats the peace issue. If he wooed the German-Americans, he left himself open to criticism from Roosevelt, to Democratic attacks on his patriotism, and to embarrassing questions about where, in fact, he would improve on Wilson's accomplishments. Expected to be a firm, upright, courageous alternative to the president, Hughes had to weld the disparate factions together in a four-month campaign and yet avoid charges of weakness, straddling, and equivocation. The task proved to be beyond Hughes's modest powers as a party politician.

In contrast to the Republican predicament, Wilson and the Democrats had the necessary ingredients of a coherent campaign in place when their convention met in St. Louis in mid-June. Since the end of 1915 the president had been evolving a progressive program, embracing parts of the New Nationalism, that would enable him to outbid the Republicans for the votes of Democratic and Progressive reformers. Wartime conditions and political necessity played some part in Wilson's shift toward a broader role for the federal government, but the flexible and amorphous quality of his political philosophy, expressed in his belief that he had always been a progressive, allowed the president to persuade himself that he was not altering but only continuing previous Democratic doctrine. To some degree progressive publicists read into Wilson's individual actions and ambiguous public statements a greater element of unity and rationality than they actually possessed. In 1916 Woodrow Wilson advanced toward progressivism without becoming an advanced progressive.

The exact timing of Wilson's transition into a reformist, nationalist chief executive remains in dispute. His open endorsement of woman suffrage in the states in October 1915 owed much to a desire to soften the public shock of a second marriage a little more than a year after his first wife's death. Nonetheless, it also indicated a Wilsonian sensitivity to this burgeoning progressive concern that he had not previously displayed. The nomination of Louis D. Brandeis to the Supreme Court in January 1916 led to a long confirmation struggle between the Boston attorney's reform allies and the conservative, Republican, and anti-Semitic coalition that regarded Brandeis as a danger to the republic. By championing his nominee and winning the confirmation victory in the spring through his personal intervention, Wilson reinforced his progressive claims for the campaign ahead.

During the first half of 1916, Wilson also reversed his earlier opposition to rural credits legislation, and a bill to establish twelve federal land banks was on its way through Congress as the Democratic convention assembled. Wooing business support as he courted the farm vote, the president accepted the idea of a nonpartisan commission to recommend tariff rates, worked for laws to prevent foreign manufacturers from dumping surplus goods on American markets, and even agreed to higher rates on industrial products that faced European competition after the war ended. The pace of Wilson's conversion to the idea of additional national action to achieve social justice and to satisfy the interests of the varied pressure groups within the economy would quicken still more when the campaign itself opened. As Secretary of the Interior Franklin K. Lane informed the president: "The Republican party was for half a century a constructive party and the Democratic party was the party of negation and complaint. We have taken the play from them. The Democratic party has become the party of construction."[26]

---

[26] Franklin K. Lane to Wilson, June 8, 1916, Wilson Papers.

The national convention fused the component themes of the Democratic appeal in 1916 in a dramatic manner that gave the party the initiative for the rest of the canvass. The platform supported an assortment of progressive solutions such as national child labor legislation, rural credits, federal aid for highway construction, and approval of state action on woman suffrage. Southern commitment to state rights precluded approval of national woman suffrage. The president also wished to have the platform contain a strong stand against what were described as "all alliances and combinations of individuals in this country of whatever nationality or descent, who agree and conspire together for the purpose of embarrassing or weakening our Government or of improperly influencing or coercing our public representatives in dealing or negotiating with any foreign power."[27] The administration, well before American entry into war, was exploring how to restrict dissent and to use "Americanism" as a political weapon. In 1916 it remained a persistent subtheme behind prosperity, progressivism, and peace.

The assertion of the peace appeal as the most prominent Democratic campaign argument crystallized at the convention. In the keynote speech and other addresses, party orators evoked an enthusiastic and emotional response when they elaborated on Wilson's peace record. The platform expressed the language that Democrats repeated on the stump as it applauded "the splendid diplomatic victories of our great President, who has preserved the vital interests of our Government and its citizens, and kept us out of war." For the Democrats the peace issue was, as a cabinet officer remarked, "the strongest card we can play."[28]

After his renomination Wilson intensified his courtship of the Progressive vote. When the Republicans sought in mid-July to place the blame on the southern Democrats for stalling the child labor bill in Congress, the president acted "to urge the immediate passage" of the measure on southerners with state rights objections. The bill passed six weeks later, and reformers praised Wilson's willingness to endorse "Federal or National control" as "the best

[27] J. Bruce Kremer, comp., *Official Report of the Proceedings of the Democratic National Convention, 1916* (Chicago: Democratic National Committee, 1916), p. 123.

[28] Ibid., pp. 98–99, 130; Albert S. Burleson to William Jennings Bryan, July 1, 1916, Albert S. Burleson Papers, Eugene C. Barker Texas History Center.

method to put an end to certain evils or advance certain rights." In August Congress also enacted a workmen's compensation law for federal employees. The administration, said a national magazine editor, could make a strong campaign appeal "for the votes of the social-reform elements of the Progressive party, for the farmer vote, and for the vote of the wage-earning classes, whether organized or unorganized."[29]

The Democrats solidified their appeal to the labor vote when Wilson compelled Congress to pass the Adamson Act to avert a national railroad strike in early September. Giving railroad workers the eight-hour day, the law embodied what the president labeled "the whole spirit of the time and the preponderant evidence of recent economic experience." After Wilson had acted, Democratic workers reported inroads into the labor vote. Within the national leadership of the American Federation of Labor, Samuel Gompers campaigned for Wilson and called on his members to cast Democratic votes. More than in any previous election, the unions and the Democrats came together in the alliance that was a keystone for the party's electoral success of this century.[30]

In his acceptance speech at Shadow Lawn, New Jersey, on September 2, President Wilson skillfully asserted his party's claims to reform support. "We have in four years come very near to carrying out the platform of the Progressive Party as well as our own; for we are also progressives." Later he told a convention of woman suffrage advocates, without endorsing their specific aims, that "when the forces of nature are steadily working and the tide is rising to meet the moon, you need not be afraid that it will not come to its flood." He praised the Progressive party "because it had the real red blood of human sympathy in its veins and was ready to work for mankind and forget the interests of a narrow party," and he informed the young men of the Democratic party: "I am a progressive. I do not spell it with a capital P, but I think my pace is just as fast as those who do."[31] By implication more than by internal debate and overt decision, the Democrats had, at least for the mo-

---

[29] Wilson to A. J. McKelway, July 19, 1916, Benjamin B. Lindsey to Wilson, August 9, 1916, Wilson Papers; *The American Review of Reviews*, 54 (1916), 140–141.

[30] Link, ed., *The Papers of Woodrow Wilson: Volume 38, 1916* (Princeton, N.J.: Princeton University Press, 1982), p. 97.

[31] Ibid., pp. 131, 163, 304, 305.

ment, given up "a regime of incoherent, indiscriminate, competitive, localistic individualism," and become "the better instrument of formative national growth."[32]

By the time Wilson made his acceptance speech and the Adamson Act cleared Congress, the inherent difficulties of the Republican campaign had emerged. Hughes quickly proved a disappointment as a campaigner. From his acceptance speech on July 31 through a lengthy swing across the country in August, the Republican candidate seemed mired in trivial criticism of Wilson over appointments and civil service policy. The stress he placed on the tariff pleased the regulars, but left the progressives unhappy. He was never able to get a grip on the Mexican problem in a way that convinced the voters he could have done better than Wilson. His efforts to rebut the key issues of the Democrats were lame. "The Democrats claim the credit for the prosperity which the country is enjoying," he told a Spokane crowd, "Do they think that the Democratic administration is synonymous with the European war?" The Democrats said that "Mr. Hughes apparently is touring the country telling the people small, petty things which amount to nothing." One reporter concluded that "Hughes is dropping icicles from his beard all over the west and will return to New York clean shaven."[33]

The Republican campaign organization and the presidential candidate had no more success in bringing harmony to the party. Hughes's choice for campaign chairman proved inept and weak, and the headquarters, though well supplied with funds, provided no positive direction. Literature did not go out; press relations were poor; and scheduling of speakers was erratic. The decision to dispatch a trainload of Republican women to stump for Hughes backfired when the press dubbed it the "Billionaires Special" because of the affluence of some of the ladies. Progressives complained when conservatives received recognition, and the party's right wing bridled at any "restoration of Rooseveltism." The "imbroglio in California" where Hughes accepted conservative guidance and appeared to snub the Republican senatorial candidate

[32] Herbert Croly, "The Two Parties in 1916," *The New Republic*, 8 (1916), 286.

[33] *New York Times*, August 10, 15, 1916; John C. O'Laughlin to Roosevelt, August 29, 1916, Roosevelt Papers; Samuel G. Blythe, "The Political Panorama," *Saturday Evening Post*, 189 (October 14, 1916), 9.

and progressive hero, Governor Hiram Johnson, was the most celebrated of the quarrels in the decisive states.[34]

The most delicate problems for Hughes were Theodore Roosevelt and the German-Americans. Since German-Americans disliked
Wilson for what they perceived as his pro-British bias, the Republicans expected to win handily among this voting bloc. While offering as little ammunition as possible to the Democrats on the
hyphenated vote issue, the GOP wanted to exploit the willingness
of the Germans to back Hughes. The Republican candidate tried to
have the matter both ways by talking with German-American leaders and making sympathetic references to the need for neutrality in
his speeches. Roosevelt would not let Hughes escape that easily.
Believing that there should be a strong offensive against Wilson's
foreign policy, Roosevelt deplored, in a Maine speech of August 31,
that the United States had been "an idle spectator of the invasion of
Belgium, of the sinking of the *Lusitania,* of the continued slaughter
of our own citizens, and of the reign of anarchy, rapine and murder
in Mexico."[35]

From then onward, with Hughes's congratulations on this address and without the candidate's public disapproval, Roosevelt
became ever more strident and bellicose. In his later campaign appearances, the former president spoke of Wilson's summer home in
New Jersey. "There should be shadows enough at Shadow Lawn;
the shadows of men, women and children who have risen from the
ooze of the ocean bottom and from graves in foreign lands," and he
spoke of the "shadows of deeds that were never done; the shadows
of lofty words that were followed by no action; the shadows of the
tortured dead."[36] Whether Roosevelt hoped for Hughes's defeat to
clear his path for 1920 is not demonstrable. What is evident is that
his part in the campaign caused sizable German-American defections and played a role in the Republican loss comparable to what
Roosevelt had done in 1912.

The enactment of the Adamson law provided the harried Republicans with a specific, well-defined issue, and Hughes immediately sought to exploit it. Privately and publicly he described

[34] Medill McCormick to Roosevelt, August 27, 1916, Roosevelt Papers; Hilles to
Taft, September 7, 1916, Taft Papers.

[35] *New York Times,* September 1, 1916.

[36] *The Works of Theodore Roosevelt: America and the World War: Fear God and
Take Your Own Part,* XVIII, pp. 451–452.

Wilson's actions as "the most shameful proceeding that has come to my attention since I have entered public life," and told his audiences that, unlike Wilson, he "would not submit to dictation from any power in the country, no matter what the consequences." Other Republicans took up this criticism. The strongly negative response to this pro-labor measure among Republicans underlined their conservative faith and belied Hughes's claim that it was "a great liberal party." Still, when Maine went Republican by an impressive margin in early September, the party's hopes revived.[37]

The Democratic campaign organization and electoral strategy had more coherence and a clearer purpose than that of the Republicans. The manager of the canvass, a former Progressive from Pennsylvania named Vance McCormick, supervised efficient machinery that fused the contributions of Progressives and regular Democrats. The time had passed, Wilson said, "when either of the old parties constitutes a normal majority of the electorate," and the national campaign had an Associated Progressive Committee and a Woodrow Wilson Independent League to reach out beyond the Democrats.[38] In the central battleground of the Middle West, Senator Thomas J. Walsh of Montana ran the western headquarters with notable success; his understanding of ethnic politics made him effective among his fellow Catholics. The Democrats put the electoral votes of the South in the certain column for Wilson and looked for a winning coalition from the Midwest and Far West, where peace and progressivism had a powerful appeal.

More than any previous Democratic canvass, the 1916 campaign looked for votes from interest groups that had benefitted from the party's legislative accomplishments or that found the platform's promises attractive. Wilson wooed the farm vote in an August public letter that outlined what the Federal Highway Act, the Federal Reserve Act, and the Farm Loan Act would do for rural America. Across the midwestern states the hearings of the Federal Farm Loan Board about the location of its banks offered a convenient way to rally agrarian support. Democratic campaign literature boasted that "For the first time in history the financial needs

[37] Hughes to Taft, September 16, 1916, Taft to Hilles, September 21, 1916, Taft Papers; *New York Times,* September 5, 1916; *Republican Campaign Textbook, 1916* (Republican National Committee, 1916), p. 3.

[38] L. Ames Brown, "The President on the Independent Voter," *World's Work,* 32 (1916), 494.

for the American Farmers have been recognized as of equal importance with the insatiable demands of Wall Street and the Big Interests."[39]

Similar appeals went out to business, labor, and the advocates of social justice. The president, the business community was told, had been able "to adjust with disorganizing, to reform without destroying," as the Federal Reserve, Federal Trade Commission, and Tariff Commission acts showed. "The workingmen of American have been given a veritable emancipation," Wilson said in his acceptance speech as he listed the labor provisions of the Clayton Antitrust Act, the La Follette Seamen's Act of 1915, and other legislation. To the progressive voter, Wilson was depicted as a candidate who "as President during the last four years . . . has steadily moved with the patriotic concurrence of his party, in the direction of Progressive ideals." As the glue of their wide-ranging hunt for support, the Democrats employed a "class-consciousness" that revealed how the ideological alignments associated with Franklin D. Roosevelt and the New Deal were in gestation in 1916. "Wall Street wants Hughes. Wall Street hates Wilson," argued Democrats in North Dakota in a characteristic statement. "Do you want Wall Street—or Wilson?"[40]

In their literature, the Democrats struck forcefully at the weak spots in Hughes's canvass and highlighted Wilson's record. The Republican's middle name was "E-vasion," and his party had selected him "in the hope of perpetrating a hoax upon the American people so gigantic that it compels admiration." On the other hand, Wilson had "Kept Faith With the Farmer," had freed the nation "from the Blight of Child Slavery," and had established a "Foundation of Permanent Prosperity" for business. It came down, contended a last-minute Democratic advertisement, to two questions: "Wilson and Peace with Honor? Hughes with Roosevelt and War?" The Republicans had about $900,000 more to spend than their rivals, an advantage that, in the evaluation of a British reporter, came to nothing. "No American campaign that I have seen has been worse

[39] *How Wilson Has Kept Faith With the Farmer*, n.p., 1916, p. 29, pamphlet in Perry-Castañeda Library, University of Texas at Austin.

[40] *Wilson and Permanent Prosperity* (New York: Wilson Business Men's National League, 1916), p. 3; *President Wilson A True Progressive*, n.p., 1916, pamphlet in Perry-Castañeda Library; Meyer Nathan, "The Presidential Election of 1916 in the Middle West," Ph.D. dissertation, Princeton University, 1966, pp. 69, 70; Link, ed., *The Papers of Woodrow Wilson: Volume 38*, p. 130.

managed than the Republican one; and none better than that of the Democrats, under the auspices of the silent House, who really must be something of a man," the London *Times* correspondent told his editor; "Yet the Republicans have lots of cash; the Democrats not much."[41]

The centerpiece of the Democratic campaign and the real architect of victory was Woodrow Wilson. During the last six weeks of the contest, he provided the momentum to overcome whatever gains the Republicans had secured from the Adamson Act and the Maine election. As always, the president would have preferred not to have campaigned, but from mid-September on he made speeches that restored Democratic morale. His most effective single strokes were first the telegram he sent on September 29 to an Irish-American leader who criticized him as pro-British. "I would feel deeply mortified to have you or anybody like you vote for me. Since you have access to many disloyal Americans and I have not I will ask you to convey this message to them." Then the next day he told an audience at his summer home "that the certain prospect of the success of the Republican party is that we shall be drawn, in one form or other, into the embroilments of the European war" and to a deeper involvement in Mexico. Wilson did not use the peace issue with the stridency of his party's managers, and he did suggest that greater world responsibilities lay ahead for the nation. Nevertheless, he said continually "I am not expecting this country to get into war," and he did not dispel the assumption that his administration could fulfill the implicit pledge in his words.[42]

As the campaign proceeded through October, it was apparent that both parties were committed to the advertising techniques that had become popular since 1904. Advertisements in newspapers received more attention than traditional rallies, and appeals also appeared on outdoor billboards and in streetcars. Campaigns devoted more time to responding to the advertising of the opposition and less to answering the charges of rival orators. Films depicted "The President and His Cabinet in Action" for the

[41] *Charles 'E-vasion' Hughes* (New York: Democratic National Committee, 1916), p. 9; *Children's Emancipation Day* (New York, 1916); *New York Times*, November 4, 1916; Arthur Willert to Geoffrey Robinson [Dawson], October 14, 1916, Archives of the *Times*, London.

[42] Link, ed., *The Papers of Woodrow Wilson: Volume 38*, pp. 286, 306; *The New Democracy*, II, p. 371.

A 1916 campaign film of
President Wilson, *The World's
Work*, October 1916.

Democrats; the Republicans showed theater audiences pictures of
Theodore Roosevelt as evidence of a "Reunited Party." By 1916
media events and photo opportunities existed, though they had not
yet received their modern labels.

With victory hanging in the balance in a tight struggle, the opposing sides expanded the range of their campaign tactics. Republicans made as much as they could privately of scurrilous gossip
about Wilson's private life, but this technique of innuendo cost as
many votes as it won. Charges that the Wilson administration was
pro-southern in its appointments and policies did not counteract
Democratic inroads in the farm states. The Democrats quietly
courted the German vote, even as they denounced Hughes for
being subservient to it. Betting odds on the outcome fluctuated as
election day neared. One Republican reporter predicted that
"Wilson will be elected" in part because Hughes "has offered
nothing constructive, and has been trying to carry water on both
shoulders."[43]

[43] McGerr, "The Decline of Popular Politics," pp. 236–237; John C. O'Laughlin
to Hiram Johnson, November 2, 1916, Hiram Johnson Papers, Bancroft Library,
University of California, Berkeley.

Campaign buttons from 1916. Author's collection.

In an age where paper ballots and the absence of radio and television made compiling and publicizing the election returns a long process, the results came in slowly on November 7, 1916, and at first appeared to reveal a Republican trend. Hughes carried the industrial Northeast, including New York, New Jersey, and Pennsylvania, and the Republican surge seemed unstoppable when the large midwestern states of Michigan, Indiana, and Illinois fell to the GOP. Early in the morning of November 8, returns from the West disclosed Democratic gains that put usually Republican states in doubt. Two days after the election, as the state of California went safely for the president, it became clear that Wilson had won. Final returns gave him 9,129,606 popular votes and 277 electoral votes from 30 states, to 8,538,221 ballots and 254 electoral votes from 18 states for Hughes. Wilson was still not the choice of a majority of the electorate, with 49.3 percent to Hughes's 46.1 percent. Turnout rose almost 4 percent in the North over 1912, but the 59.7 percent of the eligible voters who participated in the region still fell more than eight points behind the same figure for 1908.

The Democrats held onto control of the Senate by 12 seats, but only barely retained a grip on the House with the help of votes from independents and minor parties.

The fortuitous union of prosperity, progressivism, and peace in ascending order of importance enabled Wilson in 1916 to take the Democrats to the limits of their political resources during the Republican electoral ascendancy between 1896 and 1930. The president ran 2,830,000 votes ahead of his own total four years before. He made impressive gains among labor voters in California and other western states; his record lured away more than 300,000 votes from the Socialist total in 1912; and he ran strongly among former Progressives. The peace issue cut Democratic losses among German-Americans in the Midwest, and helped the party with ethnic groups such as the Poles, Scandinavians, and Italians. Like all winning coalitions, the Wilson victory drew on a diverse range of support—women who could vote went Democratic; farmers in the Middle West responded to peace, administration farm programs, and rural prosperity. At the base of the Democratic effort lay the South. Together with the trans-Mississippi West, it allowed Wilson to achieve the union Bryan had sought in 1896.

The instability of the Democratic coalition in 1916 ensured that in electoral terms Republican dominance would soon reappear. Wilson's narrow margin in several states (56 votes in New Hampshire, 1,735 in North Dakota, 3,773 in California) and enduring Republican strength at the congressional level underscored the true character of the 1916 contest. It was an election that foreshadowed future electoral alignments, but only began, in a tentative and preliminary way, to create the shift in voting allegiances that would surface in the 1930s. In the next four years the farm vote returned to the Republicans, the northern and southern wings of the Democratic party divided over prohibition and woman suffrage, and Wilson's domestic and foreign policies alienated the immigrant votes and progressives who had endorsed him in 1916. By 1920 the Wilson coalition was in shambles, progressivism was in retreat, and Republican ascendancy had been restored.

Epilogue

Wilson's victory in 1916 was in the short run only a fortunate Democratic interruption of a Republican era, but it climaxed an important formative period in the history of modern American politics that had significant consequences for the policy positions of the two parties. Though they left the electoral shape of the country essentially unchanged, the partisan struggles of the Progressive era produced lasting alterations in the way policy was made, the public's business conducted, and American elections fought. In a larger sense, the outlines for domestic political life were fixed for more than six decades.

Dominant at the start of the period, the Republicans retained their electoral supremacy despite Wilson's reelection. In the congressional races of 1918, they regained control of the Senate and House, and completed their return to power with Warren G. Harding's victory two years later. They did so as the advocates of conservatism and the opponents of federal power to regulate the economy and relieve social problems. The turbulence of the reform years did not move the GOP in the direction of the moderate activism that Roosevelt espoused. Instead, the party decided to emphasize smaller government, individual initiative, and the diffusion of the benefits of corporate capitalism. This mix of issues commanded the allegiance of the voters until Franklin D. Roosevelt and the Great Depression, and the Republican creed reasserted itself in the 1950s. But there was a discernible shift from the positive, nationalistic party of the 1890s to the conservative, antigovernment Republicans of midcentury that began in these years.

Theodore Roosevelt's legacy to the Republican party was an ambiguous one. The Republicans did not follow his concern for the equitable balance of competing forces in society. Though he returned to the GOP fold by 1916 and would have been the party's candidate in 1920 had he lived, Roosevelt's break with his Republican past in 1912 was a lasting rupture. He did more to revitalize the presidency and to offer an example to Democratic chief executives who succeeded him than he did to change the shape of national politics.

The Democrats experienced the most substantial transformation of the era. Throughout the first decade of the century, the party, especially in Congress, moved slowly away from the individualism and localism of its nineteenth-century doctrine. The strength of the party in the South meant that a perennial check existed against efforts to use national power to deal with social concerns, lest a government strong enough to ban child labor also assault racial segregation. Under Woodrow Wilson, however, the need to govern and to respond to interest group pressures brought about an enhancement of federal authority in which the South acquiesced because the Wilson administration never breached the color line.

As the Republicans moved rightward after 1910, the Democrats saw electoral advantages to becoming a liberal party of an assertive national government. The 1916 election showed the possibilities in a coalition of the South, the West, labor, women, and progressives. At the time of Wilson's victory, the Democrats had not yet unequivocally decided to become the party of strong national authority acting as a regulatory broker among competing economic, social, and cultural interests. The intellectual advocates of increased government power had the initiative in intraparty debates from 1920 onward, and in that sense Franklin D. Roosevelt and the New Deal were the natural legatees of what Wilson's first term had accomplished.

Within the national government itself, the presidency showed the most lasting effects of the political changes in these years. While McKinley laid the basis for the modern executive between 1897 and 1901, and William Howard Taft added important institutional alterations in his single term, Theodore Roosevelt and Woodrow Wilson gave the office its essential character for the century ahead. Roosevelt pioneered in making the president a positive participant in the economy in the Northern Securities case and the anthracite coal strike; he showed how the White House could formulate, advocate, and enact a legislative program in the Hepburn Act, Pure Food and Drug Act, and the meat inspection measure of 1906. The president became a celebrity and a major news source in Roosevelt's time, and building on McKinley's precedent, he brought in academics and professionals to staff the executive branch and government agencies. In foreign affairs, Roosevelt wielded executive authority to acquire a Canal Zone in Panama, participate in European diplomatic conferences, and govern the American empire. He also revealed some of the possible excesses of a strong president in the Brownsville episode and in his stricter enforcement of antitrust laws against corporations that displeased him.

Woodrow Wilson extended and elaborated the departures Roosevelt had made. Though he later dropped the practice, he held regular press conferences during most of his first term. Addressing Congress in person in 1913 broke a century of previous custom and focused greater attention on the presidency as a source of guidance and policy. Wilson also traveled and spoke to sway public opinion, kept policy initiatives in his own hands, and functioned as a powerful party leader. His actions during World War I would further increase his executive authority, but his first four years showed plainly that he intended to make his office as large an element as possible in the American system of government.

The range and scope of problems the national government addressed also grew dramatically in these sixteen years, as did the size of the government. The number of civilian employees rose from around 239,000 in 1901 to more than 349,000 sixteen years later. The informal government budget totaled expenditures of $587,-685,000 when Theodore Roosevelt became president. The expenditures of Woodrow Wilson's last peacetime year reached $782,535,000. Though the adoption of a budget process was still four years away, surplus revenues were recorded in eight of the sixteen years, and the politicians of that day did not have to choose between programs and fiscal integrity.

The distinctive changes of the era's politics most clearly emerged in the use of agencies and bureaus to deal with economic and social problems. The Federal Reserve Board (1914) regulated monetary policy; the Federal Trade Commission (1914) oversaw business practices. The Department of Commerce (1903) and the Department of Labor (1913) spoke for industry and workers, respectively, with varying degrees of effectiveness. By 1916 there were also in Washington such agencies as a Bureau of Efficiency, a Shipping Board, an Eight Hour Day Commission, a Board of Mediation and Conciliation, and a National Advisory Committee on Aeronautics. On the state level, regulatory agencies proliferated after 1905 to supervise insurance, industry, alcohol, social welfare, and working conditions.

Americans in the early twentieth century did not yet distrust the regulatory agency or see bureaucracy as the enemy of individual liberty. Many believed that trained, nonpartisan experts could best manage the subtle and difficult social questions of the modern world. Some cost to democracy might occur, they recognized, but the prospective gains in efficiency made the risk acceptable. Having seen the results of unbridled industrialism, they thought that individuals in government could adjust the market to lessen injustice without jeopardizing the gains of enterprise. If the choice lay between free enterprise unchecked or government ownership and socialism, progressives sought the middle way of regulation.

Self-interest and self-delusion lay behind some of these calls for increased government activity, and Americans in this period were surer that their interest and the public interest coincided than historians and economists have been in recent years. Skepticism about some of the results these reformers produced does not mean that the social problems they confronted or the alternatives they faced were unreal. The effort to mitigate the impact of industrialism addressed genuine inequities that market forces had not alleviated. The harm that child labor, industrial accidents, and an unorganized workforce caused understandably attracted reform attention. Because regulation did not solve all the nation's social ills does not justify the conclusion that it did no good whatever. The United States was a more humane and just nation in 1916 than it had been a decade and a half earlier.

The political party was a central target of the reform attack in these years, and in that sphere the progressive impulse achieved most of its aims. The direct primary, the direct election of senators, and the initiative, referendum, and recall shifted power over candidate selection and legislative programs away from the major parties. Proliferation of interest groups with highly focused agendas made the Republicans and Democrats, as organizations, less significant players in the policy-making process. By Wilson's second term, the partisan nature of American government had been markedly lessened.

In campaigns, the parties also lost some of their autonomy as advertising replaced spectacle. Individual candidates became more important than the party apparatus, and public relations men, cinema experts, and professional consultants took over as shapers of campaign strategy. Party appeals receded in significance, and elections lost some of their distinctive character and mass attraction.

The causes of the decline in voter interest and participation in American politics that marked this period are still in dispute. More restrictive registration procedures depressed the size of the electorate to some degree. Alternative forms of diversion—vaudeville, professional sports, the movies—competed for national attention. Perhaps the absence of a viable Socialist alternative to the major parties thwarted expressions of popular discontent with the state of politics. Given the generally conservative character of Americans in this century, that explanation seems implausible. A combination of elements produced the long-term slide in political participation as expressed in voting, but the erosion of party strength and autonomy lay at the heart of the matter. Dismantling the mechanism for voter mobilization led to lower turnout and lessened interest, instead of creating greater democratic activity and openness.

National politics between 1900 and 1916 represented neither the fulfillment of democracy nor its abandonment. In its strengthening of regulatory power and enhancement of the presidency, it accomplished changes that improved the society's capacity to deal with issues and problems. The reforms of the parties themselves remedied abuses, but also impaired their ability to involve citizens in the life of the nation. This mixed outcome bequeathed problems to the future, many of which remain unresolved. In the age of reform and regulation, American politics established the agenda for the century to come and devised approaches to the nation's domestic issues that have not been superseded or replaced in the intervening decades. Few periods in the national past have done so much or produced consequences of such enduring importance.

Suggestions for Additional Reading

A comprehensive bibliography on American politics and public policy between 1900 and 1916 would be too bulky for practical use. The following comments indicate the most useful and informative books, articles, and theses on the subject of this volume.

The best brief introduction to the historical issues of this period is Arthur S. Link and Richard L. McCormick, *Progressivism*, Harlan Davidson, Arlington Heights, Illinois, 1983. Older, general treatments are Arthur S. Link, *Woodrow Wilson and the Progressive Era, 1910–1917*, Harper & Bros., New York, 1954; and George E. Mowry, *The Era of Theodore Roosevelt, 1900–1912*, Harper & Bros., New York, 1958.

The combined efforts of historians and political scientists to examine politics between 1900 and 1916 in the context of shifting electoral alignments in the 1890s can be followed in E. E. Schattschneider, *The Semi-Sovereign People: A Realist's View of Democracy in America*, Holt, Rinehart and Winston, New York, 1960; Paul T. David, *Party Strength in the United States, 1872–1970*, University Press of Virginia, Charlottesville, 1972; Howard W. Allen and Jerome Clubb, "Progressive Reform and the Political System," *Pacific Northwest Quarterly*, 65 (1974), 130–145; and Walter Dean Burnham, "The System of 1896: An Analysis," in Paul Kleppner et al., *The Evolution of American Electoral Systems*, Greenwood Press, Westport, Connecticut, 1981, pp. 147–202.

For the nineteenth-century background of national politics, see H. Wayne Morgan, *From Hayes to McKinley: National Party Politics, 1877–1896*, Syracuse University Press, Syracuse, 1969; Richard Jensen, *The Winning of the Midwest: Social and Political Conflict, 1888–1896*, University of Chicago Press, Chicago, 1971; J. Morgan Kousser, *The Shaping of Southern Politics: Suffrage Restriction and the Establishment of the One-Party South, 1880–1910*, Yale University Press, New Haven, 1974; and the best one-volume study of the 1890s, R. Hal Williams, *Years of Decision: American Politics in the 1890s*, John Wiley, New York, 1978.

General works that help to understand the setting of Progressive era politics include Richard L. Watson, Jr., *The Development of National Power: The United States, 1900–1919,* Houghton Mifflin, Boston, 1976; Richard L. McCormick, "The Discovery That Business Corrupts Politics: A Reappraisal of the Origins of Progressivism," *American Historical Review,* 86 (1981), 242–274; and Dewey W. Grantham, *Southern Progressivism: The Reconciliation of Progress and Tradition,* University of Tennessee Press, Knoxville, 1983.

There are no satisfactory general treatments of the national parties after 1896. J. Rogers Hollingsworth, *The Whirligig of Politics: The Democracy of Cleveland and Bryan,* University of Chicago Press, Chicago, 1963, is thin and derivative. John B. Wiseman, "Racism in Democratic Politics, 1904–1912," *Mid-America,* 51 (1968), 38–58, and John J. Broesamle, "The Democrats from Bryan to Wilson," in Lewis L. Gould, ed., *The Progressive Era,* pp. 83–113, Syracuse University Press, Syracuse, 1974, are solid brief accounts. David Sarasohn, "The Democratic Surge, 1905–1912: Forging A Progressive Majority," Ph.D. dissertation, University of California, Los Angeles, 1976, argues that the Democrats were the progressive party even before Wilson, and the voters responded to them.

On specific issues that relate to the Democrats, the following articles are helpful: Edgar A. Hornig, "The Indefatigable Mr. Bryan in 1908," *Nebraska History,* 37 (1956), 183–199; Richard M. Abrams, "Woodrow Wilson and the Southern Congressmen, 1913–1916," *Journal of Southern History,* 22 (1956), 417–437; Anne Firor Scott, "A Progressive Wind from the South, 1906–1913," *Journal of Southern History,* 29 (1963), 53–70; Frank Burdick, "Woodrow Wilson and the Underwood Tariff," *Mid-America,* 50 (1968), 272–290; Claude Barfield, " 'Our Share of the Booty': The Democratic Party, Cannonism, and the Payne-Aldrich Tariff," *Journal of American History,* 57 (1970), 308–323; and Wythe W. Holt, Jr., "The Senator from Virginia and the Democratic Floor Leadership: Thomas S. Martin and Conservatism in the Progressive Era," *Virginia Magazine of History and Biography,* 83 (1975), 3–21. John D. Buenker, *Urban Liberalism and Progressive Reform,* Scribner, New York, 1973, traces the rise of an urban, activist wing of the party from 1905 onward.

For studies of Democrats in individual states, see Sheldon Hackney, *Populism to Progressivism in Alabama,* Princeton University Press, Princeton, 1969; Lewis L. Gould, *Progressives and Prohibitionists: Texas Democrats in the Wilson Era,* University of Texas Press, Austin, 1973; Robert W. Cherny, *Populism, Progressivism, and the Transformation of Nebraska Politics, 1885–1915,* University of Nebraska Press, Lincoln, 1981; and Evan Anders, *Boss Rule in South Texas: The Progressive Era,* University of Texas Press, Austin, 1982.

On the Republican side, George E. Mowry, *Theodore Roosevelt and the Progressive Movement,* University of Wisconsin Press, Madison, 1946, is now badly dated. Horace Samuel Merrill and Marion Galbraith Merrill, *The Republican Command, 1897–1913,* University Press of

Kentucky, Lexington, 1971, is critical of the GOP, but is filled with factual and analytic errors and must be read with great caution. A treatment that takes a similar interpretive position but is far more reliable is William H. Harbaugh, "The Republican Party, 1892–1932," in Arthur Schlesinger, Jr., ed., *History of U.S. Political Parties*, 4 vols., Chelsea House, New York, 1973, Vol. III, pp. 2069–2125.

The midwestern insurgents among Republicans are covered in Kenneth W. Hechler, *Insurgency: Personalities and Politics of the Taft Era*, Columbia University Press, New York, 1940, and more satisfactorily in James L. Holt, *Congressional Insurgents and the Party System, 1909–1916*, Harvard University Press, Cambridge, 1967. Patrick F. Palermo, "The Midwestern Republican Tradition," *Capitol Studies*, 5 (1977), 43–56, also looks at the insurgents. David P. Thelen, *The New Citizenship: Origins of Progressivism in Wisconsin, 1885–1900*, University of Missouri Press, Columbia, 1972, is stimulating on the origins of Republican discontent in a key state. John D. Baker, "The Character of the Congressional Revolution of 1910," *Journal of American History*, 60 (1973), 679–691, takes a fresh look at the revolt against Speaker Cannon. Norman Wilensky, *Conservatives in the Progressive Era: The Taft Republicans of 1912*, Florida State University Press, Gainesville, 1965, discusses the right wing of the GOP; and Richard B. Sherman, *The Republican Party and Black Americans from McKinley to Hoover*, University Press of Virginia, Charlottesville, 1973, examines the Republican effort to resolve their ambiguous posture on the race issue. Lewis L. Gould, "Theodore Roosevelt, William Howard Taft, and the Disputed Delegates in 1912: Texas as a Test Case," *Southwestern Historical Quarterly*, 80 (1976), 33–56, deals with one aspect of the 1912 debacle.

Valuable books on the workings of Republican parties in single states are George E. Mowry, *The California Progressives*, University of California Press, Berkeley, 1951; Richard M. Abrams, *Conservatism in a Progressive Era: Massachusetts Politics, 1900–1912*, Harvard University Press, Cambridge, 1964; Robert F. Wesser, *Charles Evans Hughes: Politics and Reform in New York, 1905–1910*, Cornell University Press, Ithaca, 1967; Herbert F. Margulies, *The Decline of the Progressive Movement in Wisconsin, 1890–1920*, State Historical Society of Wisconsin, Madison, 1968; and Robert Sherman La Forte, *Leaders of Reform: Progressive Republicans in Kansas, 1900–1916*, The University Press of Kansas, Lawrence, 1974. Richard L. McCormick, *From Realignment to Reform: Political Change in New York State, 1893–1910*, Cornell University Press, Ithaca, 1981, skillfully places the history of the Republican party in the context of recent scholarship on electoral behavior and partisan realignment.

Extensive work on voting behavior in these years is just beginning. The presidential contests are covered in Arthur Schlesinger, Jr., and Fred Israel, eds., *History of American Presidential Elections*, 4 vols., Chelsea House, New York, 1971, Volume III. For general treatments of the whole period, see Roger E. Wyman, "Middle Class Voters and Progressive Reform: The Conflict of Class and Culture," *American Political Science Review*, 68 (1974), 488–505; Allan J. Lichtman, "Critical Election Theory and the Reality of American Presidential Politics, 1916–1940," *American Historical Review*, 81 (1976), 317–351; and Jerome M. Clubb, "Party Coalitions in the Early Twentieth Century," in Seymour Martin Lipset, ed., *Emerging Coalitions in American Politics*, Institute for Contemporary Studies, San Francisco, 1978, pp. 61–79. Michael Edward McGerr, "The Decline of Popular Politics: Political Style and Participation in the North, 1865–1928," Ph.D. dissertation, Yale University, 1984, is a thorough and fascinating examination of the shifts in campaigns and elections that marked the period. Oxford University Press will publish McGerr's book under a similar title in early 1986.

Individual studies of the elections of 1900 and 1916 have appeared, but the intervening contests still need attention. For 1900, see Goran Rystad, *Ambiguous Imperialism: American Foreign Policy and Domestic Politics at the Turn of the Century*, Esselte Studium, Lund, Sweden, 1975. S. D. Lovell, *The Presidential Election of 1916*, Southern Illinois Press, Carbondale, Illinois, 1980, looks at Wilson's re-election. On particular contests, see Edgar A. Hornig, "The Religious Issue in the Taft-Bryan Duel of 1908," *Proceedings of the American Philosophical Society*, 105 (1961), 530–537; David Burner, "The Breakup of the Wilson Coalition of 1916," *Mid-America*, 45 (1963), 18–35; Michael Rogin, "Progressivism and the California Electorate," *Journal of American History*, 55 (1968), 297–314; and David Sarasohn, "The Election of 1916: Realigning the Rockies," *Western Historical Quarterly*, 11 (1980), 285–305. Meyer Nathan, "The Presidential Election of 1916 in the Middle West," Ph.D. dissertation, Princeton University, 1966, and Fred Shoemaker, "Alton B. Parker: The Images of a Gilded Age Statesman in an Era of Progressive Politics," M.A. thesis, Ohio State University, 1983, are helpful unpublished studies.

The literature on the various policy issues of this period is vast. For the tariff, however, the best works in a sparse field are L. Ethan Ellis, *Reciprocity 1911: A Study in Canadian-American Relations*, Yale University Press, New Haven, 1939; Richard C. Baker, *The Tariff Under Roosevelt and Taft*, Democratic Printing Co., Hastings, Nebraska, 1941; David W. Detzer, "Business, Reformers, and Tariff Revision: The Payne-Aldrich Tariff of 1909," *The Historian*, 35 (1973), 196–204; Lewis L. Gould, "Western Range Senators and the Payne-Aldrich Tariff," *Pacific Northwest Quarterly*, 64 (1973), 49–56.

The railroad problem has stimulated much controversy. Gabriel Kolko, *Railroads and Regulation, 1877–1916*, Princeton University Press, Princeton, 1965, argues that the railroads actually supported national regulation, but a close reading of his sources casts doubt on his thesis. Albro Martin, *Enterprise Denied: Origins of the Decline of American Railroads, 1897–1917*, Columbia University Press, New

York, 1971, contends that regulation crippled the rail companies. K. Austin Kerr, *American Railroad Politics, 1914–1920,* University of Pittsburgh Press, Pittsburgh, 1968, deals with the Wilson years. Stanley P. Caine, *The Myth of a Progressive Reform: Railroad Regulation in Wisconsin, 1903–1910,* State Historical Society of Wisconsin, Madison, 1970, considers regulation on the state level.

For general economic policy, Robert Wiebe, *Businessmen and Reform: A Study of the Progressive Movement,* Harvard University Press, Cambridge, 1962, makes clear the diversity of business views on regulation, but is less helpful on how these divisions affected public policy. Gabriel Kolko, *The Triumph of Conservatism: A Reinterpretation of American History, 1900–1916,* Free Press, New York, 1963, sees business as advocating regulatory policy, but tends to play down or dismiss evidence that contradicts his argument. Melvin I. Urofsky, *Big Steel and the Wilson Administration: A Study in Business-Government Relations,* Ohio State University Press, Columbus, 1969, is informative. Though it makes up only about a quarter of the book, the section on Louis D. Brandeis and regulation in Thomas K. McCraw, *Prophets of Regulation: Charles Francis Adams, Louis D. Brandeis, James M. Landis, Alfred E. Kahn,* The Belknap Press of Harvard University Press, Cambridge, 1984, is one of the most lucid and perceptive discussions of the economic history of these years that has yet appeared.

On the politics of resource policy, see Samuel P. Hays, *Conservation and the Gospel of Efficiency: The Progressive Conservation Movement, 1890–1920,* Harvard University Press, Cambridge, 1959; and James L. Penick, Jr., *Progressive Politics and Conservation: The Ballinger-Pinchot Affair,* University of Chicago Press, Chicago, 1968.

Various aspects of the changes in political practices and procedures are discussed in Samuel P. Hays, "The Politics of Reform in Municipal Government in the Progressive Era," *Pacific Northwest Quarterly,* 55 (1964), 157–169; Howard W. Allen, Aage R. Clausen, and Jerome M. Clubb, "Political Reform and Negro Rights in the Senate, 1909–1915," *Journal of Southern History,* 37 (1971), 191–212; Larry J. Easterling, "Senator Joseph L. Bristow and the Seventeenth Amendment," *The Kansas Historical Quarterly,* 41 (1975), 488–511; Bradley R. Rice, *Progressive Cities: The Commission Government Movement in America, 1901–1920,* University of Texas Press, Austin, 1977; and Martin J. Schiesl, *The Politics of Efficiency: Municipal Administration and Reform in America, 1880–1920,* University of California Press, Berkeley, California, 1977.

Although there have been numerous studies of Theodore Roosevelt, no full-scale biography based on the rich manuscript sources available has yet appeared. Henry F. Pringle, *Theodore Roosevelt: A Biography,* Harcourt, Brace, New York, 1931, is still stimulating, and William H. Harbaugh, *Power and Responsibility: The Life and Times of Theodore Roosevelt,* Farrar, Straus and Cudahy, New York, 1961, is thorough. John M. Blum, *The Republican Roosevelt,* Harvard University Press, Cambridge, 1954, began the modern reappraisal of Roosevelt, and remains the best single book on his life. Elting Morison et al., eds., *The Letters of Theodore Roosevelt*, 8 vols., Harvard University Press, Cambridge, 1951–1954, is a superb selection from Roosevelt's immense correspondence. Edmund Morris, *The Rise of Theodore Roosevelt*, Coward, McCann & Geoghegan, New York, 1979, treats Roosevelt's prepresidential career as its subject would have liked to have had it written. David McCullough, *Mornings on Horseback*, Simon and Schuster, New York, 1981, is a perceptive look at Roosevelt's youth. John Allen Gable, *The Bull Moose Years: Theodore Roosevelt and the Progressive Party*, Kennikat Press, Port Washington, New York, 1978, is a thorough and informed treatment of Roosevelt's third-party phase.

Taft has attracted less attention than Roosevelt. Henry F. Pringle, *The Life and Times of William Howard Taft*, 2 vols., Farrar and Rinehart, New York, 1939, is the standard biography. There are two studies of Taft's presidency, but neither Paolo E. Coletta, *The Presidency of William Howard Taft*, University Press of Kansas, Lawrence, 1973, nor Donald F. Anderson, *William Howard Taft: A Conservative's Conception of the Presidency*, Cornell University Press, Ithaca, 1973, meet the need for a careful, modern examination of Taft's political role. More satisfactory are Stanley Solvick, "William Howard Taft and the Payne-Aldrich Tariff," *Mississippi Valley Historical Review*, 50 (1963), 424–442, and Solvick, "The Pre-Presidential Political and Economic Thought of William Howard Taft," *Northwest Ohio Quarterly*, 43 (1971), 87–97. James C. German, "Taft, Roosevelt and United States Steel," *The Historian*, 34 (1972), 598–613, looks at a crucial episode in Taft's administration.

Woodrow Wilson means Arthur S. Link to American historians. Link's biography, *Woodrow Wilson*, 5 vols., Princeton University Press, Princeton, 1947–1965, takes Wilson to April 1917. The first two volumes have more discussion of Wilson's political career; the last three emphasize the problem of American entry into World War I. Arthur S. Link et al., eds., *The Papers of Woodrow Wilson*, 48 vols., Princeton University Press, Princeton, 1966–1985, will eventually bring out all of Wilson's writings. Other Wilsonian biographers include James Kerney, *The Political Education of Woodrow Wilson*, The Century Co., New York, 1926; John M. Blum, *Woodrow Wilson and the Politics of Morality*, Little, Brown, Boston, 1956; Patrick Devlin, *Too Proud to Fight: Woodrow Wilson's Neutrality*, Oxford University Press, New York, 1974; and Edwin A. Weinstein, *Woodrow Wilson: A Medical and Psychological Biography*, Princeton University Press, Princeton, 1981. John Milton Cooper, Jr., *The Warrior and the Priest: Woodrow Wilson and Theodore Roosevelt*, The Belknap Press of Harvard University Press, Cambridge, 1983, is a provocative comparative study of the two presidents.

The biographical literature on other political figures is so rich that only a small sample can be given here. Nathaniel Wright Stephenson, *Nel-*

son W. *Aldrich: A Leader in American Politics,* Scribner, New York, 1930, is the life of an important Republican conservative, while John Braeman, *Albert J. Beveridge: American Nationalist,* University of Chicago Press, Chicago, 1971, traces the emergence of a GOP progressive. Louis W. Koenig, *Bryan: A Political Biography of William Jennings Bryan,* G. P. Putnam's Sons, New York, 1971, is the best one-volume biography, and Kendrick A. Clements, *William Jennings Bryan: Missionary Isolationist,* University of Tennessee Press, Knoxville, 1982, examines Bryan and foreign policy in a fresh way. David P. Thelen, *Robert M. La Follette and the Insurgent Spirit,* Little, Brown, Boston, 1976, is an interpretive study, but La Follette still needs thorough and dispassionate analysis. Herbert F. Margulies, *Senator Lenroot of Wisconsin,* University of Missouri Press, Columbia, 1977, shows what a biography based on thorough research in primary sources and balanced judgment can do for politicians in this period. John J. Broesamle, *William Gibbs McAdoo: A Passion for Change, 1863–1917,* Kennikat Press, Port Washington, New York, 1973, looks at one of the most intriguing of the men around Wilson. Elting E. Morison, *Turmoil and Tradition: A Study of the Life and Times of Henry L. Stimson,* Houghton Mifflin, Boston, 1960, offers many insights into Roosevelt and Republicanism. John M. Blum, *Joe Tumulty and the Wilson Era,* Houghton Mifflin, Boston, 1951, is very useful on Wilsonian politics. Finally, Louis R. Harlan, *Booker T. Washington: The Wizard of Tuskegee, 1901–1915,* Oxford University Press, New York, 1983, captures as much as any book can a sense of the political limits and emotional burdens of black Americans in the era of reform.

Students whose interest in this fascinating period goes beyond the titles mentioned here should consult Link and McCormick, *Progressivism,* pp. 119–140, or William M. Leary, Jr., and Arthur S. Link, comps., *The Progressive Era and the Great War, 1896–1920,* 2d ed., Harlan Davidson, Arlington Heights, Illinois, 1978, for more of the available literature.

INDEX

About the Author

Lewis L. Gould is Eugene C. Barker Centennial Professor of American History at the University of Texas at Austin. He is the author of *Progressives and Prohibitionists: Texas Democrats in the Wilson Era* (1973) and *The Presidency of William McKinley* (1980). He is currently writing a study of Mrs. Lyndon B. Johnson and her campaigns for beautification of the environment in the 1960s, and is doing research for a book on the presidency of Theodore Roosevelt. He is also the editor of *The Progressive Era* (1974) and co-editor of *The Black Experience in America* (1970).

A Note on the Type

The text of this book is set in a computer typeface, equivalent to the linotype Caledonia, a typeface designed in 1939 by W. A. Dwiggins. That typeface is inspired by the Scotch types cast about 1833 by typefounders A. Wilson & Sons of Glasgow. To name it, Dwiggins chose the Roman name for Scotland—Caledonia. Its distinctive calligraphic qualities are the vertical stress of the letters and the horizontal but not thin serifs.

Composed by American–Stratford Graphic Services, Inc., Brattleboro, Vermont. Printed and bound by R. R. Donnelley & Sons Company, Harrisonburg, Virginia.